FRENCH CONNECTION BLUES

FRENCH CONNECTION BLUES
Memoirs of a Narc

How $70 Million in Drugs Wound Up Back On the Street.

By Peter Bono

Published by Inherent Flaws Press, New York, NY
inherentflaws@gmail.com

To my friend, KMS
for without his help this story
would not have been told.

Cover design by KMSCB
Copyright 2014 by Inherent Flaws Press
ISBN 978-0-9912866-4-5

Prologue

In 1962 two New York City Detectives assigned to The Special Investigations Unit (SIU) of the NYPD Narcotics Bureau, arrested a French Television personality. He had his car shipped to New York from Marseilles France. Hidden in secret compartments was 110 pounds of pure heroin, 50 packages weighing 2.2 pounds each. A kilo each. The FRENCH CONNECTION, as it was referred to, would be the largest single seizure of drugs for many years. A book and then a movie glorified the police work, but what happened afterward has been a dark secret of the New York City Police Department.

As with all evidence the drugs were taken to 400 Broome Street the NYC Police Department's Property Clerk's Office. The following year it was taken to a Federal Laboratory in order to determine its origin.

From there Federal Marshals escorted the 50 kilos to Washington DC for a senate hearing on heroin trafficking. In 1964, with an estimated street value of 50 million dollars, it was returned to the NYPD and sent to 400 Broom Street to be locked away under the protective gaze of the Property Clerk's Office. Our story begins about this time.

Less than 10 years later, it ended for me at 240 Centre Street. That grand building was Police Headquarters, once upon a time. It was just past midnight, my life going to hell just like this city. I was born here and now it is under siege by crime. Streets empty, silent and dark. Seems like perfect version of hell.

A line of cars were parked across from 240 Centre Street, under this row of ugly brick buildings going two, three, five, seven stories up. Rickety fire escapes dripped down the front of the tallest one, like a cancer, its arched windows looking like they wanted to hide from it. Stores on the ground floor all secured behind rolling metal panels. Even here, right next to Police Headquarters, this town is not safe.

She was parked below one of those fire escapes. The top down on her brand new 1973 Eldorado convertible, even though it's close to snowing. You could smell it in the air. Smell her perfume. She wanted me to see her, wanted to make sure I knew I wasn't alone.

I should've just got in that Caddy right then and let her drive me away, anywhere. And I thought about it for half a second. It's just, I didn't realize how bad off I was. Didn't realize that if I did go into the old HQ, like I'd been doing for some time now, it would be the end of the life I had.

But I was not thinking straight, so almost zombie like, I walked across the street. Operations had almost finished shifting to One Police Plaza, several blocks south, and I was glad. This once grand dame was now past her prime, with her columns and half-hidden windows and sort-of balconies. She took up the whole narrow block. And the fat iron railings along the sidewalk, put there to keep you from dropping into the gullies that vanished into the basement's emptiness, it's like they were giving off this "stay away" vibe. The dome on top made it look like it was a capitol building instead of a place too old to work in the modern world, anymore.

Up close, it looked like what it was – nearly abandoned and disarrayed. Nothing but a couple low-key, bare-bones offices left inside, one of them way-too-happily involving me. After that was done...after I was done for...the city will try to figure out what to do with this relic. Who knew? Now a days it is a high-end condo or co-op.

Climbing the steps to the main entrance wasn't easy, thanks to the cracks and chips missing in them. I was shaking and had to hold onto the banister, I was dizzy and it seemed the revolving door was in constant motion. What's wrong with me? It didn't help that it seemed like half the lights were either busted or missing, making being there feel like a Hitchcock movie.

It was even older and darker, inside. More lights burned out. The floors were messy and shadow everywhere. The only guy I could see was the cop with inside security sitting at the half-circle of a reception desk, like always. He didn't bother to look up as I entered.

"Buono". How ya doin'?" was all he said.

"I...I been better," I said my voice soft and cracking. I could hear it, even if he couldn't. "But thanks. It has been a long, long day. All these lights missin' – don't maintenance care, no more?"

He just grunted and never took his eyes off whatever he was reading. He had a lamp on his desk and a cushion under his butt, so he was set.

I sighed and staggered down a corridor, aiming for the lockers next to the office that was crushing my life...and finally paid real attention how quiet it was. How it seemed like nobody else was around. Had they already moved the last people over to the new building? I wouldn't be surprised. That'd be one way to keep my secret safe, this secret that was finally shredding my world.

10

That corridor seemed to grow longer and darker as I went. And there were these shuffling sounds, fresh and new, echoing from everywhere. My breathing got sharp. My eyes darted about, wary. Why were so many fixtures missing light bulbs, completely? That didn't make sense, unless they'd been removed, deliberately. Make it harder to see into the darkness, past the shadows, perfect for an ambush.

I hesitated by the first door on the left. Undid the safety harness and checked my pistol then peeked into the area. Nothing but a couple rows of freestanding lockers set up for the few people left in the place. So dark and dirty and empty and quiet, only shadows filled the room. Even my breathing seemed to echo.

Or was it mine I was hearing?

I didn't want to go in there, but God, I wanted out of this uniform, even more. I'd be back in street cloths and in my girl's Caddy and safe, again, from this horror that was...that was lasting forever.

I started to shake more. I'd been doing that a lot, lately, once I'd realized what I'd got myself into. But it's too late to second-guess, now. So I carefully slipped inside and crept past row after row of lockers, getting closer and closer to mine. I saw no one, nothing.

I was sweating now, even though the building was cold. I could actually see my breath whispering in and out, like it was trying to escape. They weren't even bothering with the heat, Well...maybe they kept at 50 but it felt colder.

I finally reached my locker and leaned against it, damn near exhausted. Then I looked down at my shaking hand...and saw a thin trail of blood whisper over its skin.

Aw, no...no – I'd been shot? I'd been hit? No.

I almost fainted but caught myself by slamming my head against the locker. It hurt, but it got me back in control. I fumbled with the lock's combination, running through it three times. Blood smearing all over the lock. Then it popped open. The noise bounced off the walls and I nearly jumped out of my skin.

And the shadows grew darker and deeper.

Then I heard that shuffling sound, again. I froze, listened, nothing but silence. Not even breathing.

I slowly pulled off my coat. It didn't hurt, but something was pulling sharp against my left shoulder. I checked it and saw the shirt to my uniform was soaked with blood. I wiped my face. Blood smeared over it.

Crap, I was hit. Dammit.

What's that shuffling sound, again? It was close. I started to quake, inside. But then I thought, maybe it's my partner come looking for me. He's a good cop; he'd be worried.

"Bobby?" I called. "Bobby, Bobby is that you?"

Nothing, not even the shuffling, just silence, stone silence.

Until a whisper of a sound came from my right and I turned to find –

A gunman standing at the end of the lockers, raising a pistol!

Everything clicked into slow motion as I yanked out my service revolver, dropped to one knee and fired at him.

My first shot hit his left knee. The second ripped through his thigh. Two more hit an arm and a shoulder.

He got a couple of shots off at me and I felt something punch my side, but then he crashed against an office wall and landed in a sitting position, his leg twisted under him.

I rose slowly, carefully, kind of dizzy and in complete disbelief. This couldn't have happened. It couldn't of.

I inched up to him, pistol ready but shaking in my bloody hands, barely under control and hoping to God he wasn't gonna make another move. I heard voices, footsteps running, echoing. They were far away but getting and closer. It seemed to take forever. I wished they'd get here, already and --

The guy lifted his gun, unsteady.

I fired, again. The bullet exploded through his skull. Blood splattered over me. I was covered in blood. I dropped to my knees, about ready to pass out – and then I saw it.

I saw the gunman's gold shield.

He was a cop.

A detective!

I just killed a cop in police headquarters!

"Man, there's gonna be hell to pay for that," I thought as I quietly drifted towards darkness.

****

That was early 1973. Never heard about it? They kept it quiet because the department was still reeling from the whole Serpico fiasco. A cop killing a cop while they were both on duty in 240 Centre Street.

What was crazy about this was I never aimed to be a cop. I was pushed into it by my dad. Well, getting a city job anyway. He insisted I take all the civil service exams. He would buy "The Chief" that was the city Official publication telling about city jobs, and sure enough he made sure I took every test. My only goal in life was to find a nice, simple desk job. Put in twenty-five or thirty easy, steady years. Retire with a nice steady pension and live in Florida, nice and warm like to escape the brutal New York Winters. Just enjoy my life as I age.

Don't get me wrong – I never minded work. Hell, I was a good kid. Real good, swear on my grandmother's eyes. Yeah, she's long passed already, but you get the point. Everybody agreed I worked hard and dreamed right and had plans, and a lot of them still said I was good, even after everything went down.

But it is funny how, in most people's eyes, you can go from being a good kid one minute to like something out of a freak show the next. People don't want to understand that sometimes things happen that you got no control over. And if you don't know the circumstances of it all – well, the way people talked you'd think I was out to kill everybody that looked at me wrong. "But he was such a good kid," they would say.

Okay...that didn't make any sense when it ought to be clear as a glass of water without ice. Maybe I'm making it hard to figure out, so let me start from another direction – my name is Pietro Giovanni Buono, Pete to my friends, and I lived on the edge of Little Italy in lower Manhattan. A nice area of buildings older than my grandparents, built on tight streets with parks that are really just open spaces covered in asphalt, with a couple trees slung up for shade. At least they got plenty of benches and some even got Bocce spaces, so that's good. Of course, in that area, you wind up with an accent that's so New York you could cut it with a knife, and with looks that seem so sleek-eyed under slick dark hair, you'd think everybody's on the fast track to being a made guy wearing a diamond pinky ring.

And yes, those were my looks, too – on the sharp and slim side, but with nice eyes and a sweet smile. Hey, I'm just repeating what all the girls said. 'Cause I know I'm not the best-looking Italian-

13

American guy out there. But was Frank Sinatra ever really all that? I mean, I wasn't as skinny as him when he was starting out, and I'm pretty sure I'm close to a foot taller – but even in junior high, when you saw me strut down the school corridors you'd think either I was way too full of myself or putting on a really big front, or both. That is probably what it really was, since that's what got the girls interested. They like to think you got secrets that they, alone, can get you to reveal...and who am I to argue?

But then I wasn't like the other kids in one way. Even at Fourteen years old, you'd have thought I was about to finish high school. I was a budding hot dog. Y'see, my looks made me look older than I really was, and that can be a ton of help when you want to get away with something.

Now remember, back then you only had to be eighteen to drink in New York State but twenty-one to vote. That's the way it should still be. Eighteen is too young to vote some of the kids today never had a job at that age; there should be no representation without taxation, you know reverse of what the people in the Boston Tea Party fought for. If you have no responsibility how can you be responsible enough to figure out who needs to be in office? It is who is going to give them something for nothing, that is what they vote for, Anyway, when I was fourteen, everybody treated me like I was in my early 20's nobody looking at me twice. Even when I made time with a girl in a school hallway, they were thinking I'd been around for a lot longer than I had.

It always helped me make some time with girls who wouldn't have given me the time of day if they knew my real age. Like Carla, a senior in high school with perky breasts and nice, round hips. I got to kiss her and cop a feel in between some stacks of lockers after school, which was a big deal back in the early Sixties. Of course, a couple days later she heard I've been bragging and found out about my age so she smacked me all over the place, but by then it was too late; the whole school knew she'd made time with a freshman. But I learned something --"Don't Kiss and Tell," a very important lesson of trust and survival.

Now at 14, I was working. Not your normal paper route or making deliveries in a grocery store, no, it was working at the Fulton Fish Market. I'd got this job for myself – working for Mickey Flats. Flats was his nickname; seems everybody had one back then. The Fish Market was down in Lower Manhattan, not that far from where I lived, down almost under the Brooklyn Bridge and going from about nine pm to whenever, year round. It was this set of old buildings

14

facing the FDR overhead that seemed like they'd been there more than two hundred years. Fish would get brought in from all up and down the coast and dumped off by huge trucks dripping from ice. The streets would be packed with hundreds of strong-backed guys and heavy dollies, hand trucks and screaming forklifts shifting crate after crate after crate of seafood from here to there and back – hell, enough to feed the whole city for a week all in one night, it seemed like. You had to be really careful where you walked in that place because the cobblestone streets had this slimy layer of water and fish oil and crap, and fishy water filled potholes so that you never knew you were stepping into it till it was too late. Then you spent the night stinking of dead mackerel.

Vans and restaurant delivery trucks would park face to face on Peck Slip, a wide cobblestone street right off South Street, the main hub of the market. They would get loaded up by union guys with their dollies and hand trucks. Then they'd take their cargo off to restaurants all up and down the coast, sometimes even back to where the fish got caught in the first place...which didn't make sense to me. Why not just buy it in New Haven for New Haven restaurants, where it's fresher? I figured there was some kind of special thing about buying the food on your dinner plate in New York. Now I know it was just how things worked so everybody got a piece of the pie – including the made guys and their boys. Boys like Mickey.

Now, Mickey was hardly a boy; no, he was close to social security age, and looking every year of it, from the lines around his sleepy eyes to his broken hooked nose. He sort of shuffled along, like he couldn't pick his feet up all the way off the ground. He ran the parking scam in the market and had it for over 20 years, they tell me. You know the kind. Park here, pay me to watch your car. If you don't, who knows what might happen to it? Most of the drivers at Fulton Fish Market knew how it worked and always had a twenty ready for when Mickey'd glide up and say something like, "Hey, Frankie, how ya doin'?"

Of course, the guy'd always smile at him and say, "Good, Mickey, how's things?"

"The same ol' same ol'," Mickey'd say. "You know how it goes." Then he'd put out his hand to shake and they'd shift the note into his palm like he was a maitre d', and he'd add, "See ya later."

And the guy'd know his load would get protected while he was buying his fish order. Because Mickey, he was on record with a made guy so couldn't be touched. This was all just a cost of doing business; that was how things worked back then. My job, along with

15

about 6 to 8 other guys, was to keep an eye out for non-precinct patrol cars and give him a nod when things were clear. Every now and then a local patrol car would glide by, giving the idea that the cops were keeping a watch on the place, but that was just show; they were on the pad. The real muscle of the area was Mickey, and I was one of the guys who floated in and out. Now I got the job because even at my age I had some street smarts. I was never a tough guy, I mean I could handle myself but wasn't this bad guy that was feared like Tommy Red who was just an ox and tough as nails for a kid his age. I was able to get what was needed without violence most of the time, by talking, reasoning about the good and bad possibilities. For that -- a good talker, a lookout and a backup if anything went wrong -- I'd get twenty a shift, cash, and a weekly bonus, while Union guys got thirty-two, before taxes, to hump heavy boxes of fish around. It was easy to figure out which was better for me.

Of course, one of my plans was to take over for him when he got ready finally retire. Even then I was dreaming big...well, big for a kid who was Fourteen.

Now like I said, most of the drivers were regulars and knew the drill – but there was always somebody who didn't understand how things work. First time I saw it, I'd been working with Mickey for a week. This truck parked in the center of the street and the driver got out and headed straight for the market. I whistled at Mickey; he saw the guy and shuffled over, calling out, "Hey, bud, that's twenty to park here."

The driver was one of those big burly bastards who think because they got fists like hams they got control of the world. So he snapped, "This ain't no parking garage; take a hike." Then he headed on.

Mickey watched him go then motioned for me to keep watch for unknown cops before he nodded to a guy called Tommy Hooks. He was this monster Sicilian kid made of total beef with only half a forehead, standing over by a shed at the base of Peck Slip and South Street, a hook hanging from his shoulder. Hooks. "Tommy hooks" -- like I said, almost everybody had a nickname. He lived in the projects up the road and was way more brawn than brain...but that kind's good to have around.

He followed the driver around a corner and waved back with that big-assed hook, then started swinging it back and forth like he was just waiting for some reason to slip it into somebody's neck. One of the other kids – this older guy named Louie Eyes – told me Hooks is the

16

last person someone should ever mess with, you know I'm no genius but I had already figured that out.

Once Tommy'd taken up his post, two other guys approached the van and quickly jimmied its back door open. They loaded everything in the van onto two hand trucks and carted it away just before Mickey Flats slipped a knife into the van's right front tire. The tire quickly deflated and that is when I notice a patrol car from Manhattan South approaching and gave a two-tone whistle.

Mickey walked away to approach another truck as it arrived, his hand out, ignoring the patrol car as it passed. And they ignored him, too. Guess everybody knew what he was up to...and truth is it made the cops' jobs a lot easier.

A bit later, the Driver returned with a delivery guy wheeling some crates of fresh fish on ice, and he saw his truck standing wide open.

I heard him snarl, "So that's the way it is." But all he did was huff and have his shipment loaded in. He slammed the back closed and got behind the wheel, obviously irritated, but it wasn't till he started to drive away that he realized he had a flat tire. He bolted from the van yelling and wide eyed. He was angry and had fire in his eyes. Then he grabbed a tire iron and headed straight for Mickey.

Tommy was right at Mickey's side and I didn't even think about it; I ran over to show numbers so hopefully this guy was smart enough not to try anything, the other guys about two steps behind me. We were his backup, know what I mean?

It didn't take much to stop him cold; just Tommy hooks, flaunting his rusty hook and the others swarming around 6 of us in all, silently threatening him. Nobody even needed to touch him. While the driver was distracted, the two guys that got the first load returned and unloaded the shipment he'd just picked up; it was like a well-rehearsed off-Broadway Play.

Well, Mickey sort-of shuffle-strutted right into the guy face, us moving to let him pass like he was parting the Red Sea, Tommy at his side like a Siamese twin, swinging his hook, and Mickey said real sweet, "We got a problem?"

The Burly Driver glared at all of us – then silently dropped the tire iron and backed to his truck. That's when he saw his new delivery was gone too. He snarled at Mickey then stormed to the pay phone on the corner.

We just watched him, trying not to smirk. At least, that's how I let on. But inside I was spooked. This could have got really nasty,

17

especially with Tommy and his hook, and being that close to what threatened to cause a ton of trouble...well, I had to shove my hands in my pants to keep the other guys from seeing how bad they were shaking. But Mickey – I think he noticed, because he nudged me and handed me a cigarette and winked as he said, "You're a good kid." Then he lit the cig...and my shaking vanished into me feeling like, in that movie, "White Heat"; I was on top of the world.

A short while later, this patrol car rolled up and the cops got out to talk to the Burly Driver. This put me on edge. But something I learned later is, all they'd do is make a report; then they'd hand the guy a card for an all night tire shop...where Mickey got a piece of the jacked-up costs; then he'd split that and the swag just taken with all of us at the end of the week. So life was sweet in the market.

I kept it up for months, right into the summer. Had my own private lookout spot across the corner on Peck Slip. Even took up smoking, since that first cig had been so cool. And I got to where I really did think I'd take over when Mickey finally hung up his knife, 'cause I was way sharper than Tommy Hooks or Louie Eyes. Besides, I figured it'd be a decent living since Mickey was rumored to have a beachfront condo in Florida, and all without a ton of work behind it. Just take the money, cut in my handlers for their share, and live the life of Riley. Yeah, I had it all figured out.

Now I'd told my dad I was shaping the Market, getting work almost every night; that's how come I always had cash on me. Yeah, I lied to him. I had to. I'm not proud of that, but sometimes it's necessary to get ahead in the world. And since my grades were okay, he didn't say anything...till one of the guys at his weekly poker game mentioned he saw another incident with another driver and I was right in the middle of it. That's the problem with working in the streets – it's like being in a fish bowl, with everybody looking in. I still get that feeling, a lot, even fifty years later, like people're watching me, talking about me, making me feel...well...uneasy. Well that is another story; we'll get to that later.

'Course, I didn't find out about this till after dinner, that night. I was beat from being up till 4am working, the night before (it was my Thursday night to Friday morning), and having to deal with two drivers who had a problem understanding the rules of the street at the market. So my plan was to just work till Mickey cut the first group, and since the next day was Saturday, I could sleep in. But then dad said he wanted to talk to me.

18

So we went over to the living room and he sat in his chair and I sat on the couch as mom cleared the table. We didn't live fancy; just a two-bedroom, third floor walk-up with half a view of the Brooklyn Bridge and waterfront. The living and dining room were all in one space, the kitchen next to it, while the bedrooms and bathroom were opposite. All we had was simple furniture, the kind you find at the discount places. I mean, it worked for what it was needed for, no show; but that was my dad – honest and hard working. He worked for the same machine shop for thirty-five years and looking every day of it. Don't get me wrong – he raised two girls and me on what he made, and he had a lot to be proud of, but lots of cash wasn't part of his deal.

Mom's either. She just wanted us all to have a decent life, and saw to it we had some background in the church to give us a moral compass. She backed dad up in everything even as she kept the place looking neat and clean, and went to mass three times a week. Their whole aim was to have self-respect through hard work and sacrifice, like any good Catholic. Well, that limited kind of life wasn't part of my plan, that's for sure.

Anyway – dad. Well, he just sat there and looked at me, all hurt and stuff, and I'm wondering what I've done to bring this out of him till he finally said, "I am so disappointed in you."

BAM. Cut straight to the heart. "What you mean, dad?"

"I hear you're working for Mickey Maggioli."

"Who told you that?"

"Is it true?"

"C'mon, dad, if I was workin' for him – ."

"Pietro, don't lie to me."

Uh-oh. I could have a problem.

"So, you – you been checkin' 'round, huh?"

"Once I heard."

"He pays good money, dad."

"He'll be lucky if he lives to be sixty. He's already been beat to hell four times, hospitalized for weeks. He's got more broken bones than you got fingers and toes, and the Commission is looking into mob influence at the market. You think he'll be able to keep paying you when he's in jail? Or when you get into one of his scrapes and are declared JD? You want to start life out with a record?"

"Dad – it's just a job."

"Does he know you just turned fourteen?"

"Everybody knows me down here!"

19

"Peter, I don't want you working for him! I don't want you going that way."

"But – ."

"Listen, you want a job? I got a better one for you. An honest job, I won't need to worry about you getting mixed up in anything bad."

"Where?"

"Patty Oriano's pastry shop. He's getting busier and needs a kid to help out around the place, afternoons. Do deliveries."

"I thought his nephew was working there."

"What's his name is off to college, out of state, you'll work Six days a week till school starts up, he's closed Monday so that is your day off."

"He ain't gonna pay me what Mickey's payin' me."

"You won't get paid anything, Pietro, once I'm done talking to him. This way, you work full time during the summer and part time when school begins...so long as your grades're okay. That'll add some to your allowance, for when you really need it. It's that or nothin'."

Aw, that's it – hit me in the wallet, where it counts. But that was my dad. Most guys would get smacked upside the head a few times when they screwed up like this. Not my dad, he'd find a way to make you want to change course on your own. And he knew I had a sweet tooth, so Patty's shop was really tempting. Plus, I know girls like pastry and sweets. The selling point was I'd never have to worry about smelling of fish after a night at work. So from that point on, I had a steady job that summer, along with afternoons and weekends during the school year. That lasted till I graduated.

My dad thought this would be a nice, safe place for me to work. I mean, it's a pastry shop; what could ever happen there?

Well, let's just say...appearances ain't everything.

****

Now Patty's shop was a simple little joint just down the street from my place – glass top counter crushed against a wall to show off his baked goods, half of it refrigerated; a cash register by the door; a couple of different coffee making machines for cappuccino, demitasse or just regular coffee. There were booths and a few tables and chairs set around for people to sit in if they wanted; tile floor from a hundred years ago, some of it chipped; a small office in the back. The bakery ovens were downstairs, connected by a dumbwaiter and these rickety steps leading up through a door in the floor that was probably added fifty years ago.

Patty, he's this short, heavy, balding guy who always had smudges of flour on his face and hands, and did all his work in the morning, cooking everything fresh enough to smell like heaven. Then he'd close his shop at eight and go straight to bed. Six days a week.

Most days, soon as I was in the door Patty'd be on his stool reading the racing form like it's the Bible or a sexy novel or something. No wonder he needed a kid to take care of things and clean the place. One of his nephews that worked there told me he wouldn't touch a table if he could help it; that's what his helpers were for. That's why I'd always wind up having to clean every one of them when I arrived.

Not that it was really all that much. His early crowd was mainly people in a hurry -- coffee and whatever, to go -- but there would always be a few sitting. The afternoons were taken up by what he called the "tea crowd," that's ladies taking time out from their day and the kids and the cleaning and shopping to just sit and have a pot of tea or cup of coffee and some of Patty's killer biscotti. The shop was a hub for all in the neighborhood. Seemed like everybody knew each other; at least Patty did. He knew not only them, he seemed to know the whole family and what kind of work they did. Both men and women would confide in him he seemed to know everything about everybody. They'd waltz in with their hair brushed and faces done, their hands washed clean, and they'd sit at a table like queens. Then I'd bop over and take their order. Chat 'em up nice with little comments like, "Your hair looks good that way, Mrs. Fiorello," or "That's a pretty dress, Mrs. Memoli." And they'd laugh and blush and wave me off...and leave me a tip, too. I learned early to never ask questions, and that you can always find something nice to say about anybody, and it don't cost anything, and it is usually appreciated.

21

There seemed to be lots of things going on at the shop. Several guys would enter and exit many times during the day. Four guys would hand Patty an envelope, three times a day and there was another that Patty would hand him a slip of paper and almost every half hour. I never asked and always made like I didn't notice, but some time later I found out Patty would bet every race at the New York tracks every day and the envelopes he got was something called single action; he would place the envelopes in a drawer behind him, all without lifting an inch off that stool.

This'd go on till about 4:30, then before the kids came running in to get something for after dinner, Patty'd tell me to clean the tables, even if they were clean, and he'd stand up and pull all the envelopes out of the drawer and go into his office. It was this tiny room with a roll-top desk stuffed with papers and no place to put anything else. And he'd stay in there for about ten minutes.

When he was done, Patty'd come out, grab a white box I'd squared up and fill it with assorted goodies, and I would have to make my daily delivery to this Italian restaurant on worth street. This I would do every day, he would grab two arm-lengths of string from off this spool atop a shelf in the corner, wrap them around twice and tie them good. It was like a ritual, it was always in the exact same way. Then he'd say, "Peter my boy, it's ready."

And I'd always say back, "On my way."

Of course, every now and then, I'd have invited a girl over to have some pastries, so I'd set up a tray of cookies or Cannoli and I'd whisper, "Keep these aside, okay, Patty? I saved 'em for Maria." Or Anita or Rosa or whoever my crush of the moment was. "Just in case she comes in while I'm gone."

He'd shake his head and wave me on, and then I'd bolt from the shop. And a couple times I'd actually come back to find Maria or Anita or Rosa nibbling the pastries I'd put aside and sipping a glass of milk or some hot chocolate. And they'd smile at me and I'd grin back, like I was bringing home the bacon. Then I'd make sure they saw how hard I was working. For some reason girls like to think you're a good worker. What woman wants a guy that can't provide? That is what my cousin Fredo said, who is three years older than me and much more experienced. I was getting kisses from girls who were years ahead of me.

After a while I got to know the regulars, like almost every evening before six this one guy came in; always looking disheveled and smelling of booze, Patty would give him a small bag every evening and

I noticed the guy didn't pay daily he would pay his tab every other Thursday. I never asked but Patty eventually told me he was a cop named Vinnie La Rocco, a World War Two hero. In '43 he was involved with the invasion of Sicily and the next year was there to liberate Rome and as soon as he got stateside the NYPD was waiting since he took the test before he left for Europe. Poor guy still lived with his mother and had drinking and money problems.

Life was good for me at this time it was the summer of 1964 I was all of 16; Pumping Iron and looking good, feeling and thinking Jimmy Cagney. You know -- I was on top of the world. My bankroll was not as big as it could have been if I were still in the market but I was able to go out to the local clubs in the evening, meeting girls.

I talk about clubs, but back then going to a club was a social club usually run by a wise guy or one of his men. There was always a bar and a few tables with card games going on. If you went in the evening, you needed to be dressed. That meant pants sharply creased and a nice shirt in warm weather, and a suit when it was cooler, it was the unwritten code. No one sat down (we did not want to mess up the sharp crease in our pants) and it was customary when you walked into the club, you buy everybody at the bar a drink. Everybody did it; it was the thing to do. Now we had clubs in our neighborhood but going to the clubs on Mulberry St. -- that's where the girls were. Rumor was these girls would only go out with you if took out a shylock loan. Half their dads we either made guys or with somebody, so it wasn't easy to impress them. I went out with my friends a couple nights a week, but you can only play a part for so long and then it was back to reality and working at the shop.

Now on Thursdays the refrigerated display case glass would be cleaned in and out. A fresh batch of Cannoli cream placed inside with other specialties, topped with raspberries or drizzled with chocolate and kept cold till ready. That's the day Rizo'd come by and Patty'd stop reading the racing form and meet him practically at the door.

Rizo "The Ice Pick" Maniello worked with his dad delivering ice, years and years ago; now he's second in command to Big Joey, the Baker, AKA: boss of the neighborhood. Rizo, was the underboss and he was feared, and I heard a stone cold killer. He did what he wanted. You see, he liked gold chains around his neck and five-hundred dollar suits made special for him and slip-on shoes instead of those that tie, and when he handed Patty a stack of cash, he didn't care a bit who saw or paid attention. Now that wasn't really considered wrong so much as,

23

well...you know, when you're sort of a boss like Rizo, you can do no wrong in the eyes of your subordinates. That counts even when you're acting indiscrete. But...so long as nobody made an issue out of it, nobody cared.

Still, it rubbed Patty wrong. He'd pop the cash in an envelope and cover it by saying, "I'll make sure that electric bill is paid on time," or something off the wall like that.

Then Rizo'd help himself to a biscotti, Patty'd ask if he wanted a coffee or something and rush into the back room. Rizo'd would help himself again then turn and strut out the door. Every time, except if any of the ladies were exiting; then he'd hold it open for them, a smile on his face that was almost a leer. And never once, in all that time, did he say a word.

Then at about 4:15 Patty would ask me to box half a dozen pastries. "Assorted", he would always say. I would then bring the box in the back as instructed. Patty would later exit the back office and tie the boxes with the usual ritual. Just a little after 4:30 that day I would have two deliveries -- the usual one to the restaurant and one other. They were two different size boxes, the larger for the restaurant and the other was for.

Patty'd whisper "Pietro, the small box is for the Judge."

Calling me by my first name in Italian meant, "Don't rush, take it easy, be polite, and don't embarrass me."

So I'd reply, "I gabease."

He would tell me the same thing every week, like after the first time I couldn't remember or something.

"Very good," he'd reply, sagely. "And I mean it – be careful, especially when you're crossing the streets."

Now the first stop was Forlino's on Worth Street, drop off the box as usual and walk down to Centre Street. I would turn right on Centre Street walk a block and a half I would be in front of 100 Centre Street, the Criminal Courts Building. Walk in the front door and hop the elevator up to the twelfth floor. Now a days, it'd take forever to enter that building with security and all but back then the doors were wide open. On twelve, I'd walk down a nice, long, echo-filled corridor till I got to this room where a little sign read, Judge Darrow A. Lefkowitz.

It had a buzzer you had to push to be let in, like this was Fort Knox or something. And it's not like they ever checked to see who it was at the door. I'd just get buzzed in to find the Judge's secretary or receptionist or whatever she was called at a desk just inside. She's one

24

of those forty-something women with hair pulled back in a roll that's so tight it amazed me she could close her eyes, Cheap looking clothes kept frumpy, and no chin on her. Fredo said was probably hired by the judge's wife so he wouldn't want to mess around with her. She'd always look at me wary as I entered the room, her thin little mouth tight and uncertain, so I always made extra nice with her.

"Hello, Miss Weller," would be the first words out of my mouth. "I made it before 5 o'clock."

"Only just."

"You do something to your hair? It looks nice."

She'd sigh and shake her head as if she couldn't believe I said that, but then she'd let herself smile and motion to this Oak door to her right and say, "Go right in, Pedro. He's expecting you."

I never corrected her, that it was Pietro Italian not Spanish. . I think she did it on purpose And I'd still knock on the door. Then this authoritative voice would call, "Come in! Come in!"

Judge Lefkowitz was always on the phone, like he waited till he knew I was there to take a call or else was faking it. He'd be saying something like, "Bernie, the law is very specific," as he waved me closer then said, "Hold on," into the phone then covered it with his free hand to whisper, "Leave the box on the desk. The dollar's yours."

The buck was big and appreciated; I always got a five the first Tuesday of the month from Forlino's.

Now so far no big deal; right? Just the usual stuff you find in any small business that's doing what it takes to make a buck. And don't tell me this never happens in Dallas or Denver. No, what made this a big deal was, Thursdays was also the night Big Joey would come by. He's one of those guys my dad always told me to stay away from – a tall, slim, strutting cat who actually looked right in a five hundred-dollar sharkskin suit, even with this little moustache laying across his lip. Now I'd heard he got his nickname because he started out as a bread baker, but it actually turned out he was the one who's behind Patty's shop, the money, y'know, and (I heard) a couple of the better recipes for those Venetians – but the reputation he had? Whooh, don't let him get near you with a rolling pin if you and him had a beef. Now I only saw Joey a few times. I would go home at 6:30 every evening but it seems on a Thursday Big Joey would show up.

I did notice on Thursday nights before he'd come in, there were different people arriving at the shop, and I noticed one or two were there pretty often.

Summer passed into fall and school started. Every day except Mondays, I'd go to work right after school make my deliverers on time and work till about 6:30, again. Every day Vinnie La Rocco comes in and gets his take-out, but this one day he comes in and sits in a corner booth. I go over to take his order and he is joined by another guy, someone I have seen in the neighborhood -- Moretti. Also a Cop. A detective. He looked to be in his early 30's; Vinnie is a lot older. I gave Patty their check and left.

The next day when I returned, Patty handed me $2.00

"For me what is this about?"

"From last night Vinnie left it for you."

"Patty you sure that guy is a cop? He smells of vodka and looks, well, bad. Where does he work -- on the Bowery?

"He works in an office on Broom Street; he is in the rubber gun squad."

"Oh," is all I could say but I thought to myself "what the hell is the rubber gun squad?" I put the cash in my pocket and staring cleaning tables.

It was the same routine, day in and day out. I could not complain, after almost two years working there, leaving at 6:30 every evening. Thanksgiving had passed and Christmas lights were up all over.

One Thursday night, Patty asked me to stay late. He closed the shop at 6:30 and called the pizza shop for a couple of chicken cutlet heroes.

We chit-chatted some about general stuff – school, what are my plans how are things are going in general, how his other helpers didn't clean the tables as good as me...stuff. I didn't know why I was still there, because I had the feeling Big Joey really didn't like new people standing around while he does business, but I wasn't gonna gripe because I was getting extra for it. Then he said something that stuck with me.

"You're a good boy, ain't you, Pietro?"

I shrugged and didn't answer...mainly because my mouth was stuffed.

He smiled and patted the back of my head, "good and quiet." I thought so. Stay that way."

I wasn't sure what he was talking about till this big black Cadillac Coupe de Ville pulled up at 7:00, sharp.

It was a very dark night. The Christmas lights lit up the sidewalk and the street outside. Patty quickly walked to the front door

26

to unlock it then said, "Clean up, now, and be your best," and went into his office.

I cleared off the table and went behind the counter to start blocking boxes for the morning. Then this big brick of a guy opened the door and held it, and in walked Big Joey like he owned the place. Well, I guess he did. And I knew what was what; tonight was gonna be an important night and Patty had to stay out of it, while "good boys" that are quiet and don't run around telling tales get to help out. I wonder if I ever told Patty about getting smacked around by that girl, for kissing and telling.

I made myself focus on the box I was squaring as Big Joey walked to the rear booth and sat facing the door. Then his bodyguard, whose suit jacket had difficulty concealing what was under it, relocked the door and stood waiting by it, like a gatekeeper.

Nobody said a word, so I headed over and asked, "What can I get you?"

He looked at me with these eyes, swear to God, I could see the devil in 'em, and he said, "How long you work here?"

I shrugged. "Been with Patty almost two years"

"Pietro, right? Gabish Italiano?"

I nodded yes and said "Of course", in Italian.

He smiled and it changed his face into something human, then he said, "Be a good kid and bring me a coffee and Cannoli."

"Coffee for him, too?" I asked, motioning to the bodyguard.

"Later," he said, "but I like that you offered. Stunada (stupid) his nephew (looking at Patty's door) – you had to spell it all out for him. But you, you're a sharp kid, right?"

"Yes sir," I said. Then I went to get him his coffee and Cannoli.

That's when this guy came up to the door and the bodyguard let him in without a word. He was stocky and didn't look right in his suit, and his eyes were black with warning. I learned later his name was Dante and he was really Big Joey's main guy, straight from 116th Street. He was referred to as "Dante from Harlem."

He strutted over to Big Joey and I could just hear him say, "They're parkin'. The guy with him is that Mick or Pollock."

Big Joey nodded and finished his Cannoli, then motioned for more coffee. I got his cup and refilled it, then as I was setting it back on the table these two new guys appeared at the shop door. I mean really, I set Big Joey's cup on the table then I turned around to see the both of

27

them framed in the glass, like ghosts. It was Moretti; the other was Kowalski, that I learned later.

Kowalski was big, the size of a wrestler, had these ice-blue eyes that looked dead, and blondish hair. He carried a small cigar box with a red bow. Moretti had dark hair, was in better shape, and only a little smaller. Both wore very expensive suits, this was something I noticed because when you saw someone in a cheap suit you can tell. "Off the rack," is how Patty would put it. The bodyguard opened the door without a question, and they strolled in like they owned the joint.

Big Joey stood and smiled as they came up to him, offering the usual greetings all around, then he and Moretti embraced, exchanged a kiss on the cheek and they all sat down.

Now I knew of Moretti. Knew he'd grown up here in this neighborhood and that he's a New York City Police Detective. Got his gold shield sitting in an office; it was because of Big Joey's connections. Meaning Big Joey was not only his godfather but also his hook or Rabbi as I later learned connections were referred to. Having a Rabbi who knows the right people and pays them off to get things done with either money or favors. That just goes to prove – it's always been who you know, not so much what.

It didn't take a rocket scientist to figure that Kowalski was a cop, too.

It is one thing for people to come meet with Big Joey about favors they need done. Some stuff's just too much trouble for the cops to deal with, like some kid knocking up a guy's daughter and not wanting to marry her. Or one of the union guys getting a little carried away with adding on carrying charges for deliveries. Crap like that. But this, this was pretty heavy duty for a kid who's catching his first look at life's reality.

I must of froze or something, because Patty cleared his throat to remind me to go over to get their order. So I took a deep breath and walked up to the table, and as I got close, I overheard Moretti say, "...perfect is, we can get all you want."

Big Joey cast him a look and he shut up, then both he and Kowalski glared at me. Big Joey cleared his throat and they looked away, then he asked, "Coffee, gentlemen, anything? We got the best Cannoli in town, if I do say so myself." Then he laughed. I guess that recipe was his, too.

Both of them shook their heads no.

The Boss held up one finger and pointed down at his cup. I took it to refill it, then I headed back over, and as I got close they stopped talking. I went back behind the counter to keep squaring boxes.

"Get all that you want." What the hell could that even begin to mean? I don't care I didn't hear it. They did their whispering and nodding and stuff for another ten minutes, then all three men stood and hugged, and Dante walked Moretti and Kowalski out of the shop. Then I noticed Big Joey kept hold of the cigar box. He winked at me, said, "You are a good kid," and headed out with his boys, leaving behind a ten-dollar tip. I pocketed it and cleared off the table then Patty sent me home. And I never said a word to my folks.

But then, why would I? It'd already proven very profitable. Looked like my world was gonna be really interesting, after all.

But I gotta admit, I was thinking, "Way to go, dad; you got me out of the frying pan and into the fire."

****

Its funny how things work out. I became a cop mainly because it was the first city job to call...and because I took typing in high school. And I didn't just learn it; I was good at it. Damn good. I stuck with the pastry shop until I graduated, and when my dad insisted I take those civil service exams. I aced them, but it didn't look too promising. Didn't matter; I'd already lined up a job in a bank. They'd loved how I did a hundred-forty-five words a minute on their test with no mistakes, so hired me on the spot. Patty was cool about it; he had a grandson ready to kick me out the door the second he could and a niece who thought she could do a better job handling the tea-ladies, so it was off to a real job.

But what was this thing FICA taxes? Federal, State and City income taxes? This was like wise guys taking a piece of my pie.

Banking was OK. I got to wear a suit and tie. That was no problem because I had bought several. They were off the rack but my plan was to get a custom made one, real soon.

Seems I also had an honest face or something. At least, I did at the time. I got to handle hundreds of thousands in cash. Well I was bonded like all bank employees.

Anyway, at three pm sharp, the tellers would close down and start tallying the day's transactions. Once they were done, they'd bring all their cash to the head teller. It would be in a large envelope with the amount written on it. After she got all the cash, she would have a tally sheet and a canvas bag of cash. I would go to her cage, she would hand me first the cash then the tally sheet. And I'd carry it off.

Now the first time I did this...and saw how much was in there...well, I had this fantasy to walk out the door and catch a cab straight to the airport and hop the first plane to Las Vegas. But in reality I walked it down the spiral staircase to the vault, where I'd hand the tally sheet and the bag to the vault attendant, who would lock it away.

Some nights before going home I would stop at the shop just pick up some cookies for the house and shoot the breeze with Patty. Patty would ask about working in the bank and all and fill me on the latest. One night I was there till way past six and asked Patty.

"Is Vinnie still coming in?"

"Not anymore, he settled all his debts and left town"

"What do you mean? What about his old mother?"

30

"She passed when you were still working here and do you remember him settling his tab every two weeks?"

"Yeah."

"Well that was the vig he was paying Riz. He owed all over the neighborhood; he made a score paid everybody and left town."

"When was that?"

"Right after the holidays. He left last January almost a year and a half ago."

"January 65? Funny I saw him every day but when he was gone I never noticed for how long. About a year before I left? I never noticed."

"I know why. You can't remember, don't you?"

"No, I don't, so please tell me."

"Because of girls, that is why. You were always concentrating on them."

"Well I can understand can't you?

Vinnie was kind of a sad case, he reminded of that T/V show the Naked City and it opened with a statement "there are 8 million stories in the naked city" I guess this World War two hero was just another story.

I went home that night and just watched T/V thinking where life would lead me. I didn't think about it too long because Ronnie called and the next thing I knew I was out, having a drink at the Rizo's club. It's in the neighborhood, just a couple of blocks from the shop. Now Ronnie was on record with Rizo, who'd finally become a real earner and the heir apparent. You see, Rizo's club was Joey's club but he took it over when Big Joey got sent upstate. Now Ronnie was running a few things and doing well, and he looked it. He may've been the same age as me just a few months older, but everything about him was money. But then Ronnie'd always had this knack for looking smooth and with it, all the time, even the short time his stayed in school.

So I told him all about the job and how "I'm sorting out paperwork and writing figures in ledgers and answering the phones and making sure there are plenty of forms in the bins on the worktable. But with all that money around, I'm getting paid sixty-five a week. It's ridiculous. And what's worse is I'm bored like crazy."

He looked at me cock-eyed and said, "How long you been there?"

31

"What is it? Eight months or so," I said. "You want to know the highlight of my day? I get to carry down one-two-hundred gee's give or take a few grand – depending on day of the week.

"Maybe you could grab a bundle or two?"

"And when they come up short, they'd never suspect me. No, they'd just ship me up to Sing Sing. Get a twenty-year bit like Big Joey. Louisa wouldn't like that."

"Louisa? Hey, what's going on with you two?"

I shrugged. "We're talking about gettin' married."

"Don't kid like that! You're barely eighteen!"

"I love her. She loves me."

"Come on getting your rocks off ain't love."

"We're not doing that. It's just, well we have a lot in common."

"God bless the both of you." Then he patted me on the back and said. "How much are you really makin' there?"

"Told you, helps living with my folks. It's just; I wish things'd go faster. Me and Louisa, we don't want to get married till we can afford a house, and – ."

He cut me off with, "Y'know, Mickey Flat's is retirin'."

I grinned at remembering Mickey's little dance with the drivers down at the fish market. By this time, I knew all he had was a big old house in Staten Island, near the ferry and up a hill, but word still was that he had a great place in Florida too, right on the beach.

"Heard rumors," I said. "He did all right, looks like."

Ronnie leaned in and whispered, "I could see to it you get a good shot at the job."

That floored me. They'd actually let me take over for Mickey? "That's a big responsibility – a lot of cash to worry about. Let me ask you a question -- if I get it do I have to go be Petey Flats?"

"You making that kind of cash and being on record you can go be anything you want."

"Ronnie, I know you known me since we were little, but why me ? How do I get a shot at this?"

"Don't worry about anything right now," he shot back. "Listen, you know the drill and got a good name, no bad habits. Even Dante's got nothing bad to say about you, and he spits crap about everybody. And look at you, now – you're a banker, but you're broke." He thought that was funny so he laughed out loud. "Come on record. Two-hundred a week, that's to start, that's right to start, clear and with the swag...plenty extra on the side. You'll have your house in a year."

32

"Wow. I dunno...my dad – ."

"Listen," he sighed, cutting me off. "Mickey don't have much longer. He'll be 65 real soon and he wants to go to Florida. Let me put your name in the hat; I know you got the best shot, know what I mean? So think about it. But don't take too long. Could be any time now, and that half brain Tommy's got somebody pushing him for it."

"Tommy Hooks? His brains're in his feet." Ronnie gave me a shrug of agreement, so I said, "Yeah. Yeah. Let me think it over. Okay? When would I have to start?"

Ronnie looked at me for a long hard moment then said, "I might need your help tonight with something, all right? Means at your current pay rate three weeks pay, an' for just a couple hours." He said that last with a smirk. "200 tax free."

I eyed him. He wasn't gonna drop that kind of coin on me for walking his dog, that's for sure. But the money hopped on my shoulder and whispered in my needy ear, so I figured, Why not? I shrugged and nodded, in answer. He nodded back.

"Good. You see my new car, yet?"

"You got another car?"

"The red one it's just up the block to the left. Black vinyl roof. Take it home. Stay by the phone. If it works out I need you, I'll call by midnight. If I don't, I'll get the car, tomorrow."

What could I say? "I'll be waitin'."

The bar phone rang. Ronnie reached over and answered it. "Hello. Who's this? He'll be here. He said to come by."

Ronnie hung up and headed into a back room, and I could just see Rizo seated at a desk, inside.

And I could just hear Ronnie say, "I told him."

Rizo nodded and said, "Close up."

Ronnie came back out and clapped his hands. "Okay – good night everybody, clear out."

People got up and headed home. Ronnie motioned for me to wait till the club was empty, then he handed over the car keys.

"Stay right by the phone. I don't wanna bother your folks. And really, you don't hear from me by midnight? Hit the sack."

I nodded and headed out the door and crossed the street and the only red car with a black vinyl roof was a beautiful brand new 1966 GTO. First one I'd seen. Man, this was a killer piece of metal, with scoops on the hood, bucket seats, and automatic. I got in, slowly, like I was going to church, and breathed in that new car smell, then gave the beast a good looking over. It had power steering and brakes, AM-FM Stereo radio, cruise control.

I hit the ignition and the engine thrummed to life. Deep and ready, sounded like a 389 Tri-power. Whooh, that convinced me – he was doing real good. Thought he was blowing smoke when he started talking about getting his own place in one of the new high-rises going up, 'cause they won't be cheap. But now? What was I doing at a job that wouldn't even pay me enough to buy a second-hand shack in Hoboken?

Thing was, my dad was harsh on me even thinking about going on record. He'd worked hard his whole life and had a good reputation as an honest man, so had the kind of respect that's earned instead of comes from fear or need or greed. And he wanted that for me, too. Him and my mom and my sisters, they'd drilled it into me that I didn't need to go that way, even more after my time with Mickey. So if I took this step, it'd break all their hearts. Crush them. I was the only son, and all their dreams for me would be gone down a drain.

But then I thought about where we had to live my whole life – that third floor walk-up where you could hear the neighbors arguing and kids screaming as they played on the street or in the halls and no trees worth anything and no grass at all, except at the projects, and then you had to deal with all kinds of other stuff. Pipes knocking to keep you awake. Garbage trucks being your alarm clock at five am.

It was the same for my aunt and uncle up in Harlem, with Fredo. They couldn't afford to live anyplace else, so their whole world was built around retiring to Florida, with a little bungalow near the beach where they could slowly die as they watched the ocean. My cousin, Fredo, was doing his own thing to keep that from happening to him, and he'd been flashing nice wads, lately. Of course, I had my suspicions of what that was all about, but all that meant was, we just didn't talk about it.

What's funny is this was all an argument my head was having; my heart didn't enter into these thoughts at all. Not once. What Louisa might think didn't figure. I knew she'd back me up no matter what I did, and I wouldn't have to tell her everything that happened. I'd just have to be the kind of guy who can keep his own secrets. That wouldn't be a problem. My dad still thinks getting me on with Patty's was the perfect answer to keeping me away from Mickey's life. It was almost funny; here I was right back to that, as if I was meant to be there. As if it was written.

I dunno if I believe in fate. If you've got your life written out for you and no matter what you do, you wind up right where you're meant to be, even if you weren't planning to go there. But still, it seemed –

A new Chrysler Imperial sedan passed me and double-parked in front of the club, jolting me out of my thoughts. I put the GTO in gear and pulled up the street, going slow so I could watch in the side mirror...and I got a great view of this massive side of beef getting out from the rear seat, wearing a camelhair coat and shoes that gleamed in the light from the street lamps. I knew who he was straight off – Frankie Bats, one of those vicious guys that hits first and asks what you've done wrong after. He strutted around the Imperial as his bodyguard-driver got out, an even bigger side of beef who was probably a former boxer, the way his face looked all mashed up. He stopped and took in a deep breath, then Ronnie opened the club's door and the both of them strutted right in like they were royalty.

Frankie Bats, he was with that midtown crew. Who'd of expected him down around here? This did not bode well, especially it being so soon after Big Joey doing time on a case that their man in the courts couldn't preside over, so I drove off.

When I got home, the place was dark except for a light in the kitchen. I like it like that. Makes it easier to just sit in a chair by the phone and not think. I tried to be quiet as I got a beer from the fridge, but I still heard mom call from her bedroom, "Peter?"

"Yeah, mom. Sorry I woke you."

"Are you working, tomorrow?"

"Yeah. See you in the morning."

I sat in the chair, sipping from the beer, thinking, wondering what was going on at Rizo's club, right then. Because something about Frankie Bats coming-on-hard strut and the bodyguard breezing in and the fact the club closed half an hour early made me wary. Man, I could just see what was gonna happen.

Ronnie'd be all polite and lead the guys to the office door then motion for them to enter and return to the bar, letting Frankie and his Bodyguard strut right in, all full of themselves and sure they were in control.

Rizo'd be seated behind his desk and wouldn't get up to greet them. That would indicate weakness, and it was obvious their attitude meant nothing but trouble. Besides, Rizo never cared about standing on formality. So Frankie and his boy'd sit in a couple of chairs without being asked, to keep in control.

35

So – what would a guy like Frankie want that Rizo might have, now? Well, seeing as how Rizo and Dante'd both moved up the ranks to fill Big Joey's space, they also probably had his old contracts. And that meant only one thing.

"Here's the deal," Frankie'd say. "You got a judge on the pad. We want direct contact."

Of course, Rizo'd get just as hard right back at him. "Are you really botts (crazy) or just stupid? My people only deal with me."

"He'll deal with me if I approach him right.'

"Cut the shit, Frankie! We got everything set up, here. Don't ruin this thing we have with him. You need help with something; you go through me, like everybody else."

"And keep makin' you rich? Fuck that. You don't share, maybe nobody got him."

"You're not stupid, you're a fuckin' idiot," Rizo'd say, and then he'd bolt to his feet, pistol in hand, and shoot the bodyguard before he blew Frankie away. Bam, bam, bam, bam like that kid on the "Flintstones." Then calmly walk around the desk to shoot each man in the head just to make sure. I've been in that back room and noticed all the extra padding on the thick concrete walls. Nobody'd hear a thing. And even if they did, even if they knew exactly what was happening, they'd just shrug it off as business that's between those guys and nobody else.

Of course, all of this was just thoughts coming out of my head, because it'd be a major violation of good manners. You don't invite a rival over to talk business then scatter his brains all over the floor, not if you don't want to start a war.

Unless you got the okay from the boys up high, something like, "This guy, Frankie Bats, he's causing too much trouble. Thinks he's gonna tell us what to do." And Rizo'd been given the job because he was stone cold, like that ice he used to deliver as a kid.

Oh, man. That was not what I wanted to be thinking about. I kept sitting in the chair in the dark, watching the phone, a fresh beer bottle pressed to my temple. It was a quarter past eleven, and I was getting nervous.

What if that was what happened? What if this was what Ronnie was involved with and now I'm involved? He'd always been more of a hard-ass than me, a nose-to-nose kind of guy who wouldn't take anything off anybody. Me on the other hand...I felt why fight it if you can work around it? Yet here I was agreeing to back Ronnie and I guess Riz when I had no idea what I was getting involved with. Could I do this? Could I?

No question in my mind, if that was what went down Ronnie'd just saunter into the room, gun in hand as he looked over the damage.

"Get his car keys," Rizo'd say, "then the tarps."

Ronnie'd carefully dig into Frankie's pocket for the keys, trying to avoid the blood. He'd clean them off then go to the back of the office, pull on gloves, and get two old tarps.

I started on my third beer, still by the phone, not even beginning to feel a buzz. Twenty till. I'd have to come up with an explanation for all these empties in the morning, if this kept up.

Ronnie'd lay the tarps out on the floor, next to each body, then he and Rizo'd lift each guy onto a tarp and roll him up.

Then Ronnie'd stroll outside, get in the Frankie's Imperial, back it up and leave it running. He'd slip over to Rizo's Lincoln, parked in front, taking up two spaces, and move it forward, then return to Frankie's car back it up onto the sidewalk and parallel park it right in front of the door to the club. He'd head back into the club, then he and Rizo'd carry each tarp to the huge Imperial's trunk and –

The phone rang. I jolted and grabbed it halfway into the first ring and whispered, "Yeah?"

"Where'd you park?" Ronnie asked me.

"Front of the building, just down the block."

"Meet you there."

I looked at the time. It was ten to midnight.

A few minutes later, I was waiting in the GTO when Ronnie drove up in that Imperial. Its passenger window glided down and he leaned over to say, "Follow me."

Ronnie drove on. I followed.

We headed over the Brooklyn Bridge, grabbed the first exit and drove down to the Brooklyn waterfront, and I think I saw maybe five cars once we were across the river. We wound up in an area that was nothing but unused warehouses and docks and nonstop emptiness, but there was a great view of the Manhattan skyline across the river, with a couple of tugs towing barges.

Ronnie held out his hand to stop, so I did. He drove right to the water's edge, rolled all the windows down, shut the car off, left the keys in the ignition and got out. Then he walked back to the GTO, got in the passenger seat and we drove away.

37

As he removed his gloves, Ronnie said, "Did you know that from eleven-forty-five to, say, a quarter after twelve, no cops are workin'?"

"What do you mean?" I asked, knowing full well, but I wanted something to talk about instead of just driving, with nothing but my brain filling my head with more and more crap.

"I mean," he said, like he was weary with the world, "the guys that started at four o'clock are sittin' by the precinct waitin' for the new guys at midnight, and the midnight guys are gettin' coffee for at least 15 minutes."

Like the change in shift anywhere. "That – that's good to know."

"Devil's in the details," he sighed, gazed out a window.

I filled my head with images of the cops sitting in their patrol cars outside the station house looking at their watches waiting for the next shift to take over, while the midnight crew exits the station house with containers of coffee in their hands, talking about their day and what was going on and not even thinking about how easy they were making it for guys like Rizo.

I learned from Mickey just about anybody can be bought, and sometimes for a lot less than you'd think. He had twenty-year guys on the pad in his sector for nothing more than fifty a week. And it was just the guys who'd be on duty while he was handling the fish market, not even the whole station. When this one fresh new cop'd thought he'd shut Mickey down, he'd only wound up getting himself reassigned and bawled out by one of the sector's sergeants, who'd probably screamed something like, "We got enough crap to deal with in this town without going after some little shit who's not hurtin' nobody!"

Which was a lie, I'd heard stories of guys getting beat to within an inch of their life. But the image is all that really mattered. So Mickey'd kept on going and the guy who'd give a damn'd been kicked in the balls.

I was next to Mickey when he heard about the guy's fate and he'd shaken his head, sad. "Stupid kid," he'd said. "I'd of paid him a hundred a week, maybe one-fifty to shut up." Then he'd looked at me and smiled as he said, "It's the honest ones who make you pay what they're worth; all you gotta do is find out what it is. Never forget that."

It wasn't till my life crashed and burned I realized he wasn't talking about just money.

Anyway, we got to my folks' place and I double-parked, leaving the car running, then we both got out and met in front of the

GTO, its headlights giving Ronnie's eyes these spooky shadows. He shook my hand and palmed a couple of c-notes into it as he said, "That thing, it could be real soon. And remember, you'll be on record with Rizo."

"Right," I said.

"See you later."

"'Night," was all I could come out with.

Ronnie drove away. I watched after him then glanced around to see if anyone had seen us. Shadows moved. Wind whispered. I could hear traffic on the FDR. But nothing else was around. I steeled myself and headed into the apartment. And somehow, I don't know how, I was asleep the second my head hit the pillow, and I didn't think about what we'd done, again.

Well, not till about a week later, when the newspapers said GANG WAR bodies found in Bedford-Stuyvesant. With a typical "New York Post" headline – MOB RUB OUT! TWO BODIES FOUND IN CAR TRUNK. Beside it was a photo of Francesco (Frankie Bats) Batelli and his associate Carlo (Chuckie Squeaks) Reno.

My first thought was about the poor dude who though he scored the Imperial only to find Bats and company all bloody in it.

Except, they probably still had rings and gold chains on, and I'm sure they'd of had plenty of cash in their pockets. So maybe the guy, you know the one who scored the car, maybe he didn't spook; maybe he made himself a nice score, because nothing was said about jewelry or cash or –

The phone rang. I jumped.

"First City National Bank, Peter Buono speaking – may I help you?"

"Peter Buono!" then this laugh in Ronnie's voice. "It does have a nice ring but Pietro would sound better."

"Bank policy, Mr. Ronnie. May I be of some assistance?"

"Yes you certainly may, I'll take a hundred-thousand in hundreds and a hundred-thousand in twenties, thank you very much. Did you hear?"

"Hear? Hear what?"

"Mickey had a problem, last night," Ronnie said. "Got his arm broke."

"Oh, wow. How'd it happened?"

"Some jerk tried to crush his melon with a steel pipe. He blocked it with his arm, thank God. That thing could be real soon, now."

39

"Is he all right?"

"Yeah, he's doing fine. Listen up – tonight, I'm droppin' somethin' off in Staten Island. I could use your help. We'll be on the midnight ferry and back by two, the latest."

"Ronnie, I – I got work tomorrow." I waited for a response but nothing but silence. "Okay, but – but two's no problem."

"Good. Meet me at The Paris at eleven-forty."

I was at Peck Slip and South by 11:30, a cigarette lit up to help me wait. Back to my old haunts, and nothing'd changed. The fish market was still in full swing, trucks lining up on Peck Slip and loads of fish being hauled in and out. Paris Bar was open all night, it seemed, like it had been for near a hundred years. I could see the headlights flashing across the Brooklyn Bridge and the non-stop hum of cars on the FDR overpass. While waiting I noticed the piles of trash and the slickness of the cobble stone street. It was almost like I never stopped working there.

And there was Mickey, making his rounds, a sling holding his right arm, his left hand extended to collect the parking fee. There were extra guys on hand for back up, and Tommy Hooks seemed glued to him. Some job.

Louie Eyes was still there, too, we shared a smoke he talked about what happened.

"Mickey shouldn't even be out here," he snarled, after we'd done chit-chatting. "That fuckin' creep clipped his head, too."

"You saw it?"

"Naw, I was 'round the corner. But I remember him, from last week, when we did a number on his truck. He came back for Mickey. Walked up nice and casual"

"Jeez," was all I said.

"He oughta be home, gettin' better."

"Why isn't he?"

"Looks like the bosses don't want just anybody else handling all that cash and other responsibility."

Now I knew what my dad meant when he told me how there's no sick days or real future in it. I mean, it's one thing when you got your first job and you're working for a guy who's always got a wad on him that'd choke a horse. But then you catch onto the fact that most of that belongs to somebody else, and it also means being out all hours of the day or night, in the middle of nasty winter storms and blistering hot days, rain pouring down or sun burning you to a crisp. And it's always the same thing over and over and over, having to worry about some fresh cop or DA's assistant out to make a name for themselves while guys who never stepped out of an air conditioned office or car made demands that took nothing of your life into account. Not to even mention how many times Mickey'd been in and out of hospitals. Yeah, it looks all great and cool when you're fourteen; hell, you can handle the world, then. But now I just don't know, man. I could see that it'd be rough.

Ronnie drove up at 11:40, sharp, in a green van with a sign that read "Jimmy's Seafood." I hopped in and we drove away.

The Staten Island ferry's just a few blocks south, at Battery Park, so almost instantly he paid the fee and we were behind a bunch of cars and small trucks that were lined up to board. When it came time, after all the incoming cars disembarked the ferry workers began waving cars on. Ronnie pulled to one side to allow all the traffic behind him to get aboard first. He didn't enter till he was dead last, and he parked in the middle of the three lanes. So far he hadn't said one single solitary word.

The ferry finally pulled away and we got out of the van to go to the rear and watch lower Manhattan recede, its lights glistening. We were gliding past the Statue of Liberty, all bright and shining under her floodlights, when Ronnie breathed in deep and cried, "These midnight ferries – they're so romantic." Then he pinched my cheek.

I had to laugh, even though I was nervous as hell wondering what we were up to. "I – I was here on my prom night. Me and Louisa just stood here and watched the world drift away. She's talking about a house being affordable on Staten Island. I just laughed at her and said, 'Of course they are'."

"You know Mickey got a house there. Take his spot; buy his house"

"Yeah, it's that easy."

"Maybe you never know. By the way, on prom night did you get any?"

"Hey! No. We're waitin'."

"Yeah, they all say that." Then he leaned in close and smirked, "So – you still a virgin?"

"Shaddup!" I shoved him. He jostled me back, and things were easy, for a moment, until he grabbed me in a headlock and leaned in close and whispered, "Go open the back of the van." Then he let me go, still smiling, his voice still soft. "Get the dolly ready."

That took me by surprise. "What? Here?"

41

Ronnie surreptitiously unhooked the ferry's rope and slid the gate open.

Man, I didn't even think; I bolted to the back of the van, opened the door and removed a large flat dolly. There was a huge wooden box, inside, labeled "fresh fish". A couple of hooks just like Tommy used were placed on each side of the box. It took both of us slapping a hook into each side to pull it out. Water dripped from it like crazy. Ice was exposed through the cracks. We got the box onto the large dolly, and then Ronnie said, "I got it. Go sit."

I started for the van but stopped and turned around. I saw Ronnie adjust and shift and then run the box and dolly, both, straight off the back of the ferry. When the box hit the water, it broke apart. And I saw it. A body. Totally nude. Wrapped in chains with cement blocks attached. Then it all disappeared into the water. I quickly got into the passenger seat and in the side mirror I could see Ronnie calmly closed the gate and re-hooked the rope before he returned to the van and got behind the wheel.

"One less Scumbag to worry about," he muttered.

No question in my mind, it's gotta be the guy who went after Mickey. That was all I could think. Think about this poor son of a bitch that got ripped off and then wanted revenge but got himself killed.

I stared ahead and tried not to think about it, but I could just see it. Some dude probably ignored Mickey's demand for a parking fee, then got pissed off when he came back to find his van trashed or ripped off, then he waited till another day and walked up on Mickey from behind.

So I figure he was just beaten so badly by Mickey's guys, he died. Maybe Tommy's hooks had got him in a leg and cut open a vein or artery and he bled to death, and this is how they're keeping it under wraps.

Hell I could just see it. The guy clips Mickey and makes a run for it, Tommy in close pursuit. The guy tries to get into his getaway car Tommy swings his hook, gets him in the leg or back. It severs an artery they can't stop the bleeding or the screaming. Additional backup arrive in a van. They muffle the guy's screams and throw him into the back of the van. They punch and kick him as he bleeds out. There is no turning back, they bring him to one of Rizo's wholesale houses, clear everybody out put the body in empty fish box then fill the box with ice, just store it. The next day someone would then use an ice pick on the frozen body. This to puncture his lungs and other organs to ensure it would stay submerged. I can see Tommy enjoying it as he plunges the icepick into the torso over and over. After this is completed, the body would be wrapped in chains with a few cement blocks, then placed under the ice machine and refilled with ice. That evening load the box onto a van for deposit in the bay.

That jolted me back to the van. Thinking about this guy getting beat to death or bleeding out or both it was horrifying. Yeah, sometimes I get carried away in my thinking. But that had to be the way it went down.

Then I realized we were on our way back to Manhattan, and were passing the area where we'd dumped the body...and I had no idea what'd happened in the last hour. Talk about spooky.

I looked at the water, like I expected to see something, any indication of what we'd done, and of course, nothing showed in the endless whispering waves.

Well, I was part of it, now, and if that's how it's gonna go, that's how it's gonna go. It's too late for me to turn back. Looked to me like I was gonna take over for Mickey and have to find some way of getting his boys to protect me even better than they'd protected him.

So I started humming "Mack the Knife" – and Ronnie moaned.

"Will you stop with that fuckin' song?!" he said. "Shit, you been hummin' Bobby Darin for the last hour."

I didn't even realize I was humming.

"Sorry," I said. "I just liked it."

"It's gettin' on my nerves."

I nodded and didn't make another sound till he dropped me off. And don't think I hummed it since.

The next day was rough at work, but I made it through, barely. I didn't sleep a wink all night. I heard the trash collectors come by, the street cleaners and everything else, each in its own little melody, and finally got up when I heard dad shuffling around and had breakfast with him before he headed out. Then I got to the bank half an hour early and, of course, that day they put me at a desk. I kept thinking about the deuce I'd got from Ronnie, knowing that was three weeks pay it gave me power enough to not fall asleep. But the tellers noticed I wasn't making my usual flirty back-and-forth with them. One even felt my forehead and asked, "You feel feverish. You okay?"

Any other time I'd have leaned into her hand and played up how great it was, but this time I just shrugged and said, "Hard night. You know how it goes."

She swatted me, fighting off the giggles, and it took me a minute to figure out what she thought I meant something else. Then I blushed and she realized I hadn't so put her hand on my cheek and said, "Eat a good dinner and get plenty of sleep." Then she went back to work.

Yeah, sure, that's easier said than done.

I stopped and had a couple of drinks at the club Ronnie was all smiles and happy to see me, telling me things will be good soon. When I left I was wondering how I'm gonna explain to my mom about not having an appetite so I picked up some cookies at Patty's before going home. But soon as I got close to my door, I could smell her cooking and suddenly I was starving. I all but scrambled through the door, just floating on the aroma, and everything was just like it always is – dad sitting in an easy chair, watching television; mom cooking a killer dinner.

"Hi, Mom," I said. "Wow, it smells fantastic. What you make?"

She giggled and said, "Steak Pizziola."

"And I got the good bread." Then I bopped off to wash up.

And that was that for the next few months. I helped Ronnie out a few more times; how can I say no? But it was always done in a way so I'd never know what was really what. I started building up a nice little savings account as we waited for Mickey to finally say he'd had enough and was headed to Florida. The nice thing about having a steady girl is, you don't have to flash the cash to impress her, anymore, not when she's talking about starting a family up with you; then it's all about how much you can save for when after the ring is on the finger. So everything was copasetic – until this one night toward the end of October I came home from the bank, and it was brisk and smelled like snow, early for this time of year, and mom was cooking her Gnocchi. It was her special cold weather dish and I could eat my weight in it. But before I could do anything more than breathe it in, joyous at the aroma, she looked at me then cast a glance at dad...and a great big "uh-oh" froze in my brain.

"Pietro," he said, "we need to talk."

Double uh-oh.

I hesitated then went to him. He looked straight at me.

"It's your life and your decision," he said, "but – these late nights – what's going on?"

"Nothin'."

"Peter..."

"I – got offered Mickey Maggioli's job."

"Oh? I hear he almost got killed, couple months back."

"Broken arm's all."

"That what these late nights are?"

"Naw – this other stuff, it – it's just some things. Ronnie hooked me up, picking a little extra cash. Though I am thinking – I could do Mickey's job – for a little while."

"It won't be for just a little while. If you take that job you'll be 'with' that crew, you won't be your own man. You'll do as you're told, period."

That much, I already knew.

"Well – uh, you know – I've got this low-pay, dead-end bank job that I don't make enough to live on or get married or...or anything. What're my choices?"

He looked at me for a long moment then sighed.

"Everybody's got choices, you remember all those civil service tests I asked you to take?"

I'd put it out of my mind 'cause I did not hear about any list of any kind getting called.

Dad took a letter from his back pocket and handed it to me. I opened it, warily, and read it. It was all about the trainee program being set up by Mayor Lindsay – something that was supposed to get more Cops back on the streets. Trainees would do the clerical work that was now handled by uniforms, freeing them up, and then when we were twenty-one, we'd get our gun and shield. The new class will be sworn in November 6, Two weeks from the date of the letter. I gave it to dad to read and he smiled and nodded, proud.

"There. You see?"

"It's with the police department. It's the police trainee program. Your son'd be a flatfoot."

"Why not? You'll have health benefits vacation and sick leave. Not to mention retirement after twenty years."

"But, dad, I won't even be nineteen for months."

"And before you know it you'll be 21, son."

Thinking about that now a days makes me wonder why I was in such a hurry for those two plus years to pass. Now I wonder where the last 45 years have gone. Don't we all?

I sat down. The fact is, this was exactly what I'd wished for...except for it being in uniform and all that. But after what'd I've been involved with? Could I still do this? Would Ronnie and his people let me? I mean, would Rizo? Ronnie knows me since I was 5 and I know he trusts me but his bosses...could he vouch for me? But would that matter?

There is only one way to find out. I grabbed the phone, dialed, and waited for an answer. Someone picked up on the other end but didn't say anything.

Finally I said, "Hello is Ronnie there?"

Some guy I'd never heard before answered, "Who's this?"

"Who's THIS?" I shot back.

"Who's this!?"

"You tell me who's this, and then I tell you who this is."

"Huh? Uh. Hold on, I'll get him."

I began to pace, not deliberately, but my dad noticed it.

"Yeah," This was Ronnie's voice.

"Hey, can you teach guys how to answer the phone?"

"Like you do at the bank" he said.

"Yeah, that would be good. What's, what?"

"What's what with you?"

"Uh, a lot, a whole lot."

"Yeah?"

"Yeah." Okay, I gotta shoot straight. "Listen, I – uh, I just got an appointment letter for a city job, and, uh, my dad really thinks it's a great idea, so – so I gotta pass on that thing you offered."

Dead silence.

I started rattling, "So, thanks, Ronnie. I know it was your recommendation got it for me and I'm grateful and stuff. But I gotta take this city job, 'cause it's got a pension and it's steady and – and Mickey's life, it ain't what I want for my life, y'know, and – and I want to get married and I don't think Louisa would want me working nights, so much, know what I mean? So I – I'll talk to you. Okay? Okay?"

I could hear Ronnie sighing. Then he asked, "You still a good guy?"

"Yeah, Ronnie. Always. Nobody got anything to worry about; we go back a long time you can trust me on that."

Dad gave me a look that made me turn away from him.

"You sure?" Ronnie added.

I got offended. "Ronnie, c'mon, how long you known me?"

"Okay, do what you gotta do. What's the job?"

When I told him, he didn't say another word, just hung up. And we didn't talk to each other for a long time.

****

A few weeks later I was in the New Police Academy Gym with the entire class of 600 trainees newly appointed. Turned out it wasn't gonna be that easy a job to keep, after all. I had to go through training and prove I was fit and learn the rules and procedures a total of four months at the police academy, then probation for another six, all to be a trainee.

Now trainees weren't really cops. We were told we would go to academy just like probationary patrolman but instead of hitting the streets upon completion we would be stuck at a desk till they were twenty-one, and there was a midnight curfew while in the academy. Still, if you got good marks in class and in the gym and stayed out of trouble, the first day of the month after your twenty-first birthday, you'd get your tin and the rest of the training (meaning firearms).

Though I started the training when I was eighteen years seven months I would be nineteen when I finished the academy; which mean only a couple years behind a desk. At that point, I could choose the next step. Till then, I'd have plenty of time to scope out the life of a uniform.

The 600 trainees were separated into 20 different groups. They were called companies. Two of my classmates and were Marc and Lou – Marco Lampedusa and Louis Washington, couple of great guys and both off to be damn good cops. Marc had a hook and had no problem admitting it; he comes from a cop family – father, uncles, in-laws, brothers, sister, next-door neighbor, their dog, you name it. Talk about having your life laid out for you from day one. But you want to know the worst part of it was? He is exactly what you think an Italian-American guy ought to look like – all-knowing eyes, a smile that jumped out at you, solid muscle but not overdone. A baby face, Elvis-like with great teeth and hair. Of course, it was also great because I knew if we went out bird-chasing, even if all I got was the leftovers, that was just fine. When women go out sometimes there is a standout and he would always get the standout. Look, as much as I was committed to marring Louisa, it was getting harder and harder to keep things under control when we were together; I know most of "you guys" know what I mean?

There were times when Louisa and I were alone, I was ready to take our courtship to another level, but she would have no part it, and it became clear nothing would happen until after the wedding.

48

So from day one, I stuck to Marc like glue and, well, let's just say, around him I learned a few new facts of life...and, uh...I got a couple of misconceptions corrected in ways that made me sure I had NOT known what I was talking about, once upon a time.

Now Lou's a cool black dude from the South Bronx, which was turning into a war zone thanks to the drug epidemic. Anybody who could was getting the hell out, and his family was one of the first, though they only went as far as Yonkers. He was a cocky guy, with dark-skin and sharp eyes with a quiet smile. Looked more like a basketball player than anything else and was he quick on his feet.

I got to know a lot of other guys in the class, but Marc and Lou're the ones who stuck with me, even after they learned I was the youngest of everybody. Thanks to my looks nobody even thought about it the first month, but once they knew, it was "Junior" this and "Babycakes" that and crap. Not that I cared. It's just, this was treatment I expected from girls when they find out I'm not thirty and marriage material, yet. Girls seemed to like their guys to be a couple years older as well as look like they'll work hard for their family.

Looking back, I think the reason Louisa wound up sticking with me is because, even though we're the same age, she saw me busting my back at Patty's, the couple times she dropped by, and in that typing class.

I took it twice, you know. Junior AND senior years, because it got me more lip-to-lip action than working at Patty's ever did. Now while junior year's class was all just fun and girls – even though I proved to have "great dexterity," as Mrs. Samson put it – my senior year Louisa was in the class and it was lust AND love at first sight. She had great eyes, long black hair. A figure that looked just right in a miniskirt and flats. Never dressed for flash but always looking nice. And this perfume she wore was like flowers in a meadow after a rain. I asked her out the first day of class. She said no.

So I turned my attention to other girls who said yes, but I kept casting her little glances as we practiced.

It wasn't till homecoming that she even seemed to notice me, let alone pay any attention. But then she saw Mrs. Samson was always holding me up as an example of good typing and focus and stuff, so it seemed like I was really serious about this thing. Then one day she let me carry her books to her next class.

"Not many boys take typing," she said as we walked.

"My dad says it'll help me get a job with the city," I told her, being all sure of myself and catching a few envious eyes shot my way

49

by some of the other guys. "Get a steady check and a pension. I got plans. Don't wanna wind up in a machine shop or on the docks. Y'know, that's a very pretty dress."

She smiled, and all the other girls'd just vanished.

Anyway, the first day of training, we got this big gruff Sergeant addressing the class, almost like it's the military.

"Fill out all the information on the application," he snapped in the mike. "Then you work hard, stay out of trouble and I promise you – these four months will be over before you know it."

Marc nudged me and said, "Easier 'n high school."

"And we're getting a paycheck," Lou chimed in.

They were right about that. Granted, I wasn't making much more than I was working the bank, but for once I could see a path forward for me. What's even better is, while the folks at the bank weren't happy at my leaving, they weren't unhappy, either. The tellers gave me a party with cake and ice cream and a card with all their names, and even the manager of the bank came down from his office to wish me luck. They made me feel real good almost like I was important.

So here I was, the Monday after I left the bank I was starting my new career path, initiating steps towards the procedure...by learning procedure.

We broke into classes of thirty, each with an instructor lecturing us on how to handle suspects and evidence and what we can and can't do and the Miranda ruling (that was still getting a lot of grousing from the rank and file) and what you had to do to book somebody. One of the first lessons was to keep a daily account of everything we did, so we were issued memo books and it was drilled into us – that was our police department diary for when you check in, when you check out, who you talked to, who you didn't talk to, evidence you gathered, statements of defendants and so on.

The department had this really large book of rules and procedures; it is the department bible. It basically described how almost anything should be handled. If you ever heard the term, "Going by the book" – well, that was THE BOOK! Every day, we'd review a chapter, one after another, and in every other one it'd remind us, "Make entries in your memo book regarding everything you do while you were on duty, including taking personal time to use the restroom."

You didn't think I was kiddin', did you?

Mark, Lou and I got to be a little competitive, both in the classroom and the gym. We quickly found out we each got our abilities.

And we helped each other build on them and learn how to improve on them as well.

Now back then, we were just getting the basics down, like in self-defense. But we would work on different moves and we all seem to be able to help one another.

Thing is, we got to be a sold little trio, and would play three on three basketball with groups of other trainees. This was done on our free time usually before lunch -- I mean Meal Time. We beat almost all the other teams, thanks to Lou's shooting and Marc's defense. I was able to get a lot of rebounds by watching the trajectory of the missed shots. It was simple mathematics, even in basketball.

It was great, and the truth is, I never wanted my academy time to end. It was like getting paid to go to school, learn, meet good people, and have fun. But it did end, and when it did we all got different commands.

****

One never knows where life will lead. I mean, sure I was now going to be a cop, but how and why is the question. My first assignment was right there in the academy, in Personnel Investigations/ Seems they were "the department" going to hire several hundred school crossing guards. This was another decision by the Mayor's office to get cops back on patrol. Anyway, they all needed to be processed meaning fingerprinting, background checks, and plenty of typing for all those forms. I was almost sorry I added my typing skills to my application. Well, not almost; I am, because things would have been different very different. Have you ever thought about some of the things in your life that would have changed it you done something differently?

You see my typing skills put me on this path. I really did spend a full two years at a desk. We finished processing all the school crossing guards by July of 1967, just in time for the upcoming school year starting in September; once all the typing was done I was then transferred to Narcotics.

My second assignment at Old Slip – uh, the First Precinct station house about five blocks south of the Fulton Fish Market. Nestled on mainly the 3rd floor of this building was the division in the Police Department responsible for keeping drugs off the streets. It was just down the street from the fish Market...and don't you think I didn't think about the irony of that, lemme tell ya.

Now most guys who become cops would gripe and moan about this. They all want to wind up like Marc, who did a little bit of filing until he got this plum assignment up the chain in intelligence, all by the time he hit twenty-one, and all real hush-hush, meaning it was probably arranged by his grandfather. But c'mon, it's like that in any business or organization; you know people, you get in the door and looked at first instead of having to wait for your turn on the ladder.

Now me, I didn't care. I figured this would give me a chance to scope out the police department, get a better idea of who's what, where, how, and when. That can come in real handy when you need it. My bet was, it worked the same on this side of the aisle as the one I'd just come from.

And that's when God showed me he's got a crazy sense of humor.

My parent's apartment was just north of the fish market and the best way to get to Old Slip was to walk down South Street passing the heart of the Fish Market.

At 7:30 A M the Market was still very busy and even more of a mess. But this time instead of jeans and boots, I'm walking through in a suit and tie and my hair slicked back with a part in it. And nobody recognizes me. Seriously, Tommy Hooks strutted by without even a hint of awareness; his hooks now hung from each shoulder...and he was collecting the parking fees.

So Tommy Hooks got Mickey's spot, after all. Perfect. Several young guys were keeping watch for him; some I recognized from the neighborhood, some not. What could I do but shake my head? Life ain't never gonna change.

Now Old Slip's in one of those buildings that are big and grey and solid stone that've been used and abused for fifty-odd years, and look it. Wooden doors on the entrance that are about to fall off. Cracks in the steps with a tile floor leading up to an old wood front desk. The desk officer would man this he was in charge of everything going in and out of the station house. The desk was raised up and had a railing going from one end to the other. All Station houses were the same and my guess the railing was for drunks to hold themselves up while being booked in. What's crazy is, it's about two feet wide – well, forty-two feet, maybe – but it's the length of the block. It's just down the street from where I lived and even closer to the Market.

I was told to report at oh-eight-hundred on a Monday. As I said, I arrived in civvies – uh, street clothes – but with my uniform in a garment bag. It was already busy as hell with cops and complainants running all over the place. Real chaos but what struck me most was how authoritative the desk officer, a lieutenant, looked behind this desk that was a good five feet tall and when any one was behind it, it projected authority and control. I entered and approached and said with my deepest voice. "Good morning, Lou, Narcotics?"

He just growled, "Third floor," and nodded to these stairs that angled up and were about two people wide.

So...I started climbing. No elevator. People ahead of me and behind me and following me and heading down – it was like rush hour on Broadway.

Everything on the third floor struck me as a hundred years old – phones, typewriters, desks, chairs, lamps you name it, all of it held together by spit and prayers. At the third floor the choice was right into this one large room or left with a switchboard. Before I made the enie-

53

mini-mini-mo, choice, this thick, thirtyish year old sergeant came up to me, wired on coffee. He had a clipboard in his right hand a pen in the left and his revolver on his left hip. For the hell of it, I made note that he's a leftie – just one of those things to help me remember names with association, you know? Something else – when he talked, you heard him.

"Good morning," he blasted. "You gotta be Buono, welcome to the Bureau. I'm Sergeant Bruno."

"Yes sir" is about all I could say.

He grabbed my papers then eyed me, cold and hard as nails. "Sicilian, huh?"

"Yes, sir." Again.

"Are you on restricted duty or something?"

"Not twenty-one, yet, sir; I'm a trainee"

"No shit?" he snorted, looking me up one side and down the other. "Heard about that program. Cops must love you guys. C'mon."

He led me to the left.

"You'll be working with Detective Goldberg, this way." He was booming the whole way, "We're old school here – meaning you work hard, you get treated with respect. You don't? It's a kick in the pants. And I ain't being metaphoric in no way."

I wish I knew what that meant.

We walked past the switchboard out of some Edward G Robinson movie from the Thirties, where Darla, a kind of pretty girl, about my age, long hair in a pony-tail, dressed in the latest styles, was handling it. She was chewing gum as she worked, her pink nails the kind that were so sharp they could stab you dead with one grab. Boxes of papers were stacked about her room and I could swear I heard rats scurrying by. If she heard them, she didn't let on. I couldn't help but pop out with, "That ain't old school."

Bruno stopped and looked at me. "What's that?"

I put on my innocent face, the one I use at confession, and said, "Nothing, Sarge. I just thought cops man the switchboard."

"What makes you think they don't?" he boomed back at me.

Oh. I glanced over at Darla, and she snickered.

I shrugged and grinned.

"Buono, c'mon!" Bruno snarled then headed down a corridor.

I cast a wink over my shoulder at Darla, and she winked back, then I chased after Bruno.

The corridor was lined with small cubicles marked only as Unit #1 to Unit #7. The first one on the left had a bunch of high school

54

kids in it, smoking and muttering and working on homework, looked like. My first thought was they were in after-school detention. I later found out that was the undercover unit, most of them straight out of the academy and already working the schools to cut down on the drugs flowing in. Man, did they look good for it. The department was headed by this cool-looking, long-haired lieutenant named Roth, and it was turning into the quickest way to a gold shield.

Fact is, after being here for almost two years just before I went for firearms training, he called me in and asked me if I wanted to work undercover, which surprised me; I didn't look like I belonged in high school even when I was there.

"There's other assignments, Buono," Roth said. "All over the city."

I told him I was going to be married and needed to talk it over and I would let him know the next day, but Louisa wasn't too crazy about the idea from the start.

"I heard they have to go to nasty places and do things they normally wouldn't do," she said. "And they're gone from home for days and days, and I don't want us to start our marriage out like that, Peter. It'll be hard enough."

So I turned him down. Now I wonder if it might've saved me.

Anyway, back to my first day, and I'm still following Bruno and I'm muttering out loud, "Gonna need a map."

"It ain't that hard," Bruno snapped. "Most of this crap's just due to some dick thinkin' he could fit an office into a hallway, like some dumb shit. But walls are walls and they ain't gonna move just to make way for anything, not without a sledgehammer. C'mon."

We finally reached this back office on the left side was a wire doorway where you needed a key to enter. The sign above the door read: S.I.U. Inside it, a stairway headed up to the next floor, this back office had rows and rows of filing cabinets to one side; to the other were desks that might've been new when the building was first built but now were just ratty looking. A wire wall extended from the door down to the other wall, leaving just enough room for some benches and a cubicle with a phone.

Bruno led me over to this round, hairy, long-time civil-servant type who wore a white shirt, sleeves rolled up, wearing a tie. Man, this office was warm, and it was only 8:05 A M. His glasses were so thick, you'd think they were the bottoms of Coke bottles. He had this film of sweat on him that made you feel hot. Well, this was a hot city building; 99% of them at the time had no air conditioning. That is why civilian employees got summer hours, meaning you worked only a 7 hour day. On his desk were filing boxes lined up along one side with what looked like a hundred writing tablets filling each one. His typewriter was on a stand next to his chair.

Bruno knocked on the desk, even though the guy was already looking up at us. "Goldberg, I bring you your new assistant – Buono."

The guy barely reacted as he said, "You the typer guy? Your name Bruno too, are you related?" Bruno Smiled.

"Uh, yes, sir, to typing, and no, they are spelled and pronounced differently."

"And he's all yours, buddy," said Bruno as he clapped me on the back. "You can use him, abuse him, but don't confuse him." Then he added, with a smirk at me, "Welcome aboard," and headed off. Something about the way he said it told me he was a guy I wanted to have as little to do with as possible.

Goldberg just sighed. "Bruno didn't scare you with his old school bullshit, did he?"

"No, sir."

"Good. Stop the sir stuff; I'm not a boss, like Bruno, and I'm not old enough to be called that, yet." Then he rose and shook my hand. "Good morning, glad you're here." So let's get started here. Daily, every drug arrest in the five boroughs is recorded on this list. We type all the arrest information onto these three by five index cards."

He showed me one then led me over to the filing cabinets. Halfway there, this black detective appeared around the corner of one and said, "Joe, I was looking for information on an arrest a couple of weeks back."

Goldberg didn't miss a beat, just said, "Give us a day or two. It'll be there."

"Shit, it's been three weeks," the detective snapped as he turned to walk away.

Goldberg sighed and said, "C'mon, Jonas. I finally got fresh help. Buono, here." Then he looked at me. "Up here the guys always want everything yesterday."

Jonas cast me a quick nod and said, "Hope you can type." Then he stormed off.

Goldberg shrugged. "We're running a little behind."

He pulled out a drawer that was half full of index cards.

"Okay, cards go in here. This side, alphabetically. In that file drawer goes the stack of dupes, wrapped with these large rubber bands." He pointed to another cabinet, opposite the first one.

I nodded. So far, it didn't seem so bad; just more of what I'd got in Personnel Investigations. Goldberg led me over to a desk that made his look empty; it was so overflowing with paperwork. He reached into the "IN" basket and pulled out a yellow legal pad that was starting to go brittle with age. He turned it to the earliest date.

"Here you go, he said. "You'll now see every single drug arrest in the city, from a dime bag to fifty kilos. I mean we type everything, each one on its own card. I can't emphasize that enough."

I must've gasped because Goldberg chuckled.

"That's right – Even the French Connection bust. Fifty kilos of pure heroin. Five years ago still the biggest drug bust ever. The guys up there in S.I.U.," he said as he pointed to the wire door and stairs, "they are legends. Maybe someday you will be too."

"No kiddin'," I muttered as I set my things down. "So what do they do with all these drugs?"

"They get vouchered and stored at 400 Broome Street, Property Clerk's Office." Then he added with a shrug, "Like I said, we're kind of backed up."

"This is your desk now. It's up to you to make it neat."

Okay...that'd keep me busy till I was forty-five. I mean, it was a big desk, with an old wooden swivel chair and a rolling cart to its left, where the typewriter was set up. Very old school. I shrugged and settled in, checking that I all the supplies I needed – cards, carbon, erasers, pencils, pens, all at my fingertips. I ran a quick finger test on the typewriter since it looked like it was from the thirties, and it felt loose enough to work with but could use a good cleaning. I figured I'd do that, tomorrow, before I got to work. Then I set up the pad, slipped in a couple cards with carbons, and started typing.

Most of what I was working off of was pretty easy to read, just a couple notes I wasn't so sure about, so I put those aside till I was done with the pad and then asked Goldberg about them.

His answer? "Your best guess."

So I got back to it.

After a couple hours, Goldberg looked over at me, saw the stack of cards I had done and asked, "Are you really doing it right?"

"Check for yourself," I said.

He shuffled over and looked at a few cards and watched my fingers working the keys and chuckled. "You really are a typer guy. Where'd you learn that?"

"High school, took the class just to meet the girls, but for some reason it comes real easy to me. Got clocked at 145 words a minute. My teacher said I was the best she ever seen."

"No shit, took the class just to meet girls?"

"Hey, I was one of six guys in a class of twenty-five, and I'm still dating the prettiest one in there." And I kept typing the whole time I talked.

"So it worked?"

"Better than expected we're talking about getting married."

"Don't be stupid," Goldberg said. "Wait till you've had some life under your belt first." Then he returned to the filing cabinets. I didn't realize it at the time, but it was damn good advice...only it took hold of my heart in ways I didn't expect.

For the rest of the week, I just kept typing along; taking piles I'd completed to the file cabinet every hour or two so my fingers could have a break. And while the filing, itself, would only take half an hour or so, when cops came in to copy down info from the cards, they'd leave behind a real mess and I had to re-file those, as well. If this is what was confiscated, just how much drugs was reaching the streets and flooding the city? Not just the French Connection stuff; that bust was over 5 years ago back in 62. It's like New York was the distribution center of the world. Were we "New Yorkers" that stupid to get hooked on drugs? But to quote William Burroughs, "Junk is the ultimate product, the ultimate merchandise. No sales talk is necessary. The client will crawl through a sewer and beg to buy."

New York City has become drug user's capital of the world. Daily new stacks of notepads kept coming in, almost as fast as I polished off the old ones. And as fast as I was and as much I got through, I was still only down by about twenty percent when I ended my last pile on Friday.

Now I should point out, when I'm typing I don't pay attention to nothing unless you ask me a question direct. Goldberg didn't even have me answering the phone, once he saw how fast I was digging through the mess. "Just keep going, kid," he'd said as he grabbed a line.

Plus, it got to where it wouldn't surprise me to find a couple of detectives in the rows intently going through stacks of the files at all hours. Lots of guys'd come in here to cross-reference their case with someone else's, though usually they're in and out before I'm aware of anything, like ghosts. So when I did see some, I'd just ignore them and head for the file drawer.

But then one day, one of those detectives digging through the pile was Moretti, Big Joey's godson. I'd seen him a few too many times at Patty's not to remember him, even though he was stockier and with a crew-cut, now, instead of slicked back hair. He was with another beefy guy. They were stacking duplicates and taking notes.

I focused on my filing and kept my back to them, hoping he wouldn't recognize me. I'd put on a little weight thanks to sitting at a desk since leaving the Academy, and he hadn't shown up at Patty's my last year there; just his partner, Kowalski, a couple times with this other guy named Troiani, who I didn't know and who seemed kind of low-key for any kind of non-legal stuff.

But then I heard Goldberg shuffle up, saying, "Hey, Velasquez, Moretti – this is our new man, Buono."

Y'know, it was normal for Goldberg to introduce me as an equal but I was wishing he hadn't even got out from behind his desk.

I turned to look at Velasquez, casting the barest of glances at Moretti. "Velasquez, Moretti, how ya doing?"

Velasquez grinned and grabbed my hand, saying, "Great. So you're the fresh meat, just out of undercover?"

"Sort of, 'cause they found out I can type," I chuckled.

Usually I get taken for older, so I guess he figured I'd just came off an undercover detail. As a rule, you only get a six month to a year assignment; anything more'n that, there's too much chance you get made. That'd happened to a couple guys and things'd gotten messy (one even got the shit beat out of him), but the big reward was the gold shield, and I'd heard Marc got his already. He had very solid hook and his job in intelligence was a whole lot easier. I understand we was a full time student at Colombia, no kidding, dealing with un-American activities, hippies and anti war voices.

"Well, maybe you'll get this hairbag caught up," said Velasquez, fake-punching Goldberg in the gut. I didn't know what a hair bag was at the time. I found out later it was just a cop with a lot of time on the job and don't care much about anything except retiring.

Goldberg just said, "You may think you're joking, but he's moving things along."

Velasquez laughed and gave me a shoulder punch then headed off without offering a goodbye.

Moretti never said a thing, just nodded as they walked away; leaving the stack of index cards they were looking at on the desk. But I'd caught a glimpse of him eyeing them, like he wanted to hide them or put them back himself...and not to be nice; I could tell that from how hard is eyes were. I sighed and went over to put the stacks in order.

Something about those two didn't feel right. Dunno what, exactly – it's just that my gut was telling me, be careful here. Then I saw that several of the cards were in their own short, sloppy stack and dealt with large amounts of confiscated drugs, so I couldn't help but wonder – was this standard procedure? Looking at arrest information of drug collars that other cops made? Wait -- 5 years ago -- 1962 French Connection bust -- early 64, he was meeting with big Joey.

I cast a quick glance after them as they swaggered down the corridor to the switchboard door. And I remembered Moretti being the one who said, "We can get all you want," to Big Joey.

Y'know, I'd convinced myself that they were talking about cigars, back then. Cubans were really under embargo, still are, yet a lot of guys still wound up with them. They gave big Joey a box of cigars with a bow around it...or was the cigar box filled with something else? After this, no way in hell could I still accept that was the explanation. Still...would a cop really do what I halfway thought they were doing? I couldn't believe they would. No way.

Y'know, I did the right thing, meaning nothing. I wasn't even a cop yet and this really wasn't my business. And the truth of the matter was; I still wasn't really all that sure about what I was sort of thinking. I mean, there could be a hundred reasons for them to be digging through the files. This is how you did cross-referencing before they had computers and networks and servers and stuff. Then later I learned Velasquez was in Plain Clothes, everybody in and out of the department knew about Plain Clothes and their reputation – it was all about the buck, being on the pad and all and making scores.

Now I know it's a dumb thing to think, these days, but I really mean it – back then nobody wanted to believe that cops would SELL Drugs. They were still supposed to be the good guys, right? Sure some guys assigned to plain clothes were looking the other way for a couple hundred a week, but only on minor stuff, like gambling, policy, that is numbers game before the state took over it was big, sports and horse bookmaking; I didn't see anything wrong with it. Everybody makes a bet or two. Drugs, however, were a different story. There were hundreds of good guys fighting to keep that crap out of the city, and I just could not believe that any cop would turn on the rest of us like that. So I let it go and filed the cards away.

But looking back on it now, I can see how that was my first step down the road to hell.

60

****

Now nothing much really happened straight off. I worked in the same place for about a year and a half, typing like crazy, filing away other cops' messes and, with 200 plus cops assigned citywide to the Narcotics Bureau, working at getting (and then staying) caught up, and that's when I wasn't relieving the switchboard. I mean, the paperwork never stopped coming, so finally it got to where that's all I really thought about when I was at work. Part of the job was to refile all the index cards that close to about 30 different cops who I referred to as regulars left out. These regulars looked at the reports that I typed and filed almost weekly. I noticed when different groups or individuals were looking, they seemed to be in competition, something I did not understand till later.

I only saw Moretti come in a few more times while I was there, though Velasquez did appear, a couple times, with another Italian guy – a low-key type in glasses, kind of unorganized and uncertain, a big wedding band on his finger. I found out his name's Borodino and he lived on Staten Island. Since Louisa was pushing for us to think about a house there, I asked him about it. He just gave me this startled look and muttered something like, "It's okay. Quiet, easy to get around."

"So do you come by the ferry all the time?"

"No, the bridge."

"Whooh, the tolls – ."

"Still faster, and Willowbrook's right there." Then he split, leaving the stacks of cards in a neat stack on the table.

I was gonna follow him and say thanks, but him mentioning Willowbrook made me hesitate. That's that school for the handicapped kids that was getting such bad press, lately. I mentioned it to Goldberg and he told me, "He's got a little girl born with problems. Sometimes it messes with him, best to let him alone."

So I put his stacks back into the drawers, only barely noticing the ones he'd put aside were of massive heroin busts, because I was just picturing him headed home, driving across the Verrazano Bridge. Passing through low-key neighborhoods that had a lot of trees and pulling into his driveway then getting out of the car and entering his house to be greeted by his wife and daughter. She'd be in a wheelchair and excited to see her dad, her hands moving as she rocked. She was trying to speak but only a soft guttural sound came from her throat.

61

He'd kneel by her and hug her and ask, "How is Daddy's girl?" Then he'd kiss her and she'd try to return the kiss. He'd wheel her over to the table and feed her as he and his wife had dinner and talked in soft voices about their days. He seemed like that kind of guy.

I guess you never know what you're gonna get when it comes to having kids. That got me to thinking about me and Louisa, and made me wonder if I was right for that or ready or anything. So I asked dad about how he felt when he found out he was gonna be a father the first time, if he felt like he was ready.

He just shrugged and said, "When it happens, you'll be ready, whether you are or not."

But that was dad; just deal with life as it comes to you and everything will work out like it should. Its okay for him, I guess, but I couldn't keep my mind easy about it. I think I was lost in thinking about that when I was covering the switchboard during Darla's meal time, because when she came back, she had to nudge me to get me to let her take her place, again.

"Contemplating the cosmos?" she asked, smiling.

Instead of heading straight back to my desk, I leaned on the switchboard and sighed, "What's gonna happen when I get married?"

She smiled and said, "Didn't your daddy talk to you?"

I huffed a little as I said, "No, not really, would you explain it to me"

She giggled a little, and said, "We'll see"

That's when I noticed the smell of her cigarette mingled with this lavender soap or perfume she used, and I popped out with, "You ever think that smokin' will mess up the baby as it's forming inside you?"

She cast me half a glance. "Your smoking or hers?"

"Either. Both."

"I'm not having kids so it doesn't matter."

"Why not?"

"Don't want any."

"All women want kids," popped out of me faster then I could think to not say it. She looked straight at me, her eyes flashing.

"Maybe for the first ten minutes," she snapped. "Then they realize they have to take care of the little brat for the next eighteen years. I've done that. I'm not interested in ever doing it again."

"Darla, c'mon," I said. "What are you, 21? Who you been taking care of for 18 years? You adopted a kid or something?"

She rolled her eyes and sighed, "I'm twenty-three, and I have a seventeen year-old brother I've taken care of since I was 13. That was plenty."

"Sorry," I said, embarrassed. "I didn't mean to – ."

"Pete, shut up. Everybody else in the building knows about my life; you may as well, too. My mother worked nights as a nurse, so I cared for the kid. My father, last we heard he's in Colorado. That was nine years ago. Darrell's a smart kid. He's going to Yale, next year. There, story told."

"So he...he turned out okay, huh?"

"As good as he can, considering."

"Well, that's a comfort, when you think of what can go wrong and all that."

She cast me a gentle look. "Petey, baby, have you been listening to gossip about Borodino?"

"I heard about his little girl and – ."

"Yeah, he got a raw deal," she said, "but it doesn't happen that often."

I sort of grinned. "My dad says I over-think things, way too much. Comes from a crazy imagination, genetics, from mom's side he says."

"Just like a man -- blame his wife. But that's better than having no imagination at all."

"So you got something against men? What're your plans, once he's off to college?"

She hesitated then took a call before she responded. "I'm a cop; that's my job and got nothing against men."

"Don't you have a guy in your life?"

"Why you asking?"

"Proving a point or...well it's just, a pretty girl like you..."
She cast me a wary glance. "Now, Peter..."

"No, seriously, Darla. You're pretty. You're still young. You ought to be going out with guys, having fun. I mean, c'mon – Darrell's old enough to stay home alone, ain't he?"

She chuckled, and then answered another call. After she was done, she gave me a pleased look and said, "I'll think about that."

"Don't think about it," I said. "There are plenty of guys here who'd like to ask you out, if they thought you'd say yes."

"That, I'm not so sure about."

"Prove it to you. Come with me after work. There's this great little pastry shop, couple blocks away. Best Cannoli in town, bar none. We can sit and talk, and it'll give guys the idea its okay to ask you."

"Why don't they have the idea now?"

"You're pretty, Darla, but you're also kind of scary – with those nails."

She laughed and popped a hand up as a claw and hissed at me. I laughed back, and after work, we hopped over to Patty's.

Then hung out. Talked and listened and held her hand.

Then I walked her home. And found out Darrell was out with some buddies. So we went upstairs and one thing led to another.

Funny thing is I'm pretty damn sure she wanted me to make my move on her. We were talking about everything and anything then she said. "You're still a kid."

"A good kid," I sneered back, then smiled.

"Are you?" I leaned into her and kissed her, and I gave it everything I had. And the electricity passing through our lips was like fire on my soul. Then I whispered, "You tell me."

She didn't answer. She didn't need to.

Other cops noticed we talked and even left the office together sometimes, but gossip never got going about us. I think because everybody knew I was getting married. She told me the reason she worked switchboard was because she was on restricted duty. Some dude tried to rip her off during a drug buy and she had to defend herself and put one in the guy. Poor creep didn't make it.

We were discrete at the office, although it seemed when I was next to her at the switchboard I wanted to touch her. It was like I couldn't help myself I would touch her hand before she left for her break and again when she returned. It's not like I loved her. Don't get me wrong she was hot, but I was committed Louisa. I just liked being with her, really I think any guy would.

This kept up for over a year, until I was closing in on twenty-one. Meaning the first day of the month following my birthday, I'd get promoted. No more with the trainee stuff; it'd be Patrolman Buono. And the wedding was set for following June. Yes, a little more than year away, but Louisa and her mom wanted it to be perfect and all that, and I just said, "Fine," to whatever they wanted.

Anyway, a month short of my birthday, Darla and I met at Patty's and soon as I saw her, I knew something was up. As usual, she shot straight from the hip.

64

"Peter you know I really like you and the time we spend together."

"So do I. What are you saying?"

"You're getting made next month. Getting a new command."

"Yeah, so?"

"It's not only that but you will be getting married, too."

"But I ain't now and it's not like her and I do anything you know, like us."

"I don't want to see you any more like we have been. Besides Roth has been asking to let him know when I was ready for the streets again, I waited this long frankly because of you, thinking maybe, but this all isn't right you getting married and all."

I reached across the table and held her hand, she pulled away. "So why does that make a difference now?"

"Pete, you gotta know I like you, and what we have been doing is not right -- not to your wife to be, anyway."

"Are you getting all holy now?"

"Yes, it's just survival, back in the street for me means I need to focus. I cannot feel guilt about anything and STAY FOCUSED."

She smiled at me, her eyes sparkling with tears. "You're a good kid, Petey boy, real good."

Then she got up and left without touching her Cannoli or me. I ate it, thinking of her as Patty's niece refilled my cup. I felt calm and thought I was fine, but my hand was shaking. Weird thing to notice of course, that's when I also noticed Patty looking at me over his racing form. He just shook his head and his eyes went back to the ponies.

And here I thought he never paid attention to anything but that newspaper.

Now as much as I liked working with Goldberg, I was ready to get more serious, especially since I'd been solid and steady and kept my occasional concerns about the drugs files to myself. Anything I saw that didn't make sense just got filed away in my memo book, just like everything before, but with more details, just like we were told to do. I used it to keep track of the guys after seeing Moretti and Velasquez do their thing a second time, even though by then I knew any detective could dig through the files if they wanted to; that's how loose it was.

Not sure why those two guys set me wrong, because other cops'd come in and look at the files. I had no idea why but it never seemed like anything wasn't right. I just couldn't believe that this was the way things worked. Yeah, maybe I didn't know for sure how serious investigations went, yet, but that didn't mean my guts were wrong.

Then ten days before I got made, I found out my gut was solid gold.

It was like five minutes to four. Summer hours were only July and August. I finished typing up some info and set it in a stack of cards to file in the morning, then like always, I put the cover over my typewriter and headed for the exit.

Now you can't see my desk from the entrance door; the only thing that tells you somebody's back there is when I'm typing; then you can hear me down the block. When I'm filing, it's like the place is deserted if Goldberg's not around.

Well, I was heading past the cubicles when in the unit marked One, I heard soft, angry voices and noticed Moretti had backed Bruno into a corner and was jabbing a finger in his face...and Bruno was letting him. This other guy was with them, his back to the door but something about him was kind of familiar.

Again, normally it'd be no big deal – a couple cops talking with a boss, that's all. But there was some serious tension going on, here, and Moretti was acting like he owned Bruno...which was weird, because I'd never have thought Bruno could be owned by anybody, not with his attitude, but Moretti had power, connections and lots of it.

Bruno was never mean or bad, just never gave an inch. It was his way or no way. He and I got along okay, mainly because I reported to Goldberg and he just ignored Bruno's crap. But to see him standing there, letting a subordinate jam his finger in his face, it felt weird.

Then the third guy shifted and I saw it was Kowalski. I'd never seen him around here, before; in fact, I hadn't seen him since my last night at Patty's, when he met with Big Joey alone, and I still remembered how cold and calculating his eyes were.

I notice Kowalski was turning to look at the door, so I made myself keep moving...even as my mind raced.

Okay...Kowalski and Moretti? They were both with Big Joey and now probably Rizo's or Dante's? Talking down to Bruno? On top of everything else, right in the narcotics bureau's office? Before I was ten feet down the hall, my brain was going ninety to nothing.

And I mean it – I really had put that cigar box out of my head, but now I know I could not. Besides, with Big Joey...his business was his business and nobody else's; you learn to accept that early.

Now Moretti, with him I could sort of explain away as just looking into busts that might have something to do with a case he's

66

working on. Even on those occasions he was with Velasquez; yeah, I didn't know that guy, but I could figure they were partners in some sort of investigation...even as I wrote down every time one or the other of them was in the rows.

But joining all three of those guys and their background with Big Joey and the fact that drugs were way too easy to get on the street, I guess once someone makes an easy score, they want that easy money to keep coming. For example, Moretti only looked at big busts of heroin. And the rumor was that Dante, up in Harlem, he'd become the biggest horse supplier and was protected by Big Joey, even though he was still away.

The world was shifting; it used to be that stuff – if your "wise guys" got involved with it, it was considered bad form. You were shunned or much worse. Nowadays there was so much money to be made off drugs, money overcomes everything, and I was pretty sure that's how my cousin Fredo was making his cash.

Last time we were together, well a few years back, me, Mom and Dad were at Uncle Gio's and Aunt Mary's, up in East Harlem, for the Mount St. Carmel Feast. Uncle Gio's one of those guys who was a round little old man even when he was my age, while Aunt Mary resembled Mom so much, it's like they're twins. Fredo was their only son, this tall, skinny guy with long hair and a moustache. He was older than me by three years, and lots edgier. Anyway, we'd had a light dinner then some pastries I brought from Patty's shop, and then Fredo and I'd busted out to the feast while our folks played cards and talked.

Fredo was more like my big brother, not just a first cousin. And he was always telling me stuff – like the first time he got laid was with this black girl named Dolores, from Brazil; and how if you checked the phone booths as you went down the street, lots of them would have coins left in them from people who forgot to take their change away; and how he had this angle or that idea about how to make a million bucks before he was twenty-five, like by selling watches that looked like brands but were made in Japan. Of course, now I think half of them were balloons floating up into the sky, but at the time I looked up to him because he always had ideas. Always had a dream and something to say about them.

Jeez, you live your life always hoping for the best, no matter what. Like with my dad and mom and sisters wanting things to be better for me so I could make them better for my kids and on and on. But you can get so locked up in that, sometimes, you just don't see what's creeping up on you. All you could see was the moment, even as

67

it threatened to destroy the beauty of the neighborhood and the people in it.

The Mount St. Carmel Feast was that beauty in all its glory. It ran ten blocks down First Avenue, from 120th to 110th, block after block after block of festival lights strung overhead and thousands of people crowded under them, hopping rides on a tiny Ferris Wheel or roundabout; eating hot sausages sandwiches, zeppoli, and calzones; playing all the contest games; getting high on wine or beer or just life.

Fredo and I wandered through it all, eating zeppoli out of small paper bags, the powdered sugar covering our fingers and faces and following us like a mist. I couldn't have been happier or felt more alive. I'd graduated high school; I was working at that bank; Louisa and I were talking about getting married. It was all so great. Then Fredo nudged me and nodded up ahead.

"Hey, cuz," he murmured in this sing-song kind of voice he used, "Look at what's coming for you."

A couple of girls were walking towards us, all tight mini-skirts and long hair and Go-Go boots, with tits that looked like bazookas and hips that wouldn't quit. They walked past us, and Fredo turned to watch them.

"Ciao, bella! Belissima!" he called after them.

The girl wearing a one-piece dress flipped him off, and they kept on walking.

He laughed at me then called after them, "Stuck-up bitches. No respect."

I just shook my head and said, "Yeah, there's nothin' but attitude from most girls, these days. That's why I'm glad I got the one I got."

"Hey, they drop the attitude when you show 'em this – ." Then Fredo pulled out a wad of bills wrapped with a rubber band, and it looked like they were all C-notes.

I think my eyes popped out of my head. "Fredo, you crazy, carryin' that much?"

He pulled me close then showed me under the C-note was a bunch of smaller bills, mostly singles. "C note on top," he said, "they won't know; and if they do catch on – fuck 'em."

He and I looked at each other and burst into laughter, we continued on.

"Fredo," I said, "when you said show em this, I wasn't sure what you were gonna pull out."

Again we burst into laughter then we headed away from the festival and into an area of burned out buildings and junkies crouching or sitting right on the sidewalks, nodding out then snapping alert as they're about to fall. One or two eyed Fredo as he passed, and it didn't feel right, the way they looked at him – like they were hungry.

Then one got up and waylaid us and said, "Freddie, how ya doing? How's the feast? Can I – can I talk to you a minute?"

"Good, okay?" Fredo replied. "Listen, Lampy, I'm with my cousin. I'll see you 'round, later." Then he pushed past the guy.

"Naw, just a minute – c'mon, Freddy!"

I wasn't supposed to notice, but Fredo gave the guy a quick nasty motion to get lost, and he kept moving.

It felt weird so I carefully asked, "Fredo, what happened to this neighborhood?"

"Reality."

"I don't get ya."

He sighed and said, "Good jobs're leaving the city, cuz, but rents ain't going down. And there's a lot of money to be made with drugs."

I looked at Fredo and asked, "Cuz – that wad you're carrying – you're not workin' so – ."

Fredo cut me off by pinching his fingers and waving his hand in front of my face, snarling, "What the fuck – can't a guy save up a few bucks to show off to his kid cousin? What's a matter for you?"

"It's just – those junkies back there, they – ."

"Shit, cuz," he snapped, "I did a little work for a guy, okay? And forget those guys back there; they're scum. C'mon, let's grab a beer at the club. It's on me. Y'know, I can't let you spend a penny in my neighborhood."

He nodded to a social club on the corner of 116th and Pleasant Avenue, this old six-story building in red brick and white trim that looked kind of like a cake. I wasn't keen on having a beer on top all the sugar I'd eaten, but I nodded and shook the crap off my hands as we ran across the street, and I cast a quick glance back at the junkies, who kept watching Fredo, like they were waiting for him.

Now I liked this club; it was dark and quiet and real homey, with a round card table for playing Goulash (a kind of Bridge) and bankers and brokers in a corner. I could spend hours watching this game where a professional-looking guy in regular clothes acted as the bank and laid out seven bundles of cards. There'd always be six players sitting around him, and each guy'd choose one of the seven stacks, then

69

one by one they'd place their bets on their selected stacks. Bankers and brokers was like in every club in the city. The banker would pay $1.00 per hand to be the house. If a player got an ace with no tie he then would be able to be the banker, but you had to make sure you had the bankroll. I never played because a tie would lose to the banker. But it was fun to make mind bets to try to guess the best stack. Again, no rocket science involved.

There were lots of other men and women at the bar or at tables – some couples, some not – drinking and listening to Roselli, Connie Francis, Dean Martin and Sinatra (seemed like you needed to be Italian got get into this juke box) as they talked, giving off this low rolling murmur of voices to mingle with the melodies. The kind of noise that made you feel at home, know what I mean?

Now the minute we got our beers, this one guy hit three hands in a row, jumped up and cried, "There's no stopping me now! Janet!" He waved at the waitress then swung his finger in a large circular motion, pointing to everyone in the room to get their attention. "Give everybody...and I mean everybody, that's everybody...my regards. Then give us good-looking guys at this table a drink!"

The whole club laughed.

A little later, Fredo and I were sitting at a table, a few beers before us. We'd been talking about nothing and I was feeling really casual and was looking at the reflections in the bottle when I saw a couple guys enter. One waited by the door while the other guy headed for the back room. As he passed us, I saw who he was.

"Was that Big Joey's Dante?" I asked.

"Yeah," Fredo said, "He calls the shots 'round here, now."

"It's him you're doing stuff for?"

"No, one of his guys. He don't talk to nobody unless he has to. And it's just now an' then, what I do – nothin' big."

"You workin' for Dante's nothin' big?"

"I ain't workin' for Dante!" he snarled at me in a whisper. "I just help the guys out with stuff, sometimes. That's it. Nothin' big, cuz. It's just – stuff." I should not have had a problem. After all I did "just stuff" with Ronnie for Rizo, but I think his "just stuff" had to do with people shooting dope into their veins; is there a line to be drawn for JUST STUFF?

I didn't know what to say. What my gut was telling me was, none of this was right. It didn't help that a few minutes later, these three black cats entered, some real "brothers" in bright shirts, leather coats, tight pants and pointed toe boots, wearing pie hats and looking dumb as dirt and twice as mean, one carrying a large suitcase. Everybody in the club eyed them, wary – until Dante's man headed over to greet them; then business returned to normal. They headed into the back room, but before the door closed behind them, I saw Dante's man shake hands with what seemed like the main guy, like they were about to do some serious business.

Yeah, Fredo, "just stuff." I could almost picture what was what, even then.

Dante'd be sitting back at this large round table, out of sight from the door, drinking a small cup of espresso. He'd barely move as he asked, "Hey, how ya doin'? How's business?"

"Real good," the main black guy'd say. "Demand is up, so we'll need an extra key for next week."

"No problem – I have it here, waitin'."

The main guy's right-hand man'd set the suitcase on the table and open it. And it'd be filled with bundles of five, ten and twenty-dollar bills; all bound with rubber bands in stacks six inches high. Dante's man'd separate and count the stacks while another guy'd bring in kilo bundles through a back door.

I had to shake off my thoughts at that point or start freaking out. I eyed my cousin. How could I talk to him about that? I was eighteen years old; why would he listen to me? He's twenty-one. Knows more. He's always been smarter'n smart. How do you tell him he's headed for a heartless hell?

I never did. I just sipped my beer and let it go. Like I let everything go. I thought at the time I was just backing him up by staying quiet. Turned into a big mistake; not my last.

Back at Old Slip, I was almost down the passageway and about to pass the switchboard, the image of Bruno being ripped apart by Moretti seared in my brain, when I realized I'd stopped walking. And then in the reflection of the window behind the switchboard, I saw why. Kowalski was peeking out the office door to watch me. He almost seemed to recognize me. But then that'd be stupid to worry about. Moretti knew who I was and that I worked here, so he'd of told the guy I was from the neighborhood. But while he didn't seem to care, anymore, Kowalski...he struck me as the careful, paranoid type who wouldn't be easy about it.

And even at that distance, I could tell the look on his face was not happy.

I headed on down the stairs, making myself seem nonchalant. But my chest was tight and it was difficult to breathe. This was not a

71

good inventory. Moretti and Kowalski talking with Big Joey, telling him, "We can get all you want," that first night. Then in another meeting, right after Christmas just before New Year, I remember now those two entered the shop with four A&P shopping bags that Dante put in the office. After a short conversation, Big Joey stood up and embraced Moretti at that time. Patty told me to get the two large pastry boxes that were sitting in the display case and put them on the counter by the door; Moretti and Kowalski took them as they left.

Now I felt I knew what it was, exactly. Drugs that'd been confiscated (or part of them, anyway) were making their way back to Big Joey's old crew, to guys like Dante and maybe even Rizo for distribution on the streets of Harlem and the rest of the City.

No, wait, that couldn't be right. How could they get them from the property room? Only the cop involved in the bust could do that, and then only when he's headed in to testify. Unless they were many cops involved, money, money, money...

Oh, man – my first thought was, let me get out of here. But then I remembered how Italian Harlem was going, and how my cousin Fredo was heavy into it. And now it's even in my neighborhood, just up the street. I couldn't let this pass, too. Not anymore. But I didn't know how they were able to get the drugs out or what to do about it.

I'd already hit the lobby and was halfway out the door when it came to me -- that old time cop that worked in Property Clerks Office. He met with Moretti a short while before that. What the hell am I doing? Just get the out of here and forget everything.

I headed outside Old Slip and stopped at the front door, then pulled out a cigarette and searched for my lighter – and noticed in the reflection in a storefront window across the street that Kowalski was leaning out an upstairs window; watching looking was it for me?

I tightened up. I noticed a patrolman exiting the station house, smoking. I hesitated – then waylaid him.

"Hey, buddy," I called. "Can I bum a light?"

The patrolman stopped and said, "Sure. Here."

He let me fire my smoke up off his own. "Thanks."

The guy shrugged me off and headed on. I shot a quick glance at the window; Kowalski was gone.

I leaned against the building, shaken. That was not bright. I'd been about as obvious as I could be at knowing something wrong was going on, and that's why Kowalski was glaring after me. I now knew I had to be more careful next time I see something like this, here.

But it didn't happen, again, not in the ten days before I got reassigned to the Ninth Precinct.

****

Talk about old and crowded, with cops, criminals, and creeps all over, that was the Ninth. I arrived in plainclothes, again, my silver badge hanging from a chain around my neck, and stopped at the desk. You had to. Every station house had the exact same setup with a boss at the desk, either a Sergeant or a Lieutenant; he's the guy who's in command of things flowing in and out of the place. And they all have the exact same attitude – I'm in control and you're nothing.

"Patrolman Buono reportin' for duty, Sarge."

He just snapped out, "Roll call's in the back, all the way. Gimme your memo book."

I slid my book across the desk. He signed it, tossed back, and I headed down a hall to an office that had a sign taped to the door – Roll Call.

I saw the usual very unhappy, very rotund roll call man pacing up in front of the tiny, hot room. I folded a twenty in the palm of my right hand and extended it to greet him.

"I'm Buono," I said. "Just got transferred here from Old Slip." Had to say that "transferred" wanted him to think I had time on the Job and not a rookie.

"Good for you," he snarled, until I shook his hand and palmed the twenty off to him, like I was paying off a maitre'd. The guy barely nodded and pointed to a chair next to his desk.

"I'll give you a seat," he said. "You'll have to fill in for now. You looking to build an arrest record?"

"Exactly."

"I got two sectors – very active – all good guys," then his voice dropped and he added, "and you'll never get a fixer." A seat would mean working in a patrol car and a fixer is a stationary assignment, a foot post that you man for your full tour with very little break time.

"Great, can you put me in group eight?"

"Group eight? Sure. Why?

"Chart shows they have Thanksgiving and Christmas off."

"You married?"

"Gonna be, next June."

He looked at me for a long, quiet moment then shook his head and said, "Your funeral."

"Already, I like you."

74

"Just don't forget my birthday or Christmas."

"Your birthday – let me guess. Next month?"

"You're pretty smart for a cop. Welcome to the Ninth."

I grinned and sat in the chair.

I know what it looks like, but this really was the best way to get set up the way you want; I'd heard it from a few too many cops to just ignore it. Also heard things like that cops think the job is on the level; some guys did, but the smart ones knew different. Besides, that's the way the world works, always has. And truth was, I was happy to be there, especially since my paycheck just doubled and I wasn't getting my face rubbed in that crap in narcotics, any more.

But what'd dad once say to me? "Never assume anything, because all that does is make an 'ass' out of 'u' and 'me'." Well I was a real ass for thinking that I could get away from that stuff. Life's got this funny way of tracking you down and slapping you around just for the fun of it. And boy was it planning to have lots of fun with me...just not right away.

Now my first few months there, I built a reputation as a guy who could get along with anybody and never had a bad word about nobody. It was deliberate, believe me. The better people think of you, the easier it is to get your way. So I worked in with seasoned guys like Bill Castle, Chuck Hurrell, and Bernie Reese, who showed me the ropes...none of them thought the Job was on the level and used it -- the job - to better our income – but more on that later.

That rep is how I wound up in a patrol car with Bobby Minguzzi, another seasoned cop...by about six years. He's one of those guys who looks like an ex-marine and still works out like one, always in total control, all the time, and next to nothing to say. I got a hint he'd been to Viet Nam when it started going to hell, though nobody I talked to knew for certain; and he'd never talk about it. Well, whatever happened, it left him with this non-stop simmering anger just under this deliberately calm surface. I found out later that I was paired off with him because a couple of the other patrolmen wouldn't go near him. The roll call man said it was just till another guy could be transferred in, but I couldn't figure out why everyone was wary because he was fine with me. Of course, I never talked much either. I think he liked that.

The 9th was the East Village. We were in Sector Charlie -- Tompkins Square Park and everything east of the park and north to 14th St. That is where they'd had the main anti-war protests and now had junkies who didn't give a damn peddling everything you could imagine. We could be ten feet away, driving by in our RMP – that's a

75

Radio Motor Patrol car – and they'd pass dime bags and pills of a thousand colors back and forth without even a glance in our direction, all for a couple bucks. Right here is where it felt like the world was swirling down this drain-hole of evil, and it made you almost sad to see all the waste. We kept partnered up like that for months, no chit-chat, no nothing more than we had to say, until one day I caught a glimpse of what Bobby was all about.

Now back then, RMPs weren't air-conditioned and it was the first really hot day of the year. So we're driving around, me behind the wheel looking out though this filthy windshield, our uniforms sticky from sweat, trying to get as close to the river as we could in case there was a breeze, when this call came in.

"Ninth Precinct. Ten-thirty-two in progress. Fourth Street and Avenue D. Tasty Bread delivery truck."

We were at Avenue D and East Ninth, so Bobby grabbed the radio and replied, "Nine Charlie, ten-four."

"Nine Boy Central also responding," crackled over the radio and Nine Adam Central.

I hit the siren and sped south, and thirty seconds later we saw the truck, double-parked, the driver limping down the street yelling as a couple people on the sidewalk yelled at us and pointed after this guy running for the corner. Then Bobby noticed he had a pistol in his hand.

He laughed and jostled me, pointing at the guy and yelling, "There! There! There!"

I hit the gas as he grabbed the radio and called, "Nine Charlie Central. Perp moving west on Fourth Street, tan shirt, blue slacks. He is armed!"

I whipped the car down sixth going in the opposite direction of the one way street. Lights and siren helped whatever traffic there was just pulled to one side. I caught up to this guy who's maybe five-foot-five and a hundred and ten pounds, dripping wet, and he's hustling, and we're pacing him. He even looks right at us and keeps running straight, like he can get away that way. I passed him and pulled the car up across the sidewalk to block him, then Bobby and I jumped out, pistols at the ready and we took positions behind the car as I screamed, "Police! Drop the weapon!"

The guy skidded to a stop, like he'd just realized who and what we were, turned, and tried to bust into a building, but when he hit the door, his gun flew out of his hand and over him and clattered to the pavement and into the gutter.

76

Bobby smacked me, hard, and snarled, "Get the pistol before some asshole does!" Then he ran over to the perp, who was now trying another door.

I scrambled over to the gutter and grabbed it up just as some dude was sneaking over, and I gave him a serious Don't-even-think-it look. He straightened up and kept on walking, like he'd never meant to anything else.

Then I heard Bobby snarling behind me, "Cut it out, you fuckin' spic! Hands against the wall!"

I turned to see him knee the perp in the back, once, twice, three times as he yanked the guy's hands behind him and cuffed him. Then he slammed the guy against the door and down to the pavement and dropped his knee into the guy's back, again.

I heard some people cry out in horror, meaning they were witnessing it all, so I yelled, "I got the weapon! Bobby! I got it!"

He looked up at me, this crazy look in his eyes, and he was about to slam his fist into the guy, but then another patrol car roared up, startling him. I jumped over and backed him away, saying, "I got him, Bobby. I got him."

He just licked his lips and swallowed and stepped back as the other patrolmen ran up.

"What's the word?" one of them asked.

I laughed and said, "This dumb bastard hijacked a bread truck! Then he – he tripped on the steps, here." And I picked him up and sat him on the stoop, then squatted in front of him. He was gasping for air and his lip was bleeding, but I couldn't see any other visible damage, so I gave him a crooked grin and added, "Y'know, buddy, when they're talkin' about bread and dough, they ain't talkin' about that kind that comes from a bakery. Got it?"

The second cop laughed and said, "What d'ya expect from a stupid fuckin' spic?"

Without thinking, I shot over my shoulder, "Same stuff I'd expect from a Nigger or Mick or Pollack even a Wop. You know how it goes." Then I guided the guy to the back of our patrol car and set him inside.

The first cop joined me and touched the guy's side. He groaned and tried to sit up, but the cop said, "Keep bent over, take short breaths. Quick and short till the pain subsides." Then he shot a nasty glare at Bobby and looked at me, this tight expression on his face.

"The guy tripped," I said.

"You gonna hand me that bullshit?" he snarled, softly.

77

I shrugged.

"Okay, fine." The cop rose to his feet, motioning for me to join him. When I did he whispered to me, "Listen up. This is my sector at least a dozen people saw what really happened, and now they're looking at me and my partner with some kind of hate. The entire lower side sucks, but here in sector Adam we need the few good people left to watch our backs. We got it hard enough, out here. This kind of shit makes our jobs a hundred times harder. So try and keep your partner in line."

"He's got a lot more time than me," I whispered back.

"Maybe, but it's obvious you got the smarts."

Then he went back to his RMP and they drove off.

We took the guy back to the precinct in total silence. Then as we walked him in, Bobby said, "I gotta wash my hands."

"Go ahead," I said, "I got this."

He nodded and cast me a furtive glance then split.

I stopped in front of the desk and told the Desk Officer, "Assault, robbery, and gun possession."

It was a lieutenant on the desk so he looked down at the perp and asked, "Name?"

The perp didn't look up, just muttered, "Cruz."

He started to sink so I helped him keep standing and asked, "You got a first name, Mr. Cruz?"

"Juanito."

"John," said the lieutenant. "Okay, go up."

As we climbed up to the holding area, I asked him, "You need to see a medic?" He just sort of half-spit a laugh at me, so I put him in a holding pen then sat at an empty desk that had a typewriter and filled in the report. Then I hauled him out and fingerprinted him. I was all done before I saw Bobby, again.

Bobby didn't want the collar so I took it.

Anyway, we get to the arraignment court and Cruz goes in with the other perps and I sit in the first row with a bunch of other cops. There were other people filling up the rest of the courtroom, and the bridge man was calling out docket numbers and the names of the defendants – and it was all so typical.

Then the case was called. "People v. Cruz."

I pulled him up and stood him in front of the judge with this A.D.A. at my left who looked like he hadn't slept in two weeks, and a public defender on Cruz's right, all in a nice little line.

78

The A.D.A. muttered, "Officer, what date is good for a hearing? In the next three to five weeks?"

Oh, dammit, my wedding. We were going to Bermuda.

"Uh, five weeks is better," I said. "I'm gettin' married in a couple weeks."

"Congrats. Thirtieth okay?"

"Yeah, we're back on the twenty-eighth."

He told it to the judge, who nodded and said, "Bail is set...at fifty-thousand dollars."

And that was that. I exited the courtroom. And Bobby's actions never entered into it.

Now I know what you're thinking – Bobby was wrong. He beat the hell out of that guy for no real reason and it needed to be investigated and he needed therapy and all that, but it just plain is never that simple. I didn't see what happened between him and Cruz. Maybe the guy swung at him or kicked him in the nuts or something to set him off. Cops have to put up with all kinds of street-fighting and attitudes, and 99% of the time we don't do jack back. It's always that one guy who pushes the right buttons and gets knocked on his butt that paints us all as bad.

And just to emphasize it, next day, things were all nice and normal with Bobby, like he'd never gone nutso. I was driving us around, again, but this time he was sitting back, relaxed, and even started talking to me.

"Didn't you just get to the Ninth?"

I looked at him, surprised by the question, and said, "Not too long ago. Why?"

"You already got good vacation time and all kinds of days off," he said, cool and casual and not looking at me. "You never got a fixers. Who's your hook?"

I didn't realize anybody really was paying attention, so I said, "Just lucky, I guess. You're asking a lot of questions, today. What are you a cop, or something?"

"When it's hot like this, and quiet, if I don't talk I get...I get sleepy."

"Maybe you should get more sleep, at night."

"Wish I could."

I nodded. "Minguzzi – both your parents Italian?"

Bobby looked at me, frowning. "Yeah, why?"

"Only a true Paisano who's heard and seen will understand what I'm about to tell you."

79

Bobby nodded and moved a hand up and down with fingers pinched. He was almost smiling.

"So there's this guy, he's walking past a bar. Inside some men are enjoying the company of some very beautiful women. He tries to enter, but is stopped at the door. He is told to enter you must be Polish."

"Polish joke?"

"My soon-to-be mother-in-law's Polish. She told me it. Just listen up. So the guy says, 'I want in. How can I become Polish?' 'Simple,' he's told. 'You find a doctor and have him take out half your brain, then you're Polish'."

Bobby chuckled. "You recitin' sociology, physiology, history, or just the truth?"

"All of the above. C'mon, listen. Now, after the operation, the doctor comes in and tells the guy, 'I got some good news, and I got some bad news.' The guy says, 'Gimme the good news, first.' 'Okay,' says the doc. 'Everything's fine. The bad news is, instead of removing half your brain; we accidentally removed three-quarters of it.' And the guy responded, 'Maude orne'." And I smacked myself on the forehead with my right hand.

Bobby laughed a hardy laugh. For those of you who didn't get the story, he became Italian -- with three-fourths of his brain out, no longer Polish.

"Okay, that was funny, you're a good kid."

"You got no idea how good," I snickered.

"Yeah, I do," he said, suddenly serious. "Backing me up, like you did."

"And I got no idea what you mean."

He eyed me then nodded. "I think that's why I like being around you. Never with the questions. Quiet. That's the way I like it, quiet."

"Who doesn't?"

"Scum out there," he said, glaring out the window at some junkies on the sidewalk. "The more noise the better, for them. Makes it hard to focus on what kind of shit they're into. What's sad is, they got no idea what that shit means, or what they got themselves into."

"Yeah," I said.

"It's these neighborhoods – East village, East Harlem, South Bronx, Harlem, you gotta be strong or the environment'll overtake you."

I shrugged. He had no idea...unless he had a cousin or somebody like that who was going down the tubes over that crap.

It got me to thinking about Fredo, and suddenly I realized I hadn't seen him in nearly three years. Not since my Academy graduation party. We had it at this nice, bright Italian restaurant, with people from both sides of my folks' families filling the place to capacity. Fredo was there, and he was flying, while Aunt Mary was about to have a stroke, she was so angry.

Fredo still thought I had the job at the bank, so you know he had to be flying since the party was because I graduated from the Academy. The second he saw me, he bolted up, his eyes joyous...and wild, and said, "Whenever I need fifty large, I know where to go. Right?"

I'd laughed, but Louisa had glared at him, and a bit later, when we were cuddling off to ourselves, she'd asked, "What's he talking about?"

"What?" I asked her, honestly not remembering his comment.

"Is your cousin going to ask you to do something stupid, like give him money to buy drugs?"

"C'mon, he's joking around. Besides, he's family so I take him and his problem with a grain of salt.

"But with people like that, when it starts it never stops."

"It was just talk so let us forget about it."

"He's a stone junkie he looks so desperate."

"That's something he needs to deal with. He is killing my aunt and uncle, and it is all because he got that monkey on his back."

Even now, I could see him sitting at a small table in his room, with its walls painted black and rock posters tacked up and a black light glowing in a corner, thick curtains over his one window, working at cutting a one-ounce bag of heroin, mixing it with quinine then scooping the mixed product into small glassine envelopes and flipping each one into a cigar box on the table next to him.

Humming, he'd take some uncut drug, place it in a spoon and add a little water and use a lighter to cook it into a liquid. Then he'd tie his arm and smack his vein and draw the liquid into a hypodermic needle and inject it into himself – and drift into another world.

"What a shame, my poor Aunt," I muttered.

"What?" Bobby asked, and I jolted back to the RMP.

I jolted and said, "Nothing."

He just nodded and said, "Y'know, my wife and I are having a party, Saturday. Bring your girl."

81

I gave him an Italian head-bop and said, "My girl or my girl friend?"

He chuckled and gave me a light backhanded swat on the shoulder. "I wouldn't joke like that around any woman."

"Hey, I may be dumb but I ain't stupid."

"Tell that joke at the party. A few real grease balls will be there; let's see if they laugh."

And he sat up in the car, honestly relaxed, and everything was good for the rest of the week. In fact, Bobby was my partner right up to the end. It seems I didn't just help keep him even and cool; on the occasions where he did lose it, I minimized the damage. Our sergeant was so happy about that, I got anything I wanted without slipping anybody another twenty. And Bobby...he didn't complain about my hook, anymore, because what I got, we both got.

But damn, he scared me sometimes. When he'd get this glazed look in his eyes I wondered if he was close to forgetting whose side I was on. And yet I have to say, when all hell tore loose, he had my back. As best he could.

Maybe it was fate put us together. A couple guys who wound up as close as brothers, and not just because of the uniform but because we sensed something in each other that needed protection from the scum out there.

After all, who else is gonna protect you better than your brother?

****

So now the wedding was just around the corner, and Louisa and her mother had planned it down to the tiniest detail, like battle plans for D-Day or something. Which spooked me, I guess.

I mean my little fling with Darla, while we were together we felt we were helping each other, not just the physical stuff, but emotionally too, obviously, it'd opened up whole new worlds to me. Let me see just how much there was, once you just let go.

For instance, I like playing the ponies. I hadn't really understood how Patty could spend so many hours sitting there and working the odds on a horse...till he showed me it's almost like working a crossword puzzle, of course the crossword has one precise answer. There is no precise answer handicapping; they don't call it a horse race for nothing, but how happy you feel when it works out. So like I said, I got to placing bets, thanks to a couple runners I knew from Patty's. (A runner is someone who takes bets on horses, sports and even boxing and brings those bets to the central office of the bookmaker).

I also started joining up with Marc and Lou, now that I had more free time with Louisa being busy with the wedding and all. Marc's connection got us into spots nobody could get into without waiting in line for a couple hours. Same for parties; he always knew when a good one was coming up. The one deal was we could never tell anybody we were cops.

"Just say you're civil servants," he warned. "Don't want word to get around."

"So Marc what do you do?" I asked.

"I'm an aide to the Mayor's office. You got me?"

"I'll be a musician," Lou said, "I can play piano you know had lessons when I was a kid."

"You grew up in the south Bronx and had piano lessons?" Mark asked.

Before Lou could answer I said, "Was there was a special, piano lessons, track and field and judo all for one price?"

"Something like that." Lou said with a big smile.

"I'd like to hear you play, because you are pretty good at the other two." I said. Lou's smile got even bigger.

"I'll say I'm an aide to you, Marco, an aide to an aide. You are my boss. You are top aide and I am band aide." I said having some fun.

83

Marc laughed. "Petey, you're better off saying you're with the mob. Get out of those pressed slacks and knit shirts and sit down and relax once in a while."

"Not a bad idea. This way I can take my off duty piece out of the front of my underwear and put in on my hip."

He swatted me...smiled and said, "Get some jeans and button down shirts and let your hair go longer." I still slicked it back on the job, so I rinsed the crap out of it afterward.

So the first party we went to, I told this one long-haired girl in this flowing, flowery caftan that I'm with the DMV, her eyes rolled and she split on me. So after that, I told everybody I taught typing. Seemed teachers were okay enough to pass, and since I could back it up, nobody got any wiser.

Now the problem with a lot of these parties was, after about ten minutes they'd break out the illegal powders and pills. Then girls in hip-huggers that barely covered their asses with hair down to their crack'd drop acid and start swaying and moaning and all that. Guys dressed the same way with hair almost as long would get coked up and manic. Then they'd lose all inhibitions. Needless to say, I got kissed by both sexes on more than one occasion. I could handle it without saying anything, but then this one guy grabbed my butt. I responded by making a joke out of it but clearly letting him know I played for the other team. Marc liked the way I handled it for it turned out that guy was the host and I later learned Marc was trying to get some information from him, all hush, hush. If it went bad, Marc would've had to start from scratch.

So I walked and wound up at the bar with a blond goddess who was so high on something, I double checked, made sure she was a girl because she kept trying to grab my crouch. For a moment I thought I left the off-duty in there. She kissed me hard enough to draw blood then slipped her hand down my jeans; we went to an upstairs bedroom. Strange this lady was really built and had plenty of practice, but I was thinking of Darla. I liked that girl. Funny where life takes you, you know, the people you meet along the way and how certain things influence or change your life path any way. I reached out for Darla, the next day, but never got a call back.

I don't think anyone can say that certain things in their life would be different when other people come into your life. Going to these parties well...that's how I met Catherine. We were in an old brownstone just after Christmas, in the East 60s. Some banker named Adam celebrating some deal, and Marc knew the guy from Columbia.

84

The place was very upscale but you could see that thru the black light and fluorescent posters in hundred-dollar frames on the walls with pillows and incense and stuff. The usual people were there – self-satisfied intellectual-types reading eastern sayings, girls with flowers painted on their cheeks and Indian beads hiding their breasts, everybody with hair so long you couldn't tell him from her, half the time. Cigarette smoke and wine everywhere as sitar music alternated with The Doors and Jimi Hendrix. It descended into the usual chaos of pot and pills and punch spiked with God knows what and puking and screaming, so I grabbed a bottle of vino and headed for the roof.

It was cold and threatening to snow, but it felt clean and real. The lights of the city seemed to be looking down on me, as if they were asking, what the hell're you doing there? Other than trying to make lightning hit twice with some stoned chick and getting my rocks off. I just sort of shrugged at my own question and sipped some of the wine straight from the bottle.

I had just about decided to split and head home when I noticed someone sitting in a folding chair off to one side, hidden in this fur coat that surrounded her face and barely reached the top of these white boots.

She held up a glass and asked, "Is that white or red?"

I looked at the bottle for show. "Red. Want some?"

"Only if you're up for sharing."

I slipped over and filled her glass then took another sip.

She smiled and said, "Do you always drink wine like its beer?"

I shrugged and said, "Not always. Wasn't a glass around and thought I would be up here alone. Besides, it tastes just as good this way as that." And I nodded to her glass.

"May I try?" she asked, holding her hand out.

I handed the bottle over and she took a dainty sip, and I got a better look at her face now that it wasn't hidden so much by the coat. Her features were totally gorgeous, she looked like Connie Stevens with light blond hair and green eyes, and her lips were a soft pink, all I could say to myself was, Wow!

She handed the bottle back, saying, "Not bad. Not the same but close enough."

"Ah, you like to let wine breathe."

"Don't you think it adds to the flavor?"

I shrugged "Well I don't usually drink expensive wine."

"Honest, even humble. I like that; it's refreshing."

85

I wasn't sure where she was coming from, so I just held out my hand and said, "I'm Peter."

She took it and smiled. "Catherine. Why aren't you downstairs, Pete? Or do you prefer Peter?"

"Either, or if you like, you may call me Pietro, but any of the above is fine. Regarding downstairs I'm not in the mood for crazy, not tonight. You either, I'm guessing.

"I'm not fond of parties."

"Then why're you here?"

"Adam asked me to come."

"Friend of his?"

"Sister. Being supportive and all that."

"Oh." I took another sip of the wine then said, "Y'know, I used to work in a bank first job out high school. It never struck me as the kind of place that'd make the kind of money that'd warrant this kind of party."

"Adam's with a private investment bank. What do you do for a living, now?"

"I'm a cop," I said, the words popping before I could think. I cast a sideways glance. She was smiling.

"Then it's no surprise you don't want to be downstairs," she said. "The happenings must drive you mad."

"Some, not all." Then I cast another glance. "But you know there's a coffee shop around the corner, on Lexington. It's warmer than up here -- what do you say?"

She eyed me then stood up, and that coat whispered up legs that went all the way to last Thursday, ending at this tiny mini that was immediately swallowed up by the fur.

"Lead the way," I said.

I rose and found she was almost as tall as me. I glanced down at her legs. "You gonna be warm enough?"

"I'm wearing tights," she said then glided towards the door.

I followed and we spent a couple hours at the coffee shop, just talking. Like about when she went to high school and the year she graduated, and the same about college...and doing the math, I figured she was almost thirty. So I lied and said I'd graduated High School a couple years earlier than I did. Her job was with an ad agency on Madison, and her folks were in St. Bart's for Christmas. And Adam was the youngest but he was also the favored child, being male. All very Upper East Side.

We also talked about my family and me working at the Ninth, and I let her believe I'd been there for a couple years. So we discussed just about anything except my upcoming wedding. It wasn't a deliberate thing on my part; it just never came up and I didn't feel the need to make it an issue.

Then she told me I wasn't like anyone she knew or was used to being around. I was hoping that was a good thing, but when I took her home to another brownstone in another part of the Upper East Side, she left me at the entrance, giving me a peck on the cheek before she headed in. And it's a good thing she did, too, because if I'd gone in with her, I seriously think I'd have called the wedding off. I mean it, something about her; I guess it was the whole package, looks, intelligence the success in her career and life. I know Billy Joel hadn't written or sang "Uptown Girl", yet, but she was that girl. She was also way over my head so I tried to kick her out of my mind.

Help came a week later; when I went with Marc to a disco and this black girl whose breasts were as firm and round as melons, with a smile that could light the whole city up, allowed me shift my total focus on things at hand.

Then a week before the big event, I had this weird dream. I wasn't even in bed; I was catching a nap on the couch.

Anyway, in this dream, I was back in high school, and there were thirty female and six male students sitting at typewriters practicing their typing in perfect unison. Miss Samson was in front of the class in her old grey suit and her hair pulled back tight in a bun and those pointed glasses like you see on wicked witches, a sample typewriter keyboard hanging from hooks atop the blackboard behind her. Written across the board was, "You're a good boy" a hundred times, in my handwriting.

Then the bell rang and we all got up to exit. I lagged behind, my eyes on the teacher. She was looking back at me but looked at me oddly, like she might be afraid.

As I got closer I could see my reflection in the window and it wasn't me, or at least it didn't look like me...not me, then -- a high school Junior at 16 or so -- it might have been me today over sixty.

I woke up to Louisa shaking me, saying, "Dinner's ready."

Dreams are interesting, what did it mean? I guess I'll never know or do I? Was it that I would at least live this long.

I went into the bathroom to wash my hands...then washed my face and drank some water and looked at myself in the mirror, and to me I looked like I was forty, already, with a mortgage and a life laid out for me like a toll road, with the next exit only being death. Then I thought of something Marc'd told me last night, "There's too much fun going on in the world, right now. Nobody ought to get married till they're forty and worn out." And I thought, "This is crazy. I'm crazy."

What Marc said made sense. I was an idiot for getting married so young. But at the same time, I cared for Louisa, was it love. I know now after all this time it wasn't, but back then I was convinced it was. Even though there was no way she was letting me do anything more than kiss and make out before that ring was on her finger, and I hadn't felt strong enough about any other girl to get to that point, so I figured it was love.

So I had dinner and forgot all about that dream.

Then came the Friday before the wedding, and I was headed out of the precinct when Marc jumped me, screaming, "Bachelor party!"

Scared the hell out of me, so I snarled, "Jeez, Marc, give me some warnin"!"

Lou and Bobby and some other cops gathered around, jostling me, playfully, as Marc laughed, "You don't give warning for a kidnapping. Come on!"

We took two cars to Brooklyn, just a short ride once over the bridge to this joint that on the outside looked like a two-bit shot-and-a-glass bar, but once you got inside and upstairs, it had women who could be models for Playboy, they were so damned beautiful. I was a little embarrassed to be there, but after a couple of shots I was grinning and throwing streamers and letting Marc and Lou and Bobby buy me drinks. Even Bobby was so busy hooting and hollering at the titty dancers, he never slipped near moody or pissed off, and pretty soon I was way into "who cares" land, having women who looked like Julie Christie do lap dances for me and shove themselves in my face and be happy with just a buck in their g-string as tassels from their pasties swung around in circles.

Look, it's obvious I've never been a saint, but that night I proved I was anything but with my own Asian chick who had these perky little breasts and lips made for sin. She took me down this back hall that angled left and right and ended at a door that had a little bed and she shoved me on it and I pulled her down and held her in every way you can think and found she had muscles where I didn't think girls had muscles.

I have tried over the years to keep things in perspective; here it is 1970, me and my closest friends having a blast before my wedding

88

day, while other cops are stealing drugs from the property clerk's office. A few years later one investigative outfit said that all the drugs were taken between 1969 and late 1972. But hey, I did not know what Bruno meant when he said "metaphoric" and I am certainly no chemist, but The French Connection bust was 1962. The drugs were taken to a federal lab and then to Washington DC and returned back to the NYC Property clerk's office in early 1964. They were swapped less than a month after they were back at Property Clerk. Everybody knew everybody in "big Joey's neighborhood" and we're not talking Mr. Rodgers here. Would the drugs still be good in 1969 after 7 years? 400 Broome Street; was not air conditioned. But there were plenty of fans circulating the hot sticky air and even in the winter plenty of steam heat is it possible the drugs were still good? Remember vacuum sealing was not available until the middle 60's. Again I am not a professional about the life and potency of drugs, but 7 years in a hot room don't sound right. I feel the comment back in 1964, "We can get all you want," was about 50 kilos of pure heroin. The arresting officers according to The French Connection Files knew the drugs were hidden and shipped in the 1960 Buick. But drugs were recovered in a house in smaller amounts on different days; therefore having several different voucher numbers. According to the Log books at the Property Clerks Office they were signed out after 1969.

There was a lot of drugs signed out after 1969 and much, much more before that but the problem the investigators had was the log books prior to 69 were either missing or had pages removed. When I worked at the Narcotics office it seemed like cops looking at the files were in competition to see who could get the information first and now I know why. One Detective from SIU it appears removed a large amount and tried to peddle it, he was killed, even though the sloppy investigation into his death ruled his death a suicide; tell me who commits suicide by shooting themselves in the chest. I and many others think he had no idea he sold worthless powder to the mob, and that cost him his life.

So let's just say, I went into that wedding more than a little hung over. Was it the perfect setup for married life?

Now, the great thing about a Catholic wedding is, the groom just needs to show up. Stand up. And be able to say, "I do," at the right moment. Everything else is handled by the bride and her mom – and believe me, you don't want to be around them when that stuff is being sorted out.

So I got dumped back home by Marc and the guys at like noon, and the wedding's happening at four with the reception at seven. Hell, I didn't dare let myself sleep. So I sat in the tub for an hour, relaxing, then hopped in the shower...and all of a sudden I'm in my tux and I got half a bottle of Pepto in me as I stagger into the church, trying to remember who's my best man. It turned out to be Bobby. I should have remembered that.

Of course, he was almost as bad off as me. Man, when Aunt Mary saw us, she just shook her head and said, "You two're gonna turn the priest's hair white with your confessions, ain't you?"

I'd have snickered and said, "Yeah," but Bobby and I looked at each other and sighed, and then I looked at her with a straight face and said, "You know I'm a good boy." And I offered her a tight little smile.

She just shook her head and went into the church.

It was beautiful. I know this because of the pictures that were taken, and because my mom and dad and sisters were there all looking great and proud and happy...and because they told me it was.

I do remember Louisa coming down the aisle in a cloud of white, lead by six girls in satin and lace with groomsmen, none of whom I knew, escorting them. Then I basically blanked out and don't remember a thing till we were at the reception, greeting all the guests as they arrived and accepting their presents.

We were in the main banquet room, the "Queens Terrace", ribbons and streamers and balloons and flowers everywhere. It was packed with over two-hundred people.

Ronnie and Rizo popped up in the line, Rizo with this wife he married probably as a teenager, a woman who was still good-looking and on her way to having their 4th child, I think. I just remember smiling at the idea that even as a boss he was not like his old boss messing with a lot of other women, it was good to know Rizzo and she were still getting it on...which gave me hope for my married life.

Now Ronnie, he was with this goddess – tall, redheaded, curves where there ought to be curves, legs all the way to there, stuck to him like glue. Every guy in the room looked at her more than once, and the smirk on his face told me he knew they were...and he loved it.

He handed Louisa an envelope and she slipped it into a silk bag, then kisses and hugs were exchanged, and he said, "Bonna fortuna." To her.

To me, first he nodded, very carefully, and then he said, "Enjoy Bermuda. The beach is like nothing you've seen before. This you won't forget...like things you've already forgotten."

Rizo was right behind him, nodding his head, slowly.

Louisa cast me a confused frown, but I just smiled and nodded back to Ronnie, whispering, "Grazie."

Not far behind Rizo I noticed Aunt Mary and Uncle Joe having a quiet, vicious argument with Fredo, and to say he was strung out would be an understatement. He obviously wanted to come join the line and give us an envelope, but he was barely able to stand up straight and his folks weren't having any part of it. Aunt Mary even slapped him and turned him around so Uncle Joe could grab his arm and march him away. They gave me the envelope, later, and when I looked inside, I saw a bunch of street money, crumbled up fives and tens and a few twenties– Two hundred in all, some of it feeling pretty greasy and dirty. Gee. Not even four years from the last time we'd been together, at the Feast, and he'd gone from being straight to a hard core addict/dealer. I gave the card to my dad; he changed out the street money.

And finally, finally, we had gone through the rice shower and now were in a hotel room filled with flowers, fruit, and champagne, and I was seated on the bed, half undressed and still off my game, as Louisa, still in her wedding gown, rubbed my shoulders.

"Oh, God, that feels so good," I moaned.

"I should let you suffer, staying out all night."

"Guys wouldn't let me go."

"All right. The flight is noon. Get a wakeup call for 8 AM. While you're taking care of that, I am going to change."

She walked into the bathroom. I got on the phone using my shoulder to hold it and stripped to my shorts. Fell back on the bed. Bounced on it. Chuckled. Closed my eyes.

And I heard Louisa say, "Peter?"

I jolted up. Looked around, a bit lost. I'd fallen asleep. Then I noticed her standing at the foot of the bed, dressed in a beautiful negligee, her hair combed down, and her look – expectant.

God, she was beautiful. Finally seeing her without clothes to hide the fullness of her breasts and the curve of her hips and the elegance of her legs – it was like I'd been reborn.

I slowly rose and went to her, in awe.

"Are – are you glad we waited?" she whispered.

I was glad she'd made me wait. For her to look like this was amazing. I kissed her. Held her tight. Pulled her back to the bed. She

91

was a virgin and it was...well...not the best experience. For either of us. Blood seemed to be all over the bed. "It's okay. Momma told me this happens."

I still needed all my control to stay tender, hesitant, and slow, even as we got closer and closer to completion. But then we were done and lying next to each other and she was shaking.

"You okay?" I asked.

She just nodded, not looking at me.

I circled my arms around her and held her tight and drifted into sleep. And we barely made the plane.

It took me only two more nights to figure out that was going to be our love life. Tender, hesitant, and slow, with Louisa. It was different, good but different. Things kept up like that for nearly a year – me working my shifts, getting off, making extra cash on the side, and finally...well, finally finding something exciting on the side, too.

Like I told you, I ain't a saint. And working around girls who give me a lot of attention tosses way too much temptation in the way of a guy who likes to have fun, know what I mean?

But that's not an important part of the story. In fact, it's kind of tedious, right? Typical everyday suburban stuff – sex with the wife becomes same-old-same-old, hubby gets bored, screws his secretary or a cocktail waitress in his favorite bar, never tells wife. They've been telling that story since the beginning of time. And the fact that I'd become part of the cliché so easily was completely lost on me...but that's how life's little twists come at you, when you're lost in thinking everything's on a one-way track to nice, normal middle-class oblivion. And I would have followed that trail without a thought for the rest of my life.

Until reality came knocking at my door. The first knock came not six months after that article about Serpico, the one in "New York Magazine", hit and sent shock waves not just through the NYPD but the whole damn city. It was all laid out – cops on the pad, beatings, planting evidence, payoffs. It all blew up and Mayor Lindsay had to set up what became the Knapp Commission to look into police corruption.

Now while it got a lot of guys spitting and moaning about traitors in their midst, it actually relieved me. This could lead them to the problem I'd had concerning Moretti and Kowalski and Velasquez and such, all without me saying a word. So I kept an eye out to see if it'd work out that way, and for a while it looked like things actually might. But that's when reality decided to slap me down hard.

It was in the middle of summer, a hot day, again. Bobby and I were tooling around in our RMP and trying not to sweat away to nothing. The good thing was it was so warm nobody else felt like doing anything, so the day was going along nice and quiet.

Then mid-afternoon, not long before my shift was over, my Aunt Mary was headed home after work, bags of groceries in hand, when she found the door to their apartment open. She should've called the cops, right then, but she went in, calling, "Fredo? Fredo, you here?"

The place looked empty, untouched, so she went to Fredo's room...and found him sitting in his chair. Stiff and white. The needle still in his arm. She called my mother, in hysterics, and my mother called the precinct. They gave a call on the radio, telling us to use a land line and call the station house. Bobby called; we had no idea what it was about he returned from the phone booth he told me to call Aunt Mary. So I did, and in breaking sobs, she told me. I called it in to Central, still not really believing he was dead. I told them it was family so I was responding in my RMP and asked them to notify the two-five and Manhattan North's radio central. Then I raced straight there, Bobby on board the whole way.

Lights and siren blasting we made it from Lower Manhattan to East Harlem in less than ten minutes.

When I arrived, the first thing I had to do was tend to Aunt Mary, so I let her cry and didn't ask her anything, even though a thousand questions were running through my brain. The two-five squad got there a few minutes before me along with a couple of their uniforms. And they basically just stood around and looked at the body and around his room till the coroner's men showed up. By then, Aunt Mary was calmed down enough to where I could take a glance at Fredo, and it chilled me to the bone. His skin was so pasty. And while he'd always been thin, sitting there so cold and still looked like something out of a concentration camp. The needle hung from his right arm, like an obscenity, and the trail of holes marched up his veins from his fingers to the nook of his elbow.

For the first time in my life, I started to shake uncontrollably. I couldn't line up the idea of how my cousin looked when we were at the feast, strong and healthy, and this...this thing that claimed to have been him. Nothing about this was adding up right.

Then the coroner's men were about to move Fredo onto a gurney, and I realized the squad already had this down as a simple overdose and just like the guys from the Ninth, the Two-Five sees this all the time.

Without thinking, I slapped this one coroner guy's hands away and snarled, "Don't move him, yet!"

They looked at me like I was crazy then turned back to Fredo, so Bobby shoved them away, snarling, "He said, don't move him!"

I grabbed one of the detectives, this guy named Schreyer, and said, "Listen I know I'm just a guy on patrol but – but just take a look at this." I pointed to Fredo's neck and wrist. They had distinctive bruises, like he was manhandled or choked. "One other thing – the front door was unlocked. That door is always locked; my aunt told me she locked it when she left as she always does."

"Those could be anything," Schreyer said about the bruises, "even a few days old. And your aunt says nothing's missing. The apartment wasn't robbed."

"But Fredo had money," I shot back. "Is any of it still around?"

"Kid, listen, this is an O-D, that's all. And maybe he had money, once upon a time, but guys like this become their best customers. And I bet ya the coroner backs me up."

I had to let the coroner's men put Fredo's body on a gurney, drape a sheet over him and wheel him out. I noticed Uncle Gio was home, now, comforting Aunt Mary. And I shook even more.

Of course it looked like nothing was stolen. Just listening in, I heard there were only a few bucks found lying around and one bag of junk in Fredo's room. But he was always flush with cash, and with him dealing, he would've had much more smack; more'n one dime bag, that's for damn sure. It stank. It had to be something else, but the squad wanted no part of it, and I couldn't get them to change their minds.

On top of it, seeing my aunt and uncle sitting there, lost in this world of hurt and sadness and confusion, that's what pulled the whole drugs issue right back to me. And I know this is crazy, but suddenly I felt responsible for Fredo's death, in some weird way. Even more-so since I now knew that cops were helping keep that crap on the streets.

Thing is, I didn't have anything in the way of proof and I didn't want to run to I A D. But the hell of it is – I did nothing. Now that I was on patrol I just wasn't running into anything really suspicious. So as the saying goes out of sight out of mind. But the fact is, while most of the time I wound up focused on the here and now, there were times the rest of the crap in the world'd bubble up and dig deep into me – especially knowing what'd been pulled on Fredo. So as much as my world wanted me to let my cousin go, reality wouldn't let me. I kept seeing flashes of his body lying there, like quick photos in the back of my brain; and I'd see my aunt and uncle weeping over the death of their only child; and sometimes the funeral worked in; and other times, moments where he and I were at the feast filled my head; and mixed in it all were images of him at my wedding and how awful he looked. And through it all, I found I had less and less of an idea what to do about it.

That's not me. I was the guy who could always figure things out. Hell, I found all kinds of ways to make a little more cash, being a cop – take extra shifts for overtime at work, off-duty security jobs at concerts and sporting events – and I did all that. I also did things that people think aren't quite kosher. Like a certain deal concerning rental cars. Or Using the RMP to take store managers to the bank you know like the armored cars do today...while on patrol. The manager would gladly pay us so he would not get robbed, in a way we were preventing crime. When a City Marshal had an eviction, they would call central. We always took them. It would be worth a few bucks. That'd bring in a couple hundred a month and it made the difference between living okay and going bankrupt. And I'd tell myself that at least it wasn't like I was putting drugs back out on the street, like Kowalski and Moretti, and Borodino, the cop with the sick kid and who knows how many others?

Thing is, with him I could almost understand why Borodino'd do it. Word was the insurance was giving him a hard time over her. He wanted to keep her home with assistance paid for them; they wanted her institutionalized, which'd be cheaper for them. So they were refusing to pay his medical bills and he had to dig up the cash, himself. A guy gets into a situation like that, he'll do anything to try and get back in control.

But Kowalski and Moretti? Their only excuse was greed, with no moral reasoning. They liked to live big, and if that meant ruining lives and dismissing their oath, so what. With Dante and Ronnie and Rizo for them, I guess it was just business; and like somebody said somewhere, "I'm not sticking the needle in their arms." Well, I don't think that applied to the last time my cousin shot up.

The rule of the streets get as much as you can for as little cost to you as possible. "Don't matter if you ruin lives and destroy families." A more intense, more perverted version of what I was doing. But I guess its part of human nature; if you don't have to work for your living, why do it? (Though made guys would argue with you that they do work hard.)

So while I was trying to build up a nice little routine, again...thinking if I gave it enough time, I'd be fine and the world could work like it wanted to...I was really getting set up to get dragged back into the middle of everything, deep.

It was in the East Village on a nice cold day, one of those where you can smell winter in the air. I was riding shotgun as Bobby drove, and the area was looking even skankier than ever. Junked-up kids sitting on door stoops barely able to even sit up straight. Brothers and sisters with attitude and serious glares as we passed. Queers bouncing around and waving at us. Trash in the streets. It was like the city was falling apart, and every damn bit of it was reminding me of Fredo, that day.

Then this call came through. "Shots fired. Three-twelve East Tenth Street. Nine Boy responding – Nine David, Central."

I grabbed the radio, "Nine Charlie, Central," as Bobby slammed on the gas and we roared down the street, siren BLASTING.

Other police cars screamed across a street, just ahead. Something big, looked like.

We swerved around the corner and skidded to a halt near an empty lot. This chunky Latino man sat on the ground, leaning against the open door of a Mustang convertible done up in florescent paint, gunshot wounds to his shoulder and leg. Bobby, me, and four other cops carefully exited our cars, guns in hand. One of the guys from the other car, Smithy, squatted beside the man and said, "Do you know who did this?"

The guy pointed to Avenue C. "It was Loco! The motherfucker went that way!"

A couple of cops took off running in that direction.

"Hey, HEY! Buddy! What is your name?" Smithy yelled.

The guy looked at him like he was drunk. "Soto. Carlos."

"Okay, Carlos, we got an ambulance on the way. Are you hit anyplace else besides what I can see?"

"Naw, man...stupid bitch. Stupid fuckin' bitch is with him."

"He's got a girl with him," I said as Bobby and I jumped in our RMP. "C'mon!"

"You know what Loco looks like?" Bobby cried at me as he slammed it into drive.

"Yeah. Skinny, wild hair, eyes as big as his mouth," I said as we zoomed around the corner. "You remember him!"

He'd been busted a few months back, when he was caught with another kid I knew, burglarizing a store. Bobby and I happened to arrive as backup to the responding unit, and I'd recognized the kid as a cousin of Ronnie's. I'd seen him around the club a few times and he seemed like nothing but a typical screwball out to cause a little trouble for some fun. But that night, sitting there on the ground, his legs crossed and his hands cuffed behind him, I noticed his hair was a mess, his t-shirt was torn up, his jeans weren't even buttoned all the way, and his eyes were glassy, like he was strung out. It didn't sit right, so I found out who was catching – this guy named Billy, a knock around cop. I waved him over to the side. (Catching is who is making the arrest or in charge of the case.)

"What you got on that one?" I asked, pointing at the kid.

"He's Loco's mule," Billy said back. "Here to help carry shit off. Probably up to his eyeballs in what he owes."

"Okay, listen – I know this kid. He's a screw-up, but I need a favor from you. One that I won't forget."

"Like what?"

"Let me call a relative of his, have 'em come by and pick him up."

"You want me to cut him loose?"

"Like I said I won't forget it. He is a total screw-up, but his cousin is good people."

"Well...we got the main one," Billy said, thinking. Then he looked right at me, hard. "So how good are his people? Like a buck apiece for me and my partner? That good?"

"Yes," I said. "You know I'm good for it. I'll see you later, tonight."

He nodded and carted Loco off. Then I called Ronnie and told him to bring two-hundred. He showed up a short while later and got the kid into his car and looked at me, for a long moment, like he couldn't think of what to say. I didn't say anything back.

Finally, he nodded and slipped me the two c-notes. I put them in my pocket. "He's my kid cousin and we're gonna clean him up even if it kills him." Then he started peeling off more hundred dollar bills and said, "What about you and your partner?"

I gave him an Italian shrug-and-bop as I said, "C'mon, Ronnie, how long we know each other? My partner he's with me he understands, this is a favor for an old Paisan."

Ronnie just nodded and said, "Thanks," then he walked the kid back to his car turned around and said, "You know I never hugged a cop."

He smiled and waved as he got into his car and drove the kid off.

And a couple days later, Louisa got flowers from me, even though I hadn't ordered them. Boy was she happy.

What was crappy about the whole thing was how Loco was out on the street the next day, like nothing happened. I couldn't believe it. Here we were busting our butts trying to do our jobs, and all we wound up doing was chasing our tails. Only now we were chasing the little bastard down for attempted murder.

Bobby aimed the RMP up Avenue C. Down the side streets, I could see other police cruisers crisscrossing the area.

"What d'ya think?" Bobby yelled, all but laughing.

"Avenue D," I snapped back. "The Projects."

He giggled and screeched around a corner.

Two seconds later, I saw three people round a corner a block down – Loco along with this overbuilt, bald-headed guy and a woman I almost recognized. She and Loco both had guns. They had to be high; they never tried to hide the guns.

"There!" I yelled. "Two of 'em packin'!"

Our cruiser roared up the avenue. They saw us coming and bolted down a side street. Bobby roared around the corner and passed them then screamed to a halt. He and I jumped out; weapons raised, and we both screamed, "Drop it!"

Loco skidded and spun and dropped his gun as the woman chucked hers into the street, then they scrambled back to Avenue D, Bobby and me giving chase. Another cruiser cut them off before they hit the end of the block, so they gave up.

I'd caught a glimpse of the other man bolting into a doorway so I yelled at them, "Third guy ran in that building!"

Two cops blasted after the guy as I grabbed Loco and handcuffed him before Bobby had a chance to get near him. This time, he was handcuffing the girl as another patrol car arrived.

Those guys searched the scene as Bobby and I took the pair back to the RMP. First they found was Loco's long-nose pistol; the woman's gun was found under a car nearby. Then Bobby went to the building door where the third perp went in, laughing and waiting. But the other cops came back with a shrug; the third perp'd vanished. Bobby returned to the RMP and we headed back to where Soto'd been shot. He was being loaded into the ambulance when we drove up. I dragged Loco out of the car and asked, "This him?"

Soto just eyed Loco with pure hate and nodded.

"Which hospital?" I asked the ambulance driver.

"Beekman," the guy said as he hopped out of the back.

Loco tossed a kiss at Soto, who flipped him off. I just guided Loco back into the cruiser and got in the passenger seat. Then we drove back to the Ninth Precinct...and it was only then I realized I was soaked with sweat.

"Damn, I could use a shower," I muttered.

I heard Loco chuckle and snarl out, "No shit, pendejo."

Bobby glanced back at him and sneered, "He's gonna be a fun one. Wanna switch?"

"Next time, maybe," I smiled. Like I said, minimize the damage.

The light just starting to fade and the city was looking lovely. Something about this time of day makes everything so gentle and true, even though there was no way it could really be. I'd like to have just stayed out and watched the light fade and feel the first breezes from the waterfront, but no way could I find an excuse. So I guided Loco into the building and ran the marathon of cops storming around as phones rang off the hook, Bobby right behind me. I found a side desk that was open; Bobby had to take one in the middle of the room so he could do his one-finger typing to get the woman's information.

"Okay, Loco," I said, once we got settled in, "what's your real name?"

"Crazy, but it don't matter."

"Your real name."

"Fuck you, motherfucker"

I reached over and flicked him on the forehead with my middle finger. "Listen, numb nuts, I was trying to be nice but now I'll wait till you want to talk to me. Bobby this guy called you a fagot."

Bobby smiled and stood up reaching in his pants for his slap. Now a slap was not Police Department issue. As a matter of fact it was later ruled a clear violation of rules and procedures. But Bobby seemed to enjoy the effects a slap had on tough guys or girls for that matter. Loco must have seen the look on Bobby face, and before Bobby could get in arm's length, Loco was chirping like a canary in mating season.

Bobby went back to processing the girl.

She was really stoned and seemed like she was about to nod out. We both looked over in time to see Bobby jabbing his finger.

"He gonna hit her?" Loco asked, almost sounding protective.

"Naw," I said, not really sure about it, "he's just keeping her focused." Loco was talking and I was typing.

"Fuck, you go fast."

"You ain't seen nothin', yet," I said. "Where do you live?"

99

He told me. There were background noises and phones ringing and cops talking, and then I heard.

"Buono, line three."

I frowned and grabbed the telephone. "This is Buono."

This vaguely familiar voice was on the other end of the line. "Buono, I know that name and voice. Weren't you at Narcotics?"

"Uh – yeah, that was me. Who's this?"

"This is Velasquez. The Ninth Precinct – what a place to get dumped."

A Detective that falls out of grace and gets demoted back to patrolman will also usually be sent to a terrible command, a bad place. That is what getting dumped means.

"No kidding, Velasquez. What can I do for you?" And out of the corner of my eye, I noticed Loco smile at hearing the name and I just barely heard him mutter, "Told you, don't matter."

"Just checking," said Velasquez. "You gonna make night court?"

"I'm heading down in five minutes. Why?"

"Good. Maybe I'll see you there. We can talk."

"What about?"

But he hung up. Frowning, Bobby looked over. "Who's that?"

I hung the phone up and said, "Some cop from downtown."

"What'd he want?"

"Dunno, yet. Okay, Loco, what's your zip code?"

"You fuckin' kiddin' me?" Loco asked. I glared at him pointed to Bobby, so he rolled his eyes and shook his head, and he told me everything I wanted from that point.

Took me a while to remember who Velasquez was, I'd gotten so focused on the here and now, but then it hit me – a guy who's connected to a guy who's connected to Big Joey and maybe Dante just called me. That bad feeling came roaring in. I hadn't had it in so long, it sort of startled me. Now I wished I'd let Bobby handle this creep and me take care of the girl, but it was too late now; I was the arresting officer and I'd have to stick with the case from now on. Well, guess I'd eventually find out what Velasquez wanted and why he'd be on a creep like Soto – but I also knew I better stay sharp. And there was no way I'd face that guy sticky from sweating all day.

So we dropped Soto and his girl, Rosaria, off at criminal courts then I asked how long the prints were taking to get back from BCI.

100

"Runnin' late," he said. "You want a bite, grab it now. Back in two hours, for this batch."

Bobby nearly hit the roof. "Shit, we won't wrap up till tomorrow."

I gave him a light smack on the back of the head, in that good Italian way, and said, "C'mon, we'll go over my parents place, we'll get cleaned up, have a bite, a couple beers and relax for a while."

That shut him up.

Dad was already in bed; he'd been doing that a lot, lately – hitting the sack early, saying he was beat. We'd been trying to get him to see a doctor, but even the thought would piss him off. "Doctors! They just want to put you on some new pill or cut you open." So...mom was watching TV, alone, in the living room and dad was already cutting some ZZZs. I bopped over to kiss her. "Hi, Mom."

Bobby kissed her, too, smiling as he said, "Hi, Mom."

"Good to see you both," she said. "Want something to eat?"

"No, mom, stay there," I said. "We're just gonna grab a sandwich, clean up, use the phone."

"Help yourselves, boys."

"You go first, Bobby," I said.

He headed for the bathroom as I went into the kitchen, grabbed the phone and dialed. Then as it rang and rang and rang, I pulled sandwich makings from the refrigerator and made two -- one for me and the other for Bobby.

Now just to explain, there was nothing anyone could do about BCI; you just had to wait to get their butts in gear. The complaint room was a different story...if they ever answered the phone.

Finally, this sweet Asian voice came on the line, saying, "Yeah?"

"Hi, Rocky, it's Pietro, Pietro Buono. How's the prettiest girl in the Criminal Courts Building?"

"Cut it out. How many guys do you think call me named Pietro? What you want this time?"

"Listen, Doll, I'll be there in about ninety minutes – what can I bring you besides a kiss?"

"Peter..."

"You want more'n a kiss from me?"

"Not tonight, just a coffee and some Danish or something. I take my coffee with two sugars."

"I remember, and I think I know what else you like."

"You don't know any such thing!"

101

"Don't I?"

"I'm gonna tell my boyfriend about you."

"I thought I was your boyfriend." She giggled, so I said, "Thanks, Rocky. See you in an hour and a half." Bobby entered as I hung up. "Rocky's there, we won't need to wait in the complaint room."

"What happens when she is off? She don't work 7 days. Who else do you sweet talk?"

"When she is not there, Maria is at her desk. She is a doll too." I said as I headed for the bathroom. "I made you a sandwich...would you put everything away when you're done, this time, okay?"

Bobby stood by the door, letting me pass. "Sweet talk always work for you?"

"Not really," I said. "Not till I got married. Then it's like girls started thinking, 'Well, his wife bought into his story, maybe there's something there to listen to.' Rest is easy."

"Careful, some day one of those girls'll listen you right into bed."

I pulled him into a headlock, smirking. "What makes you think one isn't enough for me?"

He shoved me back, sharp and tense, and the look on his face was spooky.

I jolted. "What was that all about?"

"Nothin'," he snapped. "I – I'm hungry." Then he spun around and headed back to the kitchen.

I shrugged it off and changed into a clean uniform, and then an hour and fifteen minutes later we were headed back to 100 Centre Street. We slipped into the complaint room, where about sixty cops were waiting, sitting in rows and rows of folding chairs, lined up like they were watching a movie. We passed through the swinging exit door and headed into the typists' area and stopped at a desk – Rocky's. And let me tell you something – she was anything but a knockout; just a sweet girl that seemed to have a problem with keeping a boyfriend, if she ever really had one. But lemme tell you, people are people and like to hear nice things, so it don't cost anything to be nice and most of the time it is appreciated. I set the takeout bag on her desk and sat on the edge as Bobby sat at an empty desk. She looked up at me in this slow, half-hidden way and said, "Hello, Pietroooo, Bobby."

"Did you know I would be here when you left home this afternoon?" I asked.

"I don't knoooow. Why?"

102

"Because you look so good. I was hoping it was for me."

"I'm going to tell my boyfriend you're flirting."

"Bring him over," I said. "I'll show him a thing or two about how to treat a lovely lady."

Then I sat in the chair as she slipped the complaint form into the typewriter, and I started to tell her time and place of occurrence, punctuating every bit of it with winks at her. Bobby just shook his head. Then when mine was done, Bobby sat and he told his story.

Again, this is how life works – if you know the system and are nice to people, they help you. You treat 'em like shit? They do nothing in return. Absolutely nothing; and you wind up sitting in the complaint room till they call you instead of you calling the shots.

Lots of companies knew this. Restaurants'd give you a free meal in exchange for you keeping a bit of an eye on their place or coming faster when they had a problem. We're not talking steaks and fine wines, just a sandwich a soft drink or coffee. Just stuff to show you they care.

Same for big companies too, like car rental agencies. This was back before you had to have a credit card to rent a car, so some guys'd come in, plop down the deposit and just "forget" to bring the car back. Now the car Rental car companies didn't want to report the car stolen; if they did it might take a very long time to get them returned in case of an arrest.

We would stop and check all rentals that came into the sector, (you could tell them back then because back then the tags began with the letter Z). If the rental agreement was more than a week overdue, we called the car company the driver would be detained. The rental company would be there in less than 10 minutes, with an envelope with two fifty dollar bills. Once they picked up the car, we would arrest the driver for Grand Larceny Auto/theft of services.

And, again, the world has always worked this way, no matter which side of the law you stand on. Truth is, dealing with the rental cars not only helped my arrest record, and it also helped me get my house. Because they got what they cared about; and that was all they cared about. Nice and easy to deal with.

Problems don't start until you do favors for other cops and they've got no good in mind. Oh, they'll make promises and hand you a line to get the favor, but once you do it, they use it to control you. And sometimes they don't even try to do what they promised you. But that's also how the world works. You deal with it or you don't. What you never do is go to IAD about it. Then it's like, you messed with the brotherhood, so you're gonna get hit hard. And it don't matter how fucked up the bad cop was.

But that's what I know now. That night, I had no idea what I was getting myself into. Even with all I'd seen and the investigations of the Knapp Commission, I still didn't want to think a cop'd do bad to another cop.

Now Bobby and I were seated in the first row. Loco and Rosaria were sitting to the right of the bench, in with a crowd of other criminals. Court wouldn't start, again, till after the judge was done with his break. You could tell when it was close because a court officer'd come out of chambers and stand by the railing, and then the judge'd be a couple minutes behind him.

That's when Detective Velasquez entered. He looked exactly as I remembered him, but I pretended not to see him and I don't think he remembered me. Because it wasn't till Loco nodded in my direction that Velasquez sat next to me.

"Hey, Buono, long time no see."

"Oh, hi, Velasquez," was all I said, but I was a bit better than polite in my tone of voice. "What's up?"

"So I see you're back in the bag, now, on patrol."

The term in the bag means in uniform, when we met, he assumed I had a gold shield. This I could tell by the way he spoke.

I shrugged and nodded in response.

He smiled and said, "Can I talk to you, a minute?" Then he motioned he wanted to go outside.

"Court's about to start."

"Won't take a minute. C'mon."

Okay, here it comes, I thought, but all I said was, "Sure." Then I nudged Bobby. "I'll be right outside."

Bobby jolted and eyed me, with a frown, then he looked at Velasquez with something that was never going to be mistaken for love as the guy and I headed out. Made me feel good to know Bobby had my back, like that.

In the hallway, Velasquez led me to a corner and spoke so quietly, I almost couldn't hear him. "We can get you some good info. It'd put you on a fast track back to a gold shield."

"Who's 'we'?" I asked.

"You remember Moretti, right?"

And who should suddenly appear next to me but him. We shook hands.

"Kinda," I said. "Seems like I don't remember to good now a days. How ya doin'?"

Moretti smiled at me. Then this black cop joined us. He looked familiar.

"This is Jonas," Velasquez said.

"We've met, haven't we?" the guy asked.

"You tell me," I said, looking at Moretti. I always had a knack for faces. "How you doing?"

Velasquez clapped me on the back, grinning in a way that was obviously forced. "So everybody knows everybody. That's good. Now – your defendant, he works for us. See what I mean?"

"Oh – yeah," I said, not really understanding except in a general sense. "What exactly do you want from me?"

"He wasn't the shooter," Velasquez continued.

"His gun was recovered, it was fired – ."

Jonas cut me off with, "The girl is the victim's ex. She's the shooter. We want him to make bail."

"You sure about that?"

Moretti sighed. "Ballistics'll verify it."

I nodded and said, "I see. I – will relay that information to the A.D.A."

Moretti smiled and patted my cheek as he said to Velasquez, "Told ya he's a good kid."

And that's all there was to it. The three of them walked away.

I just stood there and watched after them, feeling a little like I was being played. But at the same time, I was thinking this might be a good way to get some more solid information on them. They'd promised me info to help me make grade; maybe I could play the same game on them.

At least, now I knew why Loco walked on that last arrest, and man, was I glad I'd got Ronnie's cousin cut loose from that. Otherwise, he'd have taken the weight, looks like. And I bet that wasn't the first time Loco walked, either.

That's the way of the world.

And you think I didn't know what Moretti really meant with his "good kid" crack? Just like Patty said, "Quiet, that's a good way to be." Thing is, you have to know what to be quiet about so you can be quiet about it.

So I let the ADA know Loco wasn't the shooter, and he got the drift. Once everything was set at the arraignment, Loco got the low

105

bail while Rosaria couldn't make hers no matter what; but then, she wasn't important to Moretti. I just needed to figure out why Loco was.

I went to Beekman Hospital to see Soto. I told him that it looked like Loco will make bail, but at least we can get the gun conviction.

"That fucker's out on bail?!" he snapped when I told him.

"She shot you. It wasn't him right?"

"How'd you know but he told that fucked up bitch to do it."

"The hearing's three weeks from tomorrow."

"There really gonna be one?"

"I got him with the gun. What d'you mean?"

"You fuckin' with me? Shit. Loco's so hooked up with the Narcs, they're halfway up his ass."

"Those're some pretty heavy charges," I said, carefully.

"C'mon, man, you know they protect him. Some of the guys say they...they even supply him."

Okay that I was not expecting so I asked.

"Why do you think that?"

"He always got enough smack – even when the streets're dry, he's the only motherfucker with supply. Velasquez, that maricon; Jonas, the Black devil; and that grease-ball wop motherfucker – no offense, man."

I shrugged it off.

"You don't believe me, do ya?" he continued.

I sighed. "Talk's talk, comes out cheap and it's worth nothing in court."

He motioned me closer, whispering, "Lemme tell ya how it works. My buddy, Chico, got ripped by them and still has to pay them – ."

And as he talked, I could just see it. The apartment so full of radios, TVs, and stereos, as he explained it, Chico was a drug dealer with a heart, if his junkie customers had no cash he would take almost anything as payment, so his apartment looked like a pawn shop. Some picture -- this sleaze of a street hustler sitting on a milk crate, handcuffed, Moretti strutting before him, saying something like, "Chico, it's your choice. We take you in you lose all your cash and supply. We might even forget to lock your apartment door and, y'know, you got a lot a nice stuff here. Stuff that's worth a lot. This is just business. I'm a guy, well, we are." Now swinging his arms towards his partners. "Know what I mean?"

106

Of course, Chico'd know how the game is played, so he'd say, "Okay, I get it – mi casa es su casa. Help yourself."

Velasquez'd find Chico's stash of cash and count it out, separating the bills into different stacks. Jonas or Kowalski'd be there counting one-ounce bags of heroin that'd been stashed in a large boot box.

Now Moretti wouldn't be greedy; that'd make for a bad relationship with the mark. "Just one other thing, next week we come by – have a grand ready. Or we take you down for good. Comprende?"

"Que si, vato," is all Chico'd say back. After all, a grand is basically the same as the tax rate on what a guy like him would bring in. He could handle it, and word would go out he's in the pocket of those guys.

Moretti'd grin and make a show of removing Chico's cuffs, and they'd walk out into the night, looking at it as tax collectors splitting fifty-two thousand dollars from this one dealer for the year. And this was back when fifty-two-K was more than double what a First Grade Detective made the entire year. And that's just one dealer. God knew how many others they were rousting the same way.

Soto spit, cutting off my thoughts.

"That puto, Loco, he pays them big and deals in the open. Sometimes he even turns guys over, if they stiff him or try to pull his territory. Fuckin' animal."

I kept non-committal. "That's even more heavy stuff you're saying. You want to talk to someone in the DA's office about this?"

"Hell, no. Who's gonna listen to me? I got tracks." Which was pretty evident, since the gown didn't cover his arms. "And I deal smack to pay for it."

"Soto," I said, "why you tellin' me? What you think I can do?"

He looked away, lost and almost human. "I dunno, man," he said. "You just seem like a good guy. Hell, maybe I oughta just move away from here. Shut it down. Stuff keeps happening on the street with that dago wop motherfucker – no offense man."

"Don't worry about it."

I put it all in my memo book and made a mental note to dig deeper into that, but the fact is, nothing more happened for the next several months. Loco's trial kept getting postponed, like the ADA was just going through the motions until he could say it was too close to the statue of limitations and just let it drop.

Then Serpico got shot, and if his spilling the beans about rotten cops had shook up the city, him nearly getting killed off in a way that looked like his partner might have set him up – that made things ten times worse. Because the dumbasses who tried to pull that one off had done worse than trying to get a fellow officer killed; they'd shattered the idea of The Brotherhood.

That's something people never understand about cops and why they get so tight with each other. It's not just because we hold the same job; it's because we got each other's back, not just out in the community but in everything. Your life is as much in your partner's hands as in your own. That's why what Serpico did was considered traitorous; he'd put a crack in the faith of all cops that they had someone they could rely on, no matter what. Never mind that he was kicking dirty cops out into the open and letting the world know the higher-ups had done nothing about it. He'd slipped a hint of doubt into the main consciousness of the Brotherhood, and sent many of us to the point where if there was only one guy we knew we could trust, who we knew without question had our back, we'd do anything we could to protect him in the same way. And I knew Bobby and I had that for each other. It was the same for Marc and Lou.

I wish I'd had them around a few weeks later, when I was getting the evidence for Loco's latest possible trial. I headed into the property room at 400 Broome Street, walked up to the clerk's cage.

"A gun," I told the guy. "Ninth Precinct voucher – ."

This guy got testy he cut me off with, "Just enter the information in the log." He nodded down at the book in front of me like I didn't know the drill or something; these rubber gun squad guys were recovering drunks and they are sometimes the worst.

So I entered it and the clerk went off to get it. He could have been back by now if he just listened. I started reading some notices on the board, just for something to do. It took me down to this corner, where I could lean against a wall but still keep an eye on the cage to get back when the clerk returned. That's when Kowalski appeared at the window. He was in uniform. The clerk handed him a large evidence pouch and he headed off, without a thought. I hadn't heard anything about him getting dumped back to the bag, so I slipped over to see, and three lines above my name was a guy named Johnston picking up a key of coke, Kowalski's name nowhere at all.

Now the Property Clerks office was a joke the way it was run. Cops there were on limited duty, could be for anything but mostly because they been to the farm and back. (Alcoholics.)

108

And if you were in uniform no I D card required.

A key of coke!? My brain took a leap from that to a thought that really made me uncomfortable when the clerk jolted me with, "Hey — Buono?"

I jolted and cast a quick glance down the hall, and I saw Kowalski hesitate — then continue on. He'd heard my name. My heart just about sank as I said, "Yeah."

"Got a call," the clerk snapped. "Guy from your precinct."

I took the phone, my hands shaking, wondering what the bastard would be up to now that he knew I'd seen him doing something screwy...but then everything froze.

It was the switchboard. Mom called there to let me know.

My dad was in the hospital.

He'd had a heart attack.

****

This is when things really changed, for me. And I don't mean in a simple way. My dad was my center. The guy I'd go to for anything. My moral compass in ways the church never could be. If he was disappointed in what I'd done, I felt I'd done wrong, no matter how justified I was in my own mind. And if he was proud of me, nobody could tear me down. He was always going to be there, y'know? But there I am, just twenty-three years-old and he's having a heart attack on me? That can't be happening.

But it did. When I rushed in, I found dad on a bed, hooked up to a hundred machines, all softly beeping, and mom beside him. She put a finger to her lips to let me know he was sleeping, so I just gave him a light kiss on the cheek we slipped outside.

"So what happened?"

"He just passed out after breakfast. They want to run more tests, in the morning."

"It's gonna be okay, mom. They'll find out all it's gonna take to fix is a couple aspirin. You go home; I'll sit with him, for a while."

It took a bit more convincing, but she finally headed back to the apartment and I just sat there, watching him breathe. Watching the monitors beep and mutter. Like they were all there was. Forty years my dad worked and now this was all there was left of him. It was scary. There should be more to a man once he reaches this stage in his life. Still having to scrimp and fight to keep your head above water, after all he'd been through – that was just wrong. I sure as hell wasn't going to wind up like this, no way.

The sun was just dipping past the horizon when he woke up and at looked at me. His eyes were dark and wary, and pierced into my heart.

"What's this?" he asked.

"What's what?" I said, giving him the Italian head bop as I moved to his side.

"You're here, now. Shouldn't you be home? Your wife's gonna have a baby, soon – ."

I cut him off with, "I'm headed out soon as mom gets back."

"Where is she?"

"Just went home get something to eat and change clothes. Put on her face. You know how women are. You okay?"

110

He sort of smiled and patted my arm and said, "I'm fine. You're lookin' good."

Not really sure about that, but I am his son and look like him. I'd put on more weight, most of it muscle but a bit around the gut, too. Louisa loved to cook heavy, like her mom, and the irregular hours kept my eating habits all screwy.

Anyway, I sat on the side of the bed and said, "Dad, what's this? You – you need an excuse to take a day off?"

Dad waved me quiet. "Doctors, you hiccup wrong and they wanna run a test. I'm fine. I'll be fine."

But his color was bad, he looked blue and cold. So I just said, "Sure, dad, strong like bull."

"So, what's what with you, what's troubling you?"

"Me? What you mean? We already had been through that."

He just kept looking at me, waiting for an answer. And I realized this was the first time he'd seen me since Fredo's funeral. Maybe the guilt over Fredo's death'd been weighing on me more than I thought. Maybe it was showing in my face. I'd have to see what I could do to stop that. Thing is, even though I tried to think of a good pile of crap to answer him with, my brain was wiped clean.

Dad put his hand on my arm and said, "Peter..."

I sighed and whispered, "I was picking up some evidence – when I got the call from here – anyway, I saw something."

Then I told him about Kowalski at the pickup window, and him being handed a large evidence envelope by the clerk.

"He was in uniform," I said, "wearing a silver shield of a patrolman. I first thought he got dumped back to the bag – uh, uniform. He was First Grade. But when I was leaving the building and headed for here, I caught a glimpse of him sitting in a car with Moretti you know that cop from the neighborhood. I think they were watching me."

"Why would they do that?"

"I dunno. I...I been noticing things and...and maybe they noticed I noticed and – and even if they were, I don't think they know I saw them, so..."

"I don't understand what the problem is," dad said, his face filled with worry.

"Kowalski took another cop's evidence, a key of coke."

"How do you know that?"

"Kowalski's name was nowhere on that list. But just above my name was the printed name and signature of a Patrolman named Johnston from the Two-Five. That – that's the precinct Uncle Gio and

111

Aunt Mary live in." I started pacing. "I know a Johnston up in the Two-Five, and he's a god cop. And seeing Kowalski do this – I finally get how it works, dad. Everything I wondered about and worried about. I know how it works, now. It's so simple, so easy; I should've figured it out years ago."

"How what works? Figured what out?"

"It's so damn simple," I said. "Bust a guy, take his junk, the info gets filed at the office then some other cop waits till it's tested and returned to property. Right after it is returned they use the arresting officer's name and sign it out, and nobody's the wiser. They don't keep serious records in that place. Don't check I D cards if you're in uniform then, when returned, the drugs are replaced with powdered sugar or cornstarch. Looks all kosher."

"So what are you saying? They take drugs out and what?"

"Dad, it's already been tested by the lab. It's not gonna get tested, again." He frowned at me, still confused, so I added, "It leaves the property room as drugs, but when it's returned, it's worthless powder. No one will know the drugs were switched unless they got a reason to do a re-test."

"How could that be?" dad asked. "I mean, how could he know what to take?"

"That info's at their fingertips," I said, then I told dad everything – about Velasquez and Moretti looking at stacks of index cards near file cabinets. The meeting Moretti and Kowalski had with Big Joey at Patty's. And what I'd overheard them say. Then later how they'd got me to help cut Loco loose and how expensive their clothes were and on and on. I just unloaded it all, almost without taking a serious breath. By the time I was done, I was a little dizzy and dad was white as a sheet. What I know now is, more than one group or single cop is involved. Gee, it could be as many as 30 from Narcotics alone. Who can tell if any others are involved? It seemed everybody was in it for themselves, (It could have been scores of cops involved). It was like who got to it first. Guys would find out where and who made the bust and try to get it as soon as possible, after it was returned from the lab.

"There's inherent flaws in the system, dad. I mean – really, when you're picking up evidence, nobody checks your I.D. card. There's not even one security camera in the entire building."

"You – you sure about all this?"

"I've been trying not to believe it – but..."

"You say anything to anybody?"

112

"Not yet. This thing's been going on for years; I'm sure of that, now. What I don't know is how many bad apples are drawing from the well. You got lots of good cops getting drugs off the street, but I bet many cops figured out how easy it is to take it out. All they need is someone to buy it from them."

"You think the bosses are in on it, too?"

That jolted me. Sure, I remembered seeing Sergeant Bruno meeting with Moretti and Kowalski, but I hadn't honestly thought beyond that. All I could do is shrug and say, "This is such big money, who knows?"

Dad frowned. "Son, do you – do you think this Kowalski guy remembers you?"

"No question," I said. "I mean, if he didn't, Moretti does. He sort of knew me from the neighborhood."

Dad gripped my hand. "You – Peter, you gotta be real careful with this. Those guys – they have a lot to lose."

"I know. That's why I've been keeping a record."

"A record?"

"Yeah. You see, at the academy they said write everything in your memo book, so that's what I did. I got a record." I showed him my latest one, with the entry I'd made in it for that day. "I got a few of these little babies, all nice and safe."

"What do you mean? How does this help any?"

"Every time I saw something weird, I made an entry about it. I started it when I was in the narc office, four years ago. Anybody pulls anything; I got these to back me up."

"You really think that'll matter? Look at your cousin."

That's when I realized my father also thought Fredo'd been murdered. Wow that was like a punch in the gut. Suddenly, I saw Fredo's body, again, but almost like it was lying across the bed instead on in that chair. I could see the bruises on his neck and arms. I couldn't look at my father as I said, "He – got caught up in drugs – ."

"Your Aunt Mary thinks he was killed."

That, I knew, but what I replied was, "She does?"

"I heard her and your mother talking. She says the heroin was too pure to use, and he'd of known that. And he had cash enough to give her for groceries, that morning, but none was left in his room."

"Dad, c'mon," I said. "Fredo was a junkie – stone hooked. He couldn't think clear. And it may've been the last cash he had and – ."

"Maybe, maybe. Just – just be careful. Okay? You've always been a smart kid, so when you reach out for help, be extra careful. You'll trust that someone with your life. Remember. Please!"

I grinned and gave dad a kiss on top the head. Then I went into the bathroom and sagged against the door. I looked at my memo book. Put it in my pocket. Then looked in the mirror...and saw this nightmarish vision of hands holding a struggling Fredo down as someone plunged the heroin into his vein. He died almost instantly, they said. So with his junk box empty and all the cash he'd had gone...it all fit too damn perfectly. Dad was right; I had to be extra careful.

When mom finally showed up and ready to stay the night, I headed down to the hospital lobby and used a phone booth to make a call.

"Louisa, it's me," I said. "Call your mom. Tell her I'm dropping something off to her."

"What do you mean?" she asked.

"Look, I'll explain later. Just let her know, okay?"

"Okay," she said, wary. "You be home, right after?"

"Stop at your mom's then right home."

"How's your father?"

"Strong as an ox," I said, sounding good but not really meaning it.

I headed back to the Ninth Precinct, aiming for my locker, trying to look casual even as I kept checking around to make sure nobody was following me. I caught shadows moving on walls, around me. Later I learned your peripheral vision can play tricks on you like that, by making even slight changes in paint color or a door you're passing seem to be moving. But the sudden noises I heard weren't my imagination. Soft banging sounds and whispers caused by god knows what. It all really put me on edge.

I finally reached my locker and undid the lock, carefully, making sure nobody was around as I spun the dial. I glanced around some more then pulled a small panel down from the interior top of the locker. It held five full memo books. I put them in order, my mind making the leap to the realization that I'd been doing this for years but hadn't done a thing to actually try and end it, yet, then I slipped them into a paper bag, replaced the panel so it looked like normal, and left.

I wasn't as worried about getting to my car because I had it in the lot and there were other cops and civilians around. So I hopped right in and drove away. Only later did I realize how dumb that was. If

114

someone'd been watching me, they'd have seen where I park and how easy it'd be to disable the car or worse.

I drove over the bridge and onto the L.I.E. (Long Island Expressway) carefully looking around. Everything looked normal. No one appeared to be following me. But just to be extra safe, I exited the expressway at the last second, pissing off a few drivers as I cut across lanes.

I stopped in front of a nice older house on a tree-lined street. Louisa's mom and new step dad had bought it a year before our wedding. Her younger brother wasn't happy about having to change schools and stuff, but now they had a yard and peace and quiet. And that'd made my wife and I decide to get something in the same area, so now I lived closer to my in-laws than to my own parents.

Anyway, I headed up to the door and a woman in a comfortable housecoat – Louisa's Mom – opened it. And did she give me a good looking over.

"Hello, Pietro," she said, emphasizing the accents in my name. "Louisa called. How's your father?"

"He's got more tests, Monday," I said. "But it looks good."

"You want some coffee or – ?"

"No, thanks, I just want to drop these off. Is that OK with you? Put them in a safe place."

I handed her the bag with all the books.

She held the bag with an outstretched arm and asked, "What's in this?"

"I'll explain another time, but it's important that I don't have them with me."

"Peter, I don't like secrets."

"They're not secrets, ma. It's just paperwork I don't want anybody to see, that's all."

She shook her head, with a smile. "Okay. You and Louisa join us for dinner, tomorrow. We can talk, then."

"Sounds good, thanks, ma."

I kissed her and left. I could just see her shaking her head after me. I get the feeling she didn't think I was good enough for her little girl, and I overheard her telling a friend of hers, "He's got too easy a tongue and too big an imagination, that one." But once the wedding was set she'd gone forward with it like a trooper. Still, I could always feel her eyes on me, like she was just waiting for me to pull something so she could tell Louisa, "I told you so." It's a weird thing to feel, but it was real.

115

I got home after midnight, so Louisa was already in bed. Probably since the time I called her. She was in the last month or so of the pregnancy and got tired really quick, sometimes. So rather than wake her, I stayed in the living room and paced, going over everything in my mind.

If Moretti and Kowalski knew I was aware of what they were doing, then so did Jonas and Velasquez and Bruno. And God knows who else. And they would have a lot to lose. Maybe a hundred-grand a year cash, maybe more. Today that's big money; think about what is was back then. For me, an extra fifty to hundred a week came in real handy. My cash, as it came in, it went out. I mean, I always had enough to make it, but it sure would've been nice to be able to afford a decent vacation once a year. They say you make your own bed. I could of got a walk up apartment somewhere in Brooklyn or Queens, but we bought the house and then needed two cars. I had a four year-old Charger and Louisa drove a barge of a Chevy wagon that flat out guzzled gas but at 35 cents a gallon almost.

I wonder if there was ever a study done as to why someone -- or not just someone but cops, politicians judges for that matter -- who swore uphold the law would do this. Was it just because it was too easy? You know the flaws in the system. Saying, "Do it; no will ever know."

I can kind of understand why a guy like Borodino might, with his back against the wall, sick family member, insurance cut off. Cops don't get paid a whole hell of a lot, not considering the job's dangers and demands. Not in comparison to CEOs who never set foot off a carpet or limo but get seven figures for sitting at a desk. And a key of coke – yeah, it'd bring a decent penny. So who's to say I wouldn't have done the same thing if I was in their shoes? No cops got to draw a line...but who am I to judge?

Except I kept seeing Fredo's body and Aunt Mary's pain and kids like Ronnie's cousin screwing themselves up with that crap. It just wasn't right, and I should've been doing something more about it and –

.

Louisa was beside me and it was morning. I jolted at the sudden shift in time.

"You all right?" she asked, a bit freaked out.

I smiled and said, "Yeah. Just a little trouble falling asleep that's all."

"You were pacing most of the night."

"I – I got a lot on my mind."

116

"Pete, baby, shouldn't you take some time off?"

"Can't – not right now."

"But you're working so hard."

"Yeah, well – the, uh – the more arrests I make – faster I make detective."

"I know – but – ."

"It's okay, Louisa. It's just lots of things are happening and I gotta keep focused."

The telephone rang. I groaned, reached over to answer it.

"Good morning," I said, and not in a very nice way. Then I heard mom's voice, cracking and choking as she tried to speak, and it slammed into me like a ton of bricks.

Dad was gone.

She didn't even have to say it. "Mom – we'll be over, right away. Okay?"

I hung up – and this huge wave of feeling lost and alone and scared slammed over me...and without realizing it, I was bawling. Louisa held me close and we sat like that till I was dried out from tears. Then we raced over to Mom's apartment.

For next few days, I drifted in this non-stop fog that seemed to surround my heart and soul, both. Because I knew I was to blame. I shouldn't have told him. The second I did, he died. Massive coronary's how they put it. But my father was gone. Because I'd scared him with my talk. I should have kept it to myself, but I didn't. And now I was on my own.

I only remember bits and pieces of that time. Like driving mom and Louisa to the funeral home, parking in front and walking them both inside. I think my sisters were there, already, but I couldn't tell you for sure. They were, eventually.

I got an image of me standing beside them and looking into the casket that held my father. I don't remember them doing it, but I know mom and Louisa each crossed herself and said a quick prayer before sitting in the first row. But they were alone, at first, so my sisters must have come later.

That's not like them, especially at an important time like this.

Then I remember being by the door to greet people; who, I don't really recall. And they all said things like, "Peter, we're so sorry," and "He was a good man, Pete, a good man," and on and on. And each one would get a handshake from me and a soft, "Thanks." I don't remember doing it; I just know that's what I'd do, and nobody ever said

117

anything about me not doing it. And believe me; Italian funerals are just as big on gossip as weddings, just meaner.

I do remember this one guy heading down the aisle was whispering, "They thought he was doing so well, too – then out of nowhere." I remember because after hearing that, my chest felt like it was about to explode, and I could barely breath. The room was dark, all of a sudden, and the light filtering through the stained glass windows was sharp like knives, and I was having trouble swallowing and actually wondered if I was about to vomit in the middle of it all and started to freak out over it because that would definitely be talked about for years if I did and –

"Hi ya, Buono," jolted me.

It was Moretti. He was standing right next to me, close enough that I could smell the bourbon on his breath. His voice was in a snarl.

"Just came by to pay my respects," he said, and it looked like he was fighting a smile. "You doin' okay?"

All I could do was nod.

"Good man, your dad," he said, both snarl and smile still hiding in the back of his voice. "Raised a good kid. What you did for us with Loco, we won't forget it."

I gulped and choked out a, "Thanks."

"Y'know, it took me a while," the smile almost back on his face, "but I finally remember everyplace I know you from. Big Joey says, Hi."

Then the smile broke across his face and he strutted out the door, leaving me to ask myself, why'd he say that? Big Joey is dead. Isn't he? Died in his sleep, I heard. But maybe that was lies being spread around. Maybe that was a cover for him to vanish. I followed – as if in a haze. As if I was really gonna ask him about it.

I exited the building into darkness. It'd gone night awful quick. The wagon was parked in the lot, to the left. I sensed movement from that direction so looked around and –

Kowalski was pouring gasoline on it! Moretti was next to him, laughing as he lit a match and flicked it.

The wagon burst into flames!

I cried out, stumbled back and fell, cracking my head on the curb. Glitters of sparkling light filled my eyes. I dunno how long I lay there before I shook off the pain and slowly rose to a sitting position and looked over to see –

The wagon was untouched. No Kowalski. No Moretti. No hint of anybody else in the area. It hadn't even gotten dark, yet; the day was still bright.

I forced myself to my feet, my head blazing, and stumbled into the funeral home. The director gave me some aspirin and a glass of water, and I had to hold it with both hands to stop the shaking. He patted my back, as if he was offering sympathy. I thanked him and headed back into the parlor.

I made myself take my position by the entrance; again, trying to act as if nothing had happened. And I kept greeting people who came to pay their respects at the coffin then to Mom. But the whole time, my mind was racing at six-thousand, trying to figure out what the hell'd just happened. Because when I walked outside, I'd have sworn it was night. I'd have sworn I saw Kowalski and Moretti torch my car. On a stack of bibles, I'd have sworn it.

But I didn't. None of it was real. And I couldn't honestly remember if I'd fallen and cracked my head before or after it all. So maybe I'd passed out and fallen and just dreamed it. And nobody'd noticed. That probably meant I'd only been knocked out for a second or two, damn.

Maybe that didn't happen, either. But then I felt the back of my head and it still hurt and there was a knot growing there with a bit of crusted blood. Maybe that was it. I'd wandered outside for second and passed out and it'd all been some kind of nightmare while I was collapsed on the ground. Yeah, that had to be it.

By the time Bobby showed up, I was in better control. But God bless him, he still noticed and put a hand on my shoulder and said, "Pete, you doin' okay, buddy?" And the look in his eyes held honest concern. It...that concern helped me.

I nodded and walked him to the coffin and showed him my dad, all in silence, then I took him over to Mom and said, "Mom, Bobby's here."

He gave me a look then took mom's hand and said, "I'm so sorry, Mom." Then he leaned in and gave her a kiss on the cheek, like he was another son of hers, like he was my brother.

Mom whispered, "Thank you for being here," her voice cracking. That brought me back to the moment.

"If you need anything," he said, "anything at all, you just tell me." Then he gave Louisa a kiss, too, and I introduced him to my sisters and he took a seat in the back, and I returned to the entrance. I had my duties to fulfill. But it helped me to know he was there, looking

119

out for me, being concerned. No question – he was my backup. And suddenly I was so glad I'd kept him from flying off the handle, again.

Marc showed up about an hour later, sporting a dark suit, longer hair and a beard, like something out of Hollywood. He shook my hand and gave me a hug.

"So sorry, man," he said. "How's your mom holding up?"

"Better'n me," I said. "You – your hair really grow that fast?"

He just shrugged. I walked with him to the coffin and then to Mom, introducing him by saying, "Mom, it's been a while but, do you recognized him?

She almost smiled as she said, "Marco."

"My condolences, Mrs. B. he was a good man."

"Thank you, Marco." Then she looked at me and said, "Yes, even with all that hair is still the baby face."

"That's why I have to have it," Marc grinned. "Without this beard, they never think I'm old enough to drive, let alone be in a bar."

We shared a chuckle, and I felt so at peace, without even thinking, I said, "Mom, I'll be outside for a while." Then I looked at Marc and said, "There's something I want to talk to you about."

I cast a look at Bobby and motioned to go the door. Marc greeted Louisa and my sisters then followed me.

We all reached the door about the same time and Bobby slapped Marc on the back, half a grin on his face. "So – Mr. Intelligence Division guy, where are you working now a days? Can you talk about it?"

"It's best I don't – but if it works out, I was promised Second Grade."

"Shit," Bobby said. "And still a kid."

"I'm legal for almost anything," giving him an Italian head bop and crooked grin and a wink.

Bobby smiled and said, "And having fun, right?"

Marc let a sly grin cross his face and shot a glance my way. "It's not all fun and games. I can't wait till it's over. I'm never home. There are other things in my office I would rather be doing; do you know our office is responsible for protecting the Mayor?"

"No kidding hard life," Bobby smirked.

"Yeah," I said, "hard life." And I had to fight to think of that much to say. I was gonna talk to them about something but I couldn't remember what. Then I noticed mom was weeping, Louisa and my sisters around her, so I said, "Wait – uh – be right back."

I hurried down to her and put my arms around her as Bobby and Marc slipped outside.

And I forgot completely about them.

I just left them out there, after waiting about and hour they'd looked into the parlor and seen I was still with mom, so they came in for the final prayer and said goodnight, then they had a drink at a nearby tavern and caught up on each other.

I didn't mean to leave 'em like that, but it seemed like all of a sudden I just couldn't think, and my head was pounding, and I was back to understanding my father was gone and I finally saw just how much I'd relied on him, and even with Bobby and Marc as my backup, I still felt so – so alone.

****

A week later, I was at the property clerk's office in street clothes, waiting to obtain the gun evidence for Loco's latest hearing. I'd forgotten about it until the ADA called me to ask some question about if it was Loco's gun or the other defendant. Took me a moment to remember what he was talking about. Anyway, I hadn't got into line, yet, because I was checking my agenda book. I had it laid out with days off and what hours I would work on certain days. This helped for court dates when Lou appeared beside me. I think I jumped.

"Sorry, Petey, didn't mean to startle you," he said, his voice gentle. "Sorry about your dad. I didn't hear till I got back."

"Thanks," I said. "Where'd you go?"

"North Carolina," he said. "Army reserves and the family reunion, we do this every year. You doin' okay?" I shrugged. "You sure you want to come back to work, so soon?"

I shrugged, again. "I sit at home, I think too much. I've been pacing a lot."

"My dad used to say that's a dangerous pastime."

"Pacing or thinking?" I said, smiling. "Louisa was close to killing me."

"I can imagine."

No, he couldn't. Me not sleeping at night and pacing endlessly, lost all day. Starting things and not finishing them. Louisa took it as long as she could, but with the bun almost cooked in the oven, it was hard on her. So back to work I went.

By now I was ready so I got in line, Lou one spot ahead of me. We kept chit-chatting, talking about who knows what. Just things in general and I liked it. The conversation kept my mind off the turmoil in my heart. Police officers ahead of us exited with evidence envelopes under their arms, and we moved closer to the window, step by step. And then I realized Velasquez was a couple guys ahead of me. In uniform, just like Kowalski had been.

I must've frozen my gaze on him, because Lou noticed and asked, "Do you know that guy from someplace?"

I jolted and said, "Yeah, I thinks so."

"You act like you owe him money," he said, smiling.

"No it's nothing like that."

Velasquez signed out a large envelope and calmly strolled out, never even looking at me, but I knew he'd seen me. I could tell by how

122

he deliberately looked away and shifted into a quietly steady gait. I didn't even pretend to not notice him.

Lou signed for his envelope then stepped aside for me.

As I filled out my information, I scanned the previous entries. Velasquez's name wasn't on it, but someone named Maxwell'd just signed out almost three pounds of heroin, two entries before Lou's.

There was no conversation as Lou and I walked away, then at the end of the hall, just out of sight from the cage, I stopped and made an entry in a new memo book. Lou noticed.

We left the building at the Broome Street entrance and headed for Centre Market Place, mostly by habit since I was so lost in thought.

Lou finally asked, "Petey what's going on? Why so quiet?"

"What do you mean?" I asked, not really hearing him."

"You saw something inside and made an entry in your memo book and – ."

"No, no," I said, cutting him off. "It's nothin'. Nothin'."

"Are you kidding? You got all tense and went whiter than you normally are and – ."

"I – I don't want to talk about it. Not here."

"Petey, you know you can tell me anything."

All of a sudden, I couldn't take another step. It was too damn much. I was too lost and confused and couldn't decide what to do, next. I stopped, dead, and looked at Lou. He was right; I could talk to him. Tell him anything. He was one of the good guys. But I said, "Not now. Not here."

"Okay. You want to meet for lunch at Val's?"

He was offering me more backup, offering to help me out. And that's when I realized half of my problem was I'd kept everything bottled up inside, since Fredo. If I'd confided in Bobby or Marc or Lou, I might not've told my dad, and he'd be alive today. Maybe this was too damn big for me to figure out, alone. So I said, "Y'know what? I'm gonna call Marc, see if he can meet us, too."

"Marc?"

"Yeah, something's gotta be done about this I must try to put a stop to it or it's gonna end me."

"What?"

"I – I'll tell you both at lunch."

We'd started walking again, without me realizing it, and had reached the back entrance to the Criminal Court Building, so we headed in different directions. Then a couple hours later we were seated

123

in a booth at the far end of this noisy and crowded joint close by, and I'd filled them both in.

Marc was looking over my new memo book as I said, "I got books like these going back to since I started this job. Some have entries that are incriminating to certain cops, and...and the entries show a pattern, Marc – cops signing out evidence that isn't theirs. All of it drugs."

Marc leaned forward, his face troubled. "But it's all just circumstantial. What do you really have in the way of evidence? Did you actually see Velasquez sign those particular drugs in or out?"

I had to shake my head and wonder why Marc was saying that. Perps had been convicted on less in a trial.

"I know," was all I said, in reply. "But it's just – it's just too coincidental. So...that's why I kept making entries in my memo book, hoping...someday I'd catch 'em in the act."

"Yeah, that's the best thing you can do, right now. That'll back you up if anything goes down."

"Couldn't we go to Internal Affairs?" Lou asked.

I shook my head. "You talk to them and people find out? You're marked. Look at Serpico. He's lucky he's alive – gettin' shot, like that."

"If there's just some way to get something on film," Marc said I know there are no cameras at Property Clerk.

Lou hopped up and down, like a kid. "My sister, Gina, is a photographer. She has all kinds of cameras. I'll ask her if I can borrow one. Keep an eye out. If we can catch one of those guys leaving with the wrong evidence envelope or folder, or meeting up with the wrong people..."

"Gina?" I sort-of laughed. "You are half-Italian."

"Not unless I was adopted," Lou smirked back at me.

Marc sighed. "Have you done surveillance, Lou?"

Lou shook his head. "Not really but come on, how hard can that be? Snap a few pictures."

"I have done it. And believe me; the hardest part is not getting spotted. It's not like the movies, you know when the cops are running around with these big cameras and the bad guys don't see 'em. In real life, they'd have been made in five seconds, and if you are, you could blow the case – or worse."

Lou nodded his understanding then said, "I just hate to see that shit get back on the street. It's ruined so many kids."

124

"And their parents," I said. "My Aunt and Uncle – they were never the same after my cousin O-D'd. Thing is – I think if they'd lived somewhere else it would have been different."

"No, man," Lou said, "drugs're everywhere now. I caught a couple of White Plains brats trying to score, a few months back. Idiots. And what's worse? Daddy's lawyer got them off and the case thrown out."

"Well we gotta do something," I said. "This has been going on for years. I mean, at least since I started over at the Narcotics Bureau. That's four – no, five years, minimum. And I'm pretty sure it was happening even before that."

"Okay, you're right," Marc nodded. "Again – we can't prove anything, but if you do get something more solid, there are people I can talk to get a real investigation going. Let's start with that."

I'd like to say unloading like that on Marc and Lou made me feel better, but I was still keyed up. I wanted the whole damn thing over and done with, not carrying on even longer. And Marc seemed to be setting pretty high standards for evidence. But then, I had to admit – if you're going after a dirty cop, your details had to be iron-solid.

So a few days later, in spite of Marc's warning Lou and I were sitting in his car down the block on Broome Street, with a perfect view of the one and only revolving door. Cops and civil servants and all sorts of other people entered and exited, non-stop, none of them knowing or thinking or caring about what went on in there. He had this kick-ass-looking 35mm camera with a lens half a foot long on the seat between us. His sister had shown him how best to use it and he'd already focused on the door so it was ready to fire in a flash.

He was almost like this excited puppy as he said, "I had myself put on steady four to twelve's, so I can sit here everyday. Carl didn't like it much, but..."

"Carl?"

"Carlo Pantucci."

"Oh, okay," Lou's partner. I'd only met him once; didn't really know him but he hit me as a guy who's a lot like Bobby.

"He's a good guy. We've been together the last four months. Anyway, he and his wife're still like newlyweds, so..."

"Tell him to make it last as long as he can," I said.

"You haven't been married that long."

"Doesn't matter," I sighed, and then got back on track. "I can't do a change this week. I got three court – well, two trials and a grand

125

jury appearance going on. But next week, I'll ask Bobby if he'll do four-to-twelves with me so I can be here, too."

"I can handle it till then."

"No, no, no, Lou, don't even think it. Wait till I – ."

"C'mon, Petey, you think I need my hand held?"

"I just don't want you here alone. Let's start this next week so I can be with you...or better yet, I'll see if Marc knows somebody who can get us a temporary assignment for a month or two. Just don't let anybody in on it."

"Ah," he whispered in that Kung-fu style. "Tell no one; do everything, grasshopper. Everything we allow you to do."

Him making light of it, pissed me off, so I grabbed his arm, suddenly scared for him.

"Lou, listen up – this ain't a game. I lived around guys like this all my life. Maybe Marc gets it. You don't. You can't, not unless you grew up around these guys. This code – it's about more than just keeping quiet about what some cop does or what some wise guy does. But when there is a cop hooked up with a powerful wise guy that could be a big problem. I know what they can do – what they will do if they have to. Because they'll see you as going up against the family and their business and they turn into tigers when it comes to that. You don't fuck with them. You just – you just don't."

"Then why're you doing it?"

Bam, that right between the eyes. He was right to ask, because that's what I was doing. I'd promised Ronnie I wouldn't do this, all those years ago, but that is exactly what I was doing. I hadn't really let myself think about that.

But then I saw my cousin, Fredo, crashed on that chair, his clothes messed up, needle in his arm, exactly like Aunt Mary found him with cops walking around and chit-chatting like he's just another screwed-up junkie who got dumb about how much horse he could handle. And I heard her weeping in the next room. And I could see him being jumped at the door and held down by a couple of goons as they shot him up. And I could see the terror in his eyes as he realized what was gonna happen and how he fought it as they held him down and let him drown in that crap. And then were heartless enough to leave him like that for his family to see. That's what this was leading to. It wasn't just that he was killed; it's that they spit on my aunt...on my family by leaving him like that. And there's where the difference was – junkies would've snuck the pure crap in on him and let him die on the floor. It was cops that did this. That left him like that. And that's who I was

126

after, some bastard cops who didn't give a damn about how much hurt they were causing. Not Ronnie or Rizo or Dante or anybody else.

"It's those bastards," I said, the words starting to spill out, "Velasquez, Kowalski, Moretti – they aren't family. No, what they're doing is – they're crushing us – all of us – our families and how can a cop be involved in this? How can a cop be helping that? Helping assholes who don't give a damn what they're doing to families and people who're part of their own? And all for greed and money. They are worse than animals, those scumbags. They're a cancer. They are a cancer eating away at everything and not giving a damn. Eventually they'll kill what they're feeding on and that'll be the end of them, too. They'll die along with the people they're feeding off of, and they don't care. All that matters is now and the hell with tomorrow. It's sick. It's fucking sick, and it's gotta stop. It's gotta."

Lou looked at me, a bit wary. "Man, I don't even want to think about how that's messing you up."

It took me a second to get back in control, then I said, "I'm just telling you – don't take any chances. Be as discreet as possible."

"Buddy, I'm black," he smirked, "so I can't be anything but smooth as a breeze."

"Cut it out! It's their ass on the line, so they'd kill us both in a heartbeat if it'll keep them out of jail."

"Don't try scaring me, Petey. I've been to Nam, and they were some killing motherfuckers, over there."

"Then that should give you a fuckin' idea what you're up against! Ask Carlo; I hear he's been in Nam, too."

"I know! Okay? Shit."

"Do you also know people think all you Nam vets are crazy. And if word got around the street, it'd make things harder for you and Carl, both."

"You know I'm the only black guy in my reserve unit in North Carolina? It pisses off a couple crackers, too. 'Damn nigger in my unit'."

"Shit, Lou!"

"Hey, I can use the word; you can't. Okay?" And his smile was backed by some serious warning. I nodded. He grinned and said, "C'mon, I'll drop you off at Court."

Then he started the car and we pulled away, and I saw at least three of the people near that door watching us leave, probably wondering what we were up to, and talking so hard.

Yeah, real smooth, that's us.

127

Of course, he didn't get it. How could he? And I knew he couldn't. I should've just called in sick. Rode herd on him till he understood. I should have insisted he wait. If only he'd waited, just a couple days. That afternoon I got a call from him, and he told me what he'd done, all sure and proud of what he thought he accomplished.

Soon as he dumped me at 100 Centre Street, he'd gone back to Broome street and parked and was about to get out when he saw Moretti exit through the revolving doors, in uniform, a thick evidence envelope in hand.

He hopped back in the car, yanked the camera from under a towel on the front seat and took pictures of him walking to the corner and turning right. Lou started his car and slowly drove around the corner to catch Moretti getting in back seat of an unmarked city car.

Moments later, Moretti exited the back seat; a jacket covering the uniform shirt then got behind the wheel and drove away, first to Houston then east to the FDR drive and headed uptown.

Lou followed at what he figured was a safe distance.

Moretti exited on 96th then turned right on First Avenue. Not even paying any attention, Lou said. No worries. Nothing, which was nonsense, and I told Lou that. He shrugged it off, because when Moretti reached 116th, he turned right and parked in front of this building.

"What'd this place look like?" I asked.

"It was pretty run down," Lou said, "but in better shape than the rest of the neighborhood. Just off the corner of Pleasant Ave and 116th street on the right side of 116th going east. No number on it."

"Was it like an old brownstone?"

"Yes and t had bars on the ground floor windows, kind of old and ugly and the one next it better shape, taller, got arched windows. You have been there?"

Back then a guy name Dante had it. Yeah, I'd been there. "Uh, My Aunt and Uncle lived up there. We went in for a beer."

My cousin and I did, years ago after the Feast.

"So it's a mafia club?"

"Aw, shit, Lou, get your brain out of the Fifties. It's not just Mafia now; its blacks and Ricans and white guys on Wall Street and queers on Christopher Street and gangs in Chinatown and everybody everywhere. Yeah, it was an Italian Social Club, but that was ten years ago. God knows what it is now."

"Ten years ago?" he asked, sounding stupidly incredulous. "They allowed underage drinking? I'm gonna have to report this."

128

"Son-of-a-bitch! Lou, will you get serious? What happened next?"

Well, Moretti got out, a red shopping bag in hand and walked straight into the side door of the building without a pause; Lou snapping away. Then he made a U-turn and waited on the other side of the street get a better view. He'd run the full 24 on his roll and had to pop in a new one, but he kept an eye on the club and watched mostly older Italian-looking guys enter and exit. So it was still Dante's; I guess they wouldn't give that place up till the money stopped rolling in and all of east Harlem was black or Hispanic, what with the Church of our Lady of Mount Carmel just down the street.

Two minutes after he got the new roll set in the camera, a Cadillac double-parked in front, and both the driver and the passenger were black. The driver stayed with car; the passenger got out and entered the club.

Lou snapped photos, including some of the license plate, but his view of it was partially obscured.

I had to blow up at that. "Shit, Lou, why not just put up a neon sign sayin', 'Hi, I'm your friendly neighborhood amateur cop here to surveillance you; smile for the fuckin' camera!'?"

"Nobody paid any attention to me! Shit, you think I'm an idiot?"

No question, because what happened next was, the passenger came out of the club, holding that red shopping bag, and got in the car. It made a U-turn in front of Lou and drove west on 116th.

That meant they'd made him and wanted a better look without it looking like they were looking. Shit. And what did Lou do? He started his car and followed them.

They turned right on First Avenue and headed north, then stopped at the next light.

Lou slowed down a good four car-lengths back and got a good shot of the license plate. And I just knew that's where the driver would've gone beyond just noticing Lou in the rear-view mirror and told his passenger, "The brother in that Pontiac's following us."

He might even have reached in his jacket to pull a gun but his passenger would've noticed there was an RMP down 125th so would've said, "No need for that. There's one of our guys."

They took their time turning left on 125th Street, forcing Lou to get caught by the light, then drove on slowly, seeming like they didn't have a care in the world. Down the block, Lou saw the Caddy do a lane shift to hide in front of some other cars. And from there it was easy as cake to see what happened.

The Caddy slowed down alongside a 28th Precinct patrol car, some cop just out doing his thing. The passenger window glided down and my bet is the passenger said something like, "Hey, Officer," or even called him by name; they could have had a contract with the sector. "Got a minute?"

Then he'd carefully shown two hundred-dollar bills, the car never stopping, completely. The cop'd would reach in and palm money, maybe not even looking straight at the guy, and he'd mutter, "What can I help you with?"

"I got eight more," said the passenger, "if you come by the office, later, and tell me who the brother is drivin' the blue Pontiac that's about to come down this street."

The cop'd say, "Twenty minutes." By that point, the Cadillac would've pulled completely away.

How do I figure this? Because after Lou turned onto 125th, the Caddy just in sight, the cop waived him over the second he saw him. Lou opened his window and held up his tin, saying "I'm on the job." Then he tried to just keep going.

But the cop stepped in from of him and pointed to the side so Lou pulled over. Then the cop strolled up and said, "You got an ID card to go with that shield?"

And Lou showed it to him.

"You did what?!" I screamed. "Are you nuts?"

"What'm I supposed to do, Petey? He's a uniform, like me!"

The cop'd looked it over and asked, "What in the hell you doing up here in the Two-Eight, Officer? You're not a tourist, are you, with that camera and all?"

Of course, Lou'd seen the Caddy was long gone, so he just sighed and said, "My wife and I're looking for a place to live, but she's working today so I'm taking pictures of buildings that look good."

"Trust me," the cop said, "you don't wanna move to Harlem. I suggest you get back were you belong."

So Lou'd gone on back to work, not even seeing what he'd done. Because twenty minutes later, I knew that cop'd entered some bar or store and said, "This is gonna cost ya an extra grand." And the cat'd handed it over like it's nothing.

Jesus.

"Lou, don't turn out," I said. "Call in sick."

130

"What the fuck, Pete. It's after four; we're on our way to post."

"But they know who you are!"

"Who's they and how?"

"You told 'em. That cop looked at your ID card and asked if you work in the Ninth and what're you doing in Harlem, right? He got your name and command! I think he sold you out."

"Cops don't do that – ."

"Lou, cops set up Serpico – ."

"We don't know that for a fact, yet."

"The hell we don't – !"

"Petey, get control of yourself. C'mon, you think that cop's gonna turn me over? Don't we have a brotherhood?"

"Well, yeah – we got a brotherhood, except when it comes to lots of cash and or going to jail. I guess in Nam they didn't worry about either one of those things, did they? You think I never heard of grunts fraggin' their officers? Well, this jungle ain't no different from that one! Guys never know what hit them till it's too late."

He just sighed and said, "Okay, cool it! I gotta get on post. My partner's waiting for me, so you – ."

"Lou, just be careful, okay?"

"I'm with Carlo, and we got the Avenue B foot post, tonight, okay? Who the hell's gonna mess with the both of us?"

"All right, all right, all right, just – just keep your eyes peeled."

He shouldn't have gone in. He should've listened to me. He should've at least given me a chance to find out who that cop was and warn the bastard off. But he didn't.

So that night, Lou and Carlo Pantucci walked their beat. It was chilly and they were bundled up. It was late January 1972,then according to witnesses, three men passed them, all wearing dark clothes, wool caps, scarves, and gloves, and the second they were behind the cops, they pulled out guns and fired into their backs. After Lou and Carlo crashed to the ground, the shooters walked up and fired several more bullets into their heads, then hid their guns and vanished into the night, like ghosts.

First word I got was a flash on the Eleven o'clock news – two cops shot, no other details. But the instant I heard I knew. I knew. And I went cold all over and completely blank. Louisa told me later that I walked out of the house like I was in a trance, didn't hear her call me as I got in my car and drove away.

131

I went straight to the Ninth and the place was in frenzy. Cops from all commands were there in addition to guys like me, who'd roared in to help in any way we could. It was chaos.

Initial word at the time was that the perps were holed up somewhere in the Precinct. A supposed witness stated they entered a building on Tenth Street; the problem was all the roofs were connected. So a door-to-door search was initiated. Of course, if nobody answered the door there was nothing that could be done. You can't smash into somebody's home looking for a killer unless you know for a fact they're in there. And nobody knew anything. So a perimeter was set up for Tenth Street from Avenue B to C, and since the building was on the north side of Tenth it went all the way around to Eleventh Street. For days no one could enter or leave without showing identification, but nothing was found. Nothing was learned. Nothing could be done. And after several days with no results, the search stopped.

Through the whole time, I stayed at the precinct. Showering there, changing uniforms and having food delivered. Louisa brought me fresh clothes and seemed to understand why I had to be in the middle of the whole mess...but how could she, really? You see, Lou was my buddy. Lou'd tried to have my back, and I hadn't been there for him. Now I was doing the only thing I could to even try and make up for it.

What she didn't know was I was also scared...and scared for her. I figured if I wasn't near her, right then, she'd be safer. And I was trying like crazy to figure out what my next move'd be. No question in my mind, Lou was killed because he'd followed that Caddy. And a cop'd turned him over. And he and I'd been seen together, out in front of Broome Street. His actions could be traced right back to me, and I could just as easily be getting both Bobby and me put down the same way. So the best place to stay was in the Ninth, making calls and sorting through information that was coming in, I avoided going on patrol, being out there making us both a target until I had a better handle on the whole mess.

I put some calls through to Mark but he was caught in the hysteria, too, out pumping his contacts and using his undercover persona to try and get a lead of some kind, so he was completely unavailable, at first. Then I figured he was flat out ignoring the messages I was leaving. I didn't know what to do.

Until I got the call. Since I was not just a fellow officer but also a close friend of Lou's, would I like to stand honor guard over his coffin? I couldn't say no. No matter how scared or freaked out I was I couldn't say no.

132

I should've. I should've.

133

****

The wake for Police Officers Franklyn and Pantucci was held in St. Patrick's Cathedral, even though Lou wasn't Catholic. It's tradition for cops who die in the line of duty to have their services there. This time, it was a closed casket with two uniformed cops flanking each one's head, as Color Guards; a portrait of each cop in his uniform was placed on the casket. The pews were full as lines of people wandered in to pay their respects, cross themselves and wander off to sit and pray or light a candle or give sympathy to Lou's mom and sister, sitting to the right of Lou's casket, then over to Carlo Pantucci's big Italian family, seated to the left.

I made myself go home, get cleaned up right and dressed proper, and I presented myself at the very moment I was called for. I stood to the left of Lou's coffin, and every tear I saw stabbed me in the heart, adding to my knowledge that I could have prevented this. I could have. I could've left the house and gone on patrol with Lou, the moment I hung up. He'd told me where he was going to be. I should've gone without even asking him. I should've had his back, that way.

Or I could've called the Two-Eight, right then, and put the fear of god into that cop. Yeah, I didn't know who it was, but I could've found out. Told him I knew what he'd pulled and would turn him over if anything happened. Made him tell me who the black guys were and gotten hold of Ronnie to get a message to Dante to make 'em back off. Let them know how bad it'd be for everyone if a cop was whacked. That would've all but guaranteed Dante would had stopped it cold.

But I didn't do any of that. Louisa was having troubles from the baby and I got busy with tending to her. Trying to make her comfortable, bringing her things. Wishing to god the kid would pop out already, even though he wasn't just yet due. And I'd hoped for the best. So now one of my partners was dead, and I felt like dirt.

I was barely under control through it all, watching the scores of men and women enter and exit the cathedral. But I made myself stand there one solid hour, at full parade rest, like we're supposed to, till a couple other uniforms relieved me and my Color Guard partner, on the half-hour; Pantucci's color guard was changed on the hour. Then we marched away in perfect sync to break formation outside. I didn't even nod at the guy before I went back inside and down to the front pew.

134

Lou's elegant mom and a pretty young woman, Gina, both in black, sat there, quietly weeping. I stopped before them, shaking, trying to figure out what to say. I could see Lou in his sister, even with all her tears. And in his mother, who seemed to have the strength of Job in her. They looked at me, expectant.

Finally, I just whispered, "I am so sorry. So sorry. I – I wish – ."

Lou's mom took my hand, firmly, and sort-of smiled at me, saying, "It's okay, sugar. Thanks."

I leaned over and hugged her. What else could I do? I'd warned Lou not to take these guys too lightly. I'd told him to be careful. Yeah, he was a man, a solider that did a tour in Viet Nam...and he came home to this. A different, more dangerous jungle. No one deserves that.

I took his sister's hand and said, "Gina? May I speak to you for a minute?"

She nodded and we slipped over to an alcove. Candles were burning in the background and the light seemed to dance and glow around her hair and face. Her eyes caught glimmers of it, giving them a thousand times more life than I had in my own. She was peaceful and graceful in the face of one of the worst things anyone can face. Suddenly I was really nervous.

"What is it?" she asked.

I finally sputtered out, "I'm so sorry, Gina, and – and I'm sorry to ask, but Lou mentioned he borrowed a camera of yours. Can I have the film? It – it could be important."

"Camera?" She frowned at me, and I felt my heart drop. Then she remembered. "Oh, right, right. I don't have it. Lou left it in his car." Then her lips twisted into a painful snarl. "It was broken into. On top of all this, his car was broken into."

I think I stopped breathing, for a moment. "When?"

"The night he was shot," she said. "Man, when it rains, it pours. But it was stolen, and now no one can find it."

Well, there it was. There was proof positive. That was in my mind, of course; nothing that would hold up in a court of law against any cop or a guy with a good lawyer. On top of it, the brass was already busy blaming this on the Black Panthers. Someone said the bastards called the "New York Times" claiming responsibility and saying they were out to kill black cops for – how'd they put it? – collaborating with the enemy. I could already see how it'd play out, now. Nothing would be found. Nobody held to blame. Lou and Carlo would wind up dead

135

and buried with no justice for either one of them. And the same night Lou's car getting busted into. That would just be a crazy coincidence that nobody wanted to pay attention to. If they did, it'd raise too many unsettling questions.

Why I was not surprised?

Soon it was time for the mass; the Cardinal of all of New York presided. I was in the front row, along with a group of guys from the Ninth Precinct. And I was barely keeping it under control. Bobby was next to me. I knew I'd have to tell him, now. And tell Marc what I knew. But they wouldn't be willing to believe me without some proof. Something to show them, without question, Lou was murdered because he'd been caught following the wrong guys – and that he'd been turned over by a fellow cop. You had to have more than proof for anybody to believe that; you had to have a confession, and no cop would ever confess to that. No way in hell.

I watched the brass sit in the front row, acting like they really gave a damn. Same for the politicians who went on and on about how these two brave young men died fighting crime, even as they went back to their offices and cut into the police budgets and complained loudly about police brutality whenever it would get them notice on the eleven o'clock news and took bribes from the guys who were ruining the city. It was sickening.

At the same time, hundreds of police officers representing every state in America waited outside. I saw them as I exited. It seemed like a total ocean of them, from the entrance at 51st street all the way to 47th street. When the coffins were brought out, they snapped to attention, row after row after row of them.

Too little too late, I thought, and I know some of you are being two-faced about it. Lou wanted to help clean up the department, and some of you bastards would've fought him every step of the way.

I mean, it's not like the NYPD's the only group that's got crooked cops in the world. I'd heard things about the New Orleans that'd make your hair curl. LAPD, Dallas and Houston. Forget about it. But this whole exhibition here, it was only meant to show the public that we're all a bunch of nice guys who love each other and just want to protect and serve. It was making me sick.

Then I noticed Kowalski and Moretti nearby, their eyes locked on me. All but screaming at me, "We know what you're up to, you rat."

My breath started coming in sharp, ragged bursts. Lou'd been murdered by guys like this. Now that I knew a cop'd finger another cop for death, I knew I could be, too. It's funny, but until Lou died, I'd never seriously paid attention to the possibility that I'd get killed. That I'd never see my child, and Louisa and the baby would have to live on without me. Keep going the rest of their lives without me. I'm not much of a religious person...I mean, yeah, I went to mass with my folks every Sunday, confessed my sins and received Holy Communion every once in a while, but I was never an altar boy or Knights of Columbus or anything. And up till now it'd always been this abstract idea that, yeah, eventually you die and stuff, but it wasn't something I honestly thought could happen to me until I was old and tired and ready for it. Not until now, when my dad was dead and I knew cops'd kill cops if they were threatened.

And who was I threatening? Moretti and Kowalski and their extra income.

And Velasquez, who was suddenly off to my other side. Who was also shooting me sharp, knowing glances.

Oh, shit.

Suddenly I felt like every cop in the funeral cortege was glaring at me. Like they all knew. That guy, he'd rat out a cop. He'd hurt the brotherhood. He can't be trusted. He's got to be got rid of, like a mad dog and –

Bagpipes blasted to my left, making me jump. There is something very humbling and sad when you hear those damned things blare. Everyone knows a cop has fallen in the line of duty, no matter what race, religion or creed they were. This wasn't my first Line of Duty funeral; by God I hope it to be my last.

Then the two caskets exited the church, carried very solemnly and very respectfully and very slowly by uniformed police officers. One after the other, down step after step after step, each with a little pause on every step to show how deeply affected we were. How we really, really cared. Then each was placed in its own flower-smothered hearse.

I was at full attention as I watched the whole thing play out, knowing full well I was marked. I might be dumb enough to point out they would never catch the guys who did this. My guess was, they themselves were killed as soon as they returned and they may be fish bait already.

I remembered being with Lou in his car and warning him, "Lou, listen up – this ain't a game. I lived around guys like this all my life."

And remembered Rizo shooting Bobby Bats and his bodyguard and seeing them crash to the floor as I'd said, "I know what they can do."

I know what they've done. What they're capable of.

But had I known? Really? No, it'd just been in my mind, not my heart. It'd always been something done to somebody else, never me and mine. Now it wasn't anywhere else but in my heart. Tears streamed down my face as I thought about the whole new world I was being forced to take notice of and the dangers now obvious in it and it's all coming to roost on my doorstep and –

Three uniformed cops marched in front of me and Bobby, completely out of order. They stopped, facing away.

This isn't right. What're they doing there? Why'd they get out of formation? This doesn't make any sense or –

All three did an about-face and everything clicked into slow-motion as they looked directly at me and Bobby and pulled shotguns up from under their overcoats!

I grabbed Bobby and yanked him back as the shotguns fired and screams were heard and people stumbled about and the smell of gunpowder filled the air and –

Suddenly I was on my back, at the top of the steps, and Bobby was pulling himself away from me.

And the three cops had vanished.

They just vanished!?

I slowly got up, dazed. Other cops helped Bobby up, and he was pissed. "What the hell's wrong with you?!"

He didn't see them? Didn't see the guns? Didn't see anything that I saw? People were glaring at me like I'd just spit on one of the coffins.

And there was no smell of gunpowder in the air. Not even a hint of it.

Oh, jeez. This wasn't good. I Gotta say something.

"I – I dunno, Bobby, I – I must've passed out," I said.

"Yeah? Really?"

I couldn't speak. I couldn't think except to get back into formation with everybody until the two hearses started down Fifth Avenue. Then all of us returned to attention and saluted. After the hearses were gone, we broke formation, and I noticed a lot of the guys were casting wary glances at me.

I was shaking like crazy, felt close to breaking down. So Bobby dragged me away from everyone into a corner of the church

138

foyer, still angry. He shoved me into the wall and got close into my face, growling, "Pete, what the fuck's going on?"

"Bobby, I – I'm sorry. I felt dizzy. I – I thought I saw something, heard something."

"Bullshit. You said, 'Watch out,' then you grabbed me. That wasn't just passing out."

"I – I didn't know, I – heard a sound and – ."

"A car backfired," Bobby snapped. "A couple people started wailing and – ."

"Are you so sure?" I snapped at him.

He looked at me for a moment then said, "Okay, Pete – listen; don't take this wrong, but – uh, you've been kind of weird, lately. Maybe you should talk to – you know, a doctor. Just check it out."

"A shrink. Yeah, right, I was just scared for you, trying to protect you, you bastard, and you say I'm nuts?"

Except...except he said I'd been acting weird, lately. He was seeing it in me, like Dad did.

My God, has it come to this a shrink? It's the modern version of your father confessor but without the absolution of your sins? Was that really what I needed?

I could see honest concern in Bobby's face. I have seen his face at times so full of hate and anger directed toward criminals and creeps. I felt he cared about me and wanted to get me help, he was worried and he was right. Maybe it was time for that. Use it to test the waters a little. See what the general reaction might be to me all but climbing onto the top of Centre Street and yelling, "Cops peddle drugs and kill cops!"

So I rubbed my face and nodded, and a week later, I was sitting in an overstuffed chair in one of those fake wood paneling offices on the forty-something floor of some mid-town high-rise. This guy who looked more like an organizer for the UAW sat at his desk, suit and tie a bit too tight on him. I'd been referred to him by one of Louisa's friends, not the union's health care reps; I wanted this kept as low-key as possible till I knew what was what with me.

Anyway, we chatted around, for a little bit, then he finally straight-out asked me why I was there. It took me a minute, but I finally told him, "I keep seeing things that seem so real and are happening, but they're not."

"Give me an example," he said in this tone that was almost soothing.

139

"Well – at my dad's funeral, I saw a couple guys pour gas on my car then burn it. Only it didn't really happen."

"That sounds rather intense."

"While I was seeing it, it was it felt so real, but now? I think I fell and hit my head, I can't even tell you for sure if I even had a conversation with one of those two guys in the first place."

"Did you see a doctor? Have it checked?"

"That's what I doing here."

"You know I meant the dizziness was there a cut or bump on your head?

"Yes and no. There was a wound. I found dry blood the next day but never did anything about it; I wanted not to talk about it only after my last incident my partner insisted I come see you, well you know a professional."

"Tell me about this incident?"

"Well – last week, I thought someone was going to shoot me and a buddy of mine, well me and my partner."

"Thought? Can you be more specific?"

"I – it's like I saw it. It played out, during the funeral of two good cops."

"I see." The doctor murmured, and then he looked at the forms I filled out. "So, you're a police officer."

"Yes, sir – that's right."

"And you said both incidents happened at funerals? Was your father's very recent?"

"Yes, sir, a few months back. And – and a friend was killed."

He straightened up, as if he'd just thought of something, and then he said, "Those two officers who were executed."

What a way to put it. I nodded.

He continued with, "I see. You know, this could be job-related stress. It's not unusual for police officers to become hyper-vigilant after such a traumatic incident. Police work would make someone overly concerned and aware of the possibility of something similar happening to them. I'll prescribe you something for it, but I don't recommend you work while taking it. This medication has a tendency to slow things down."

What? I talk to the guy for five minutes and he wants to drug me up? "But, I – I gotta work."

"Don't you have sick leave? Take some time off. And I'll want to see you sometime next week."

Next week?! He was the one who's nuts. I mean, seriously, the guy's a MD. He's got diplomas all over the wall. Probably cost a hundred-grand to get them. But he can't figure out that if I take sick leave now, they'll know? They'll know I know something and I'm using that as an excuse to give me time to take it to the brass or IAD? That much sick leave at one time is obviously a cover. Oh, I had plenty accumulated; I hadn't called in sick once in the last year and only a couple times the whole time I'd been a cop, so far. Which meant it would be seen as out of the ordinary, for me. And I'm supposed to send up a red flag, like that? He is the one who's crazy if he thinks that's a good idea.

But all I said was, "Thank you, Doctor."

He filled out a prescription and handed it to me. And I took it and left, figuring I'd never bother with it. And that was that.

But man, that night was not good. Every noise I heard was amplified ten times. A car driving past the house was going too slow for reality. Shadows seemed more like people hiding and lying in wait. I started pacing and kept going till I was nearly exhausted. Louisa put up with it for as long as she could then stood in front of me. To be honest, if she hadn't been so big and pregnant, I don't think I'd have noticed her, I was so focused on trying not to lose it. But she stopped me.

"How long did you take off?" she asked.

"Three days," I said, a little out of breath. "Can't take too long; they'd find out – ."

"Who are they? Find out what?"

Dammit, I almost let the cat out of the bag. The less she knows the better. So I just glanced at her, shrugging.

"Try these," she said. "See how it goes."

I finally noticed she had a glass of water and a pair of different-colored pills in hand. I had to laugh at seeing it; I hadn't even realized she'd gotten the prescription filled. I sighed. "Tranqs. Tranquilizers – for a cop. Perfect."

"Peter, you need to get some sleep. Good sleep. Now, I'm sure the doctor knows what he's doing, so..."

She all but shoved the pills at me. What the hell. I took them and chased them down with the water.

"Now sit down. Take it easy. Unwind."

She guided me over to the sofa and sat with me, rubbing my back.

I pulled her close and words just started flowing out; I had no control over them. "I'm sorry, so sorry, it's just, I get going and keep going and can't seem to stop and I know they're coming for me, and sometimes I'm so scared. Gotta protect you...and the baby...but I don't know how. There's so much going on, so much I can't tell you about." And on and on I went.

Finally, she shushed me and lay me back on the sofa.

"I'll get a cool washcloth for your eyes."

I nodded. She headed for the linen closet.

I kept muttering, "Can't take too long. They'll know."

But slowly, slowly, it got to where it mattered less and less, and my heart stopped thumping like crazy and my brain began to calm down, and I drifted away as the tranquilizers took control.

A week later, I was sitting before the Doctor, and for some reason I was rubbing my hand. Nonstop. And it scared me.

"The medication could cause that," he said. "How long did you take it?"

"Just two days – but then I didn't even want to get out of bed."

"Try half a pill. Then – after a week – take the full pill."

"But how about work?"

"You should take some time off, like I suggested. I'll write a letter and tell your superiors I recommend it. Then stay on the meds and after six months, you should be able to go back to work."

"Six months!? Doc, if I do that – my police department life is over. And besides, someone killed two good cops and the investigation's going nowhere – but if it's all connected – ." And I stopped talking, not at all happy.

"Connected?" he asked. "Connected to what?"

Dammit, I'd almost spilled it, again. I had to keep better control of my tongue.

"Officer Buono, may I call you Pete? – talking about things will help you in many ways, positive ways. Just to get something out in the open and off your mind – you see things from a clearer perspective."

"Maybe." He just kept looking at me, so I knew I had to have something to make him happy. I finally came out with, "You know, I – I make sure I'm not followed when I come here."

"There's nothing to be ashamed of, seeing a psychiatrist."

"It's not that. I – I just don't want – certain people – to think you know what I know."

"Our conversation is privileged."

142

I just sighed. "You don't get it."

"Get what?"

"Never mind I guess I'm just babbling."

"Maybe, maybe not, but on your next appointment here. I want to talk more about this, next time. And please consider taking some time off."

I nodded – but there was no way I was going to. This guy just didn't get it. Maybe I should've gone with a doctor who understood cops better.

What I did was go back to what I knew. I held a barbecue in my back yard and invited Marc and Bobby, along with a bunch of other people. For some reason, flipping burgers on the grill helps me focus and chatting with Marc while doing it wouldn't seem out of line, especially since he was first in line and had his plate in hand and bun all ready.

I quietly filled him in on everything that I'd seen and what Lou had done as I cooked his burger to medium-well, flipping it three, four, five times, then I said, "I'm tellin' you – Moretti, Velasquez, Kowalski, they had something to do with Lou and Pantucci."

"Pete, this is still a lot of conjecture, and some pretty wild accusations, at that," he said, keeping his voice low as mine. "I can't say anything to anybody without something in the way of proof."

"C'mon, Marc, Lou's car getting broke into the night he dies? And his sister says they can't find her camera?"

"Camera?"

"Yeah. He – he borrowed it and was taking pictures, starting in front of 400 Broome Street – that's not just a coincidence – ."

"You think there's a connection?"

"Come on, Marc, what are you -- second grade? What did they do, give you grade just because you're good-looking?"

"All right, all right, calm down."

"Gotta be connected. What are the chances of any car in that lot right across from the station house being vandalized, never mind the same day two cops getting popped? I'm telling you, it's like getting hit by lighting twice. Can you talk to your guy? I'm feeling all alone, here."

Marc frowned, not looking at me, then he said, "I'll call him, Monday, and – ."

Louisa waddled up and I motioned for Marc to be quiet.

"Who're you calling?" she asked. "Is it new girl?"

"Still stuck on you, Louisa," Marc grinned, not missing a beat.

143

"Let's see how you feel in a couple hours."

That was a weird thing to say. "What's that about?"

"It's about you calling the doctor."

The doctor? Why a – DOCTOR! Okay, if I'd been freaking out, before, that was nothing in comparison. I dropped the spatula, forgot about the burgers and in five seconds we had a caravan of cars racing through traffic for the hospital. And even though it was only five minutes away, it felt like it took hours. Then we screamed to a halt by the ER entrance and I guided Louisa from the car as everybody else piled out of the other cars to shepherd us in.

The nurses put her in a wheelchair and scooted her off to the delivery room. Everybody set up the party in the reception area, with Marc and Bobby going back to the house to get the rest of the burgers and stuff, and a couple hours later, Louisa and I were holding our son. Well, she was, because I was kneeling at her side, and I was touching the baby and beaming at my wife and well-wishes were coming from everybody.

"He's beautiful," I said, overwhelmed. Then I touched her face and said, "You did such a good job holding everything together – and – and – Louisa, baby, I – I'm gonna do everything I can – everything."

She caressed my face. I kissed her hand, and suddenly the rest of the world vanished. This is what mattered most. Just this, the rest had to go away. If HQ didn't want to deal with crooked cops, so be it. If politicians wanted to sweep corruption under the rug, let 'em. It's not like there was anything new about any of it. Cops'd been corrupt since the beginning of time; hell, even Pontius Pilate sent a man he'd declared to be innocent of any crime to death, all because of politics. And if people didn't want to demand their police force be held to a higher standard, who was I to say they're wrong?

No, all that mattered from this day forward was my wife and baby.

All the rest could go to hell.

So a few months later, Louisa was still home being fussed over by her mom and my mom and sisters and it seemed like every woman I'd ever met in my life. Which I thought was funny. It's not like my sisters hadn't already given mom grandkids, but apparently since this was the first boy from the only boy, it meant the name would carry on and everybody could breathe a sigh of relief now that I'd done what was expected.

I'd gone back to work a week after the baby came. No fear. No tranqs. No shaking. Everything great between Bobby and me and everybody else. I hadn't heard anything from Marc about what I'd told him, and I got the feeling he'd put it on a back burner. And to be honest, I didn't feel the need to push him on it. My family mattered most, right then, and it took everything I had to make sure Louisa and little William Joseph Buono had everything they needed to make their lives as easy as possible. That meant overtime and anything else I could do to bring in some cash. We had just the one paycheck, now, and Louisa was hinting like she'd prefer to stay home to be there with our son.

Thing is, our sex life wasn't back to where it had been, yet. That was to be expected. Though like I said, it wasn't all the 4th of July fireworks that everybody wishes for before she got pregnant. So I...well, I did what any creep of a husband would do and look for sex in other places. Again, I'm no saint, and the weird part is, it seemed to help me keep my mind under control. Hell, working doubles and after-hours gigs and backing up the local merchants (on top of a girl here and there), that was enough to keep my brain going so fast; I didn't have time to go crazy.

We hardly ever wrote parking tickets, but one day Bobby and I came up on this new Eldorado convertible parked in front of a hydrant across from Tompkins Park, on Avenue A. I'm talking right on the hydrant, and its top was down. Bobby just shook his head.

"Askin' for it to get 'jacked," he said.

I was riding shotgun, so I nodded and grabbed my summons book. But then this woman with long, long blond hair and the latest in Park Avenue fashions slipped out of a brownstone, briefcase in hand, and hopped into the car. And my heart skipped a beat.

It was Catherine. I must have muttered something when I saw her.

"What," Bobby said, jolting me.

"Hold on," I said. "I know her."

We pulled up beside the Caddy, blocking her in before she could drive off, and I said, "Y'know, it's illegal to park like that."

She took in a deep breath and said, "Yes, I do. I was in a rush and couldn't find a space. No excuse, but..." And then she looked at me and blinked. "Pete?"

"Hi-ya, Cath," I said, grinning, amazed she remembered me.

"You put on a bit of weight. It looks good on you."

"You haven't changed a bit."

"Mind over matter...and some high-end makeup, helps."

"I don't believe that for a second. Besides, you always did know how to dress. That's a really nice outfit."

She smiled and her face took on a thousand kinds of beauty.

"Are you going to write me a ticket?" she asked her eyes coy and dancing.

"Maybe, maybe not. You know, we can make exceptions for a pretty face. By the way this is Bobby." Bobby leaned forward and they exchanged nods. "Now getting back this offence I might be able to forget it if you give me your business card."

"You never asked me that night. I was disappointed."

"Well...I'm asking now."

I heard Bobby inhale, beside me, but Catherine didn't seem to notice. She reached into her purse and pulled out a card.

"Thanks," she whispered as she handed it over.

"Like to catch up, tonight. What do you say?"

"Tonight?"

"I'm off at four."

"I'm in my office till seven...but I'm open to sharing a sandwich with an old friend."

"You know there is a great deli here on Houston Street. What would you like?"

"Jewish deli?"

"We're on the Lower East Side; there's still a few Jew's left."

"Corned beef on rye, with mustard. I'll supply the wine, this time."

"Six good?"

"Perfect."

I held her card up then slipped it into my uniform pocket, and then we drove off. I turned to watch her pull into traffic, behind us; she turned right at the next corner. Then I looked at Bobby. He was tight, his hand gripping the wheel.

"So," he said, "you never asked before?"

"No, and I always wondered why. I was single then."

"I guess you figured it be more fun when you got married."

I settled back in the seat and stared forward. "Your wife gives you everything you need?"

"That ain't the point."

"I know this don't look good, but it's just a sandwich and a glass of wine..."

"I don't wanna know about this."

We drove a moment longer, and then I whispered, "Like I said, nobody said anything about anything except have a sandwich. We're just a couple old friends."

He didn't say another word the rest of the shift. But he got me to wondering, so I almost didn't go...until I reminded myself that the last time Catherine and I'd been together, sex had never entered into it. So who was I to say this time'd be different? We'd get together. We'd bring each other up to date. She'd get done with her work and go home, as would I.

So I showed up at the address on Central Park South, signed in, zipped up to the 22nd floor to be greeted by a frazzled secretary who ushered me into this office that overlooked the park. She was then dismissed with a simple, "Thank you, Anna. That'll be all for the day."

Talk about uptown, jeez. A desk from some Swedish designer (I didn't know that; I found out later), a chair behind it that looked like something out of science fiction, leather couch and matching chairs, objects d'art in narrow glass shelving units, a rug so thick you sank into it like you were in quicksand, all in low-key colors that blended together just right. I had the feeling she'd spent more decorating the place than I'd made all last year.

Now her coat was gone, I could see Catherine was wearing this light silk blouse that draped down over her breasts like clouds whisper over a mountain. It was tucked into a wool skirt topped by a slip of a belt that made her hips look exactly right. She motioned to a coffee table and pulled a bottle of wine from a rack in the bottom of a cabinet.

"Red," she said, "in remembrance of our first meeting. Do you want a glass?"

"Oh, I'm all cultured now," I said, nodding. "Even use a knife and fork."

She laughed and it was like hearing music. Suddenly something was whispering behind my heart and I had the first idea that I ought to leave. Instead, I tore open the bags to reveal the sandwiches and set them on the table.

"Corned beef in the white wrapper, with the mustard stains," I said. "Turkey, Russian dressing in the other."

"I've never had Russian dressing on Turkey. Do you mind if I try a bite of yours?"

"Help yourself." Then I looked around the office. "This office is quite impressive."

"Thanks. Real estate is a solid market for investing."

"That what you do, now?"

"Some. That's why I was in the East Village. A client's interested in acquiring some property in that area and wanted a better purview of its potential." All said as she poured some wine into tulip glasses and handed me one.

"What'd you tell him?"

"If he buys now, it will be a loss-leader for the next few years, but he will recoup his investment three times over by Nineteen-eighty."

"Tompkins Park's still a mess."

"For now. So Tompkins Square park is in the Ninth Precinct." I nodded as I sipped some wine. "I almost called there to ask about you," she continued as she glided onto the couch. "I was about to call when I read about those two officers that got shot. To touch base and see how you were doing or something like that."

"Wish you had; I could have use some additional support."

"I know you told me your last name, but..."

"Buono. It's pronounced like Sonny's, but my family still has it old school from the other side."

She nodded. "I guess I might have needed that, too, instead of just Officer Peter, Pietro Something-Italian."

"Well, I think there are 3 other cops named Pete there. If you would have asked for sincere Pete or Pietro, I might've got the message."

"You're sweet." Then she took a bite of the sandwich, and nodded. "This is good."

"Katz's," I said, proudly. "Nothin' but the best for my girl."

"Your girl?" she asked, her eyes laughing.

Oops, probably stepped over the line, there, so I shrugged in as off-handed a manner as I could.

"You know what I mean."

"Do I?" she said, licking a bit of dressing off her finger.

I leaned over and kissed her. I didn't even think about it and did it without hesitation. She didn't pull away.

When I finished the kiss, I moved back just a little and whispered, "Should I say I'm sorry?"

"Are you?" she whispered back.

"Not a bit."

"Good." Then she kissed me, and all my hunger shifted from my belly to my heart and soul.

We didn't leave her office till nearly midnight. And when I got home, I was so easy and calm, Louisa felt my head to see if I was sick.

Okay, again, I know what you're thinking. That I'm a rotten animal that cannot control myself, that I'm slime. Catting around on my lovely wife and kid, and letting the other woman think I'm single. A creep and a total bastard, right?

But what you need to understand is, you're right but it kept me steady. It made me feel good, not only in usual way but mentally too...and yeah, a little guilty...but that helped me fight back the suspicions and uncertainty I had about the whole situation with Lou and Marc. I felt had the support of two women, and I cared for both of them, each in her own way. With Louisa it was because she and I started a family. Catherine and I had something special, after being with her once. I felt that and I think she did too. It was fantastic.

And let's be clear, I never had Bobby cover for me. Like with Lou's murder, I'd figured out it's best to keep him out of the loop. And that made me feel like I was back in some kind of control over the situation. It lasted for a few months, anyway...like a vacation from the world.

But then Loco's trial finally came up, and it was marked final. That meant no more adjournments so the ADA wanted everybody there. I'd parked in my usual spot and was jaunting across Centre Market Place, behind HQ, aiming to cross against traffic when I saw Jonas exit 400 Broome with an evidence envelope.

Now this is a great big "so what" moment. Cops get evidence envelopes all the time, even crooked ones. And Jonas was in plainclothes, so nothing suspicious there. He probably had his own case about to go to trial. But without even thinking, I stopped behind a truck, to watch.

149

Sure enough, he met up with Velasquez and they rounded the corner, down Cleveland. Meaning they were headed away from the criminal courts building.

That was NOT a great big "so what." Still...I had other things to worry about so I told myself to let it go.

I headed on across Broome and up into the property room. The phone was ringing like crazy behind the cage, keeping the clerk busy as hell, so again without thinking, I took a look at the book. There was no Detective Jonas pulling out evidence for anything, that day – but there was an entry for P.O. Michaels, 28th Precinct for six-hundred glassine envelopes – of heroin.

Dime bags like what Fredo'd been selling.

Like what he'd been using.

Like what'd been used to kill him.

And leave him lying in that chair and –

"Hey, you browsing or picking up?" The clerk asked as he got off the phone.

I jumped and said, "Sorry; just checking if my partner got here already."

I put in the necessary information then went to a desk. I sat down. And swiveled around in its chair for a moment, the used its phone to make a call.

"Two-eight P.O. Rodgers," was the answer at the other end.

"Good morning," I said, "this is Buono from the Ninth. I'm a friend of Michaels. Is he working a day tour?"

"Hold on," The old switchboards had no music while you waited just dead silence. I did a slow rocking twist back and forth in the chair as I noticed the windows had been cleaned recently, and done good, and were offering a great reflection of everything and –

Moretti was in that reflection, glaring at me. Dammit, he'd heard me. The son-of-a-bitch had heard me. Then Rodgers came back on to bark, "Nope, not today," jolting me.

"Oh, uh – thanks," I sputtered out.

I had to fight to keep control as I swung back around. Moretti had turned away from me, like he couldn't see me.

Then the clerk blasted out with, "Buono!"

I made myself smile, pick up the evidence and leave, like I hadn't noticed him...but the whole time my mind was going nuts.

I thought I had it under control. I thought I had it all reasoned out. My wife and kid came first. I had other things in my life that were just as important. I didn't want to get back into this mess. But as I was

150

walking to court, I caught myself muttering, "Dime bags? They're switching stinkin' dime bags. Is everything else gone? How could this be going on for so long?"

When I got to the courtroom, I saw A-D-A Shannon, one of those true-believer sorts, talking with another cop. I had to wait till they were done, so my brain kept racing around what'd happened to Fredo and all the other times I'd seen cops I knew take drugs I knew weren't theirs and –

"What?" Shannon snapped, waving me over, irritated.

"Oh, I – uh, I'm here on the Mendoza case," I said. "Jose Mendoza."

Shannon shuffled through some case jackets, opened one, and read it. "Is the complainant going to be here?"

"He was notified," I said, "but truth is, I'm not sure. He wants it to go away so..."

"I need more time on this case, anyway."

"More time still?" Burst out of me before I could even think to hold it back.

Shannon looked at me with complete exasperation. "Yeah, still. I'm gettin' showered with this shit, right now. So...we don't need Soto for the gun possession, but I would like to get this Mendoza character and co-defendant on the attempted murder. Their Attorney requested a bench trial. The date suggests Judge Lefkowitz'll hear the case. Try your best to get him here."

"Me?"

"Is this your case? Yeah, you."

He slapped a business card in my hand. I wrote the latest never-gonna-be-postponed-again date on it and took the evidence back, muttering the whole way. Then I went in and did my tour. And spent the whole time making damn sure I didn't do anything that might call attention to me, like freaking out or muttering or acting tense or anything. I wanted everyone or anyone who might be paying attention to think I hadn't got a care in the world and didn't know jack from jack-off. I didn't fool Bobby, but I think he figured the hints of nervousness he caught were due to my catting around with Catherine.

Then that night, as I was driving home, I noticed a car keeping exact pace with me. It changed lanes when I did. Sped up when I did. Slowed down when I did. The other car seemed to be getting closer and closer. It had two headlights on the left side but only one on the right. I finally just hit the gas and sped away, weaving in and out of traffic, leaving the suspect car caught in traffic. Could word have gotten around that quick?

When I got home, I was hyperventilating. Louisa met me at the door, baby in hand, and noticed, so she checked me over.

"You all right?" she asked, first thing out. "You seem uptight."

"Oh...uh...damn traffic, again."

"Uh huh," she said, but it was obvious she wasn't buying it. "Oh – someone called and left a message. He said, 'Tell your husband, I hope he's still a good guy.' What's that about?"

That settled it. They knew. Their focus was now on me, and they were letting me know it was also on my family. I wondered if they knew about Catherine, but I kept myself from calling her to find out if she'd gotten any weird messages, today. That was not what I needed to know, just then. Instead, I put on a comforting face and said, "What? Nothin', honey. Uh – just one of my poker buddies kidding around."

I grabbed the phone and dialed, and Marc answered. "Hello?"

"Hey, buddy."

"Look, I was just about to call you and – ."

"Marc, the stuff we talked about – ."

"I think we just got the break we needed. Can you meet me tonight?"

"Tonight I just got home," I said, my voice beginning to shake. "I got grand jury, tomorrow. It'll be finished by noon. Could you swing by my mother's apartment she won't be home all day tomorrow, say after one?"

"Yeah. Sure, I'll be there; things will get rolling real soon."

"Marc, it's really important you come through for me."

"I'm gonna say one thing -- Police Commissioner."

"That is big, but I'm still worried."

"Stay cool. I'll be at your mother's tomorrow. Hang in there, don't worry."

Then he hung up and I saw Louisa looking at me, wary. "Peter, what's going on?"

"Nothin'."

"Like hell! You're keeping things from me."

"It's police crap, baby; you don't want to know."

"You always say that."

"What d'you mean?"

"I'm worried. You're getting to be so erratic. Secretive and – and I dunno, nervous."

152

What was she talking about? Everything had been going fine. It'd all been cool. I put on my best comforting face and pulled her and the baby onto my lap. "There are some things going on at work that I can't tell you about. That's all. I don't want you to get all nervous over it."

"Are you going to lose your job?"

"What? No! What makes you ask that?"

"The doctor you saw isn't part of the police insurance roster. And the odd hours you're keeping. I thought you might have another woman, but...but you still love me don't you? You'd never do that to me or the baby?"

Oh, damn, did she suspect something? Is it true someone can always tell or was she just fishing? All I could say was, "Never."

She put a hand on my face and murmured, "Promise you'll tell me when you can?"

"Yeah, baby, I promise."

She left it at that and worked up a meatloaf for dinner. Cooked with potatoes and carrots and smothered in tomato soup. A full-course meal, once you threw in the salad. Who said I missed momma's cooking?

The next day I was at Mom's new apartment, just blocks from One Police Plaza. She moved there after dad died because it was smaller and the building had an elevator, so things were easier on her. It also had a nice view of the East River and Brooklyn Bridge. She was out shopping, so I made a cup of coffee and was sitting at the table flipping through the paper, checking my watch every five seconds...until I saw this headline on one of the inside pages – POLICE SERGEANT COMMITS SUICIDE.

The article went on to say Sergeant Joseph Bruno was found sitting in his car at a rest area on the Belt Parkway. He was shot through the right temple, the gun still in his hand.

His right hand?

SHIT! They burned him. How could he let it happen?

I can just picture it, he gets a call from someone he trusts, (SOME ONE HE THINKS HE CAN TURST) and they make a meet. Why there why not a public place? Maybe money is to change hands. Anyway he is there first waiting outside his car smoking another car pulls up most likely two guys.

One guy would say, "Joe you know I gotta check."

153

That would be checking for a wire or recording device. Joe allows this other guy to pat him down, while doing so he removes Joe's revolver from it holster.

Joe complains, "What's this about?"

"You'll get it back when we leave."

They get in Joe's car, Joe behind the wheel the other guy gets in passenger side he says something or points to get Joe to look to his left out the window, Joe turns the guy puts the gun to Joe's right temple and fires. He then places the gun in Joe's hand and leaves the car. Had to be someone he trusted, like dad said, "You'll trust them with your life; be careful, son."

My mind started playing tricks on me. I started asking myself about Marco. Can I truly trust him? He has been distant lately; did they get to him with a large amount of money? Is he coming here to kill me? What am I saying? What is wrong with me? Marco is a friend, a trusted friend...or is he? Yes, yes, stop this.

A knock on the door made me jump. I crept over to it so carefully; you'd think I was sneaking up on a cat I'm trying to catch. "Bobby" I asked. Trusting them with your life kept playing over and over in my head.

"It's me Mark."

I wasn't expecting Bobby but I wanted to let Mark think I was just in case he was here to kill me, stop it he is with you, meaning me since I'm talking to myself. I unlocked the door and opened it. Marc entered.

"I asked Bobby to meet us here. I told him you were coming about one."

You know why I told him this? Just in case I would be dead, he would think someone else knew he was here. I am feeling so confused and I must have looked it. He gave me one of his wary looks and asked, "What's wrong?"

"Shit, Marc, they called my house, yesterday, and today in the paper – about Bruno."

"Yeah, I heard about him. You know him?"

"Well enough to know he's left-handed."

"Left handed? What're you saying?"

"Marc, the article says he shot himself in the right temple. He was left-handed. Think about it. And think about this – he met a couple times with Moretti and Kowalski. It's in one of my memo books."

Marc sat at the table, letting it sink in. I silently offered him some coffee but he shook his head. Of course, he did notice my hand was shaking. I couldn't stop it.

"Pete, I can get you an appointment with the C.O. of P.C.C.I.U. That is coming from the PC, himself."

"I don't care how you did it, but I'm ready."

"A Detective from the 17th Squad got locked up in Nassau County, a couple of months ago."

"And how is this related?"

"It seems they, Nassau County Cops were following him. He was suspected of raping women in their homes"

"A New York City Detective a serial rapist?"

"They caught him in the act and after they locked him up got a search warrant for his house."

"Is there a point here?"

"Believe it or not that is the break we, YOU needed, they found in his home drug evidence envelopes that were opened and the contents missing."

"So even cops outside of Narcotics are drinking from the well. Marco I told you this was big. I bet they got it all."

"All."

"One time I was there they were even taking dime bags, all the Keys and ounces and everything in between most likely already had been switched."

"They will find out soon enough the P.C. is sending scores of cops down to 400 Broom Street to test every drug evidence envelope. The C O of P.C.C.I.U. wants you to put names and or faces with anything you can."

"Do you want to go ahead with this?"

"Yeah, it...it's been eating me up and – wait – Police Commissioner's Confidential Investigating Unit? That's been shut down a couple years."

Marc smiled at me. "Publicly, yes. You know my brother-in-law's an Inspector, who knows this Assistant Chief who never took a free cup of coffee. He's your man. Here's his phone number." He handed me a slip of paper. And as I took it, again, it was obvious my hands were shaking. "Call them tomorrow – around seven."

"Zero seven hundred?"

"Yeah, they start very early over there. And, buddy calm down – this'll work out. Don't worry. Now I gotta get back to the office."

155

He gave me a hug and left. He'd been with me maybe for five minutes. Why was he leaving so quickly? His office wasn't that far away. I feel so bad that I was worried about Marc. He is good cop and a better man. Marc was on my side. I know it, I knew it. I was just being dumb. Marc was on my side, wasn't he?

Now I was feeling antsy, feeling the need for someone to just be around, so Catherine was my choice. She had this way of just sitting and talking that soothed me so nicely. Or maybe we'd go driving in her convertible with top down, even though it's cold. She's got that coat with a hood that'd keep her warm and I could just let the wind blast all the craziness out of me. God that sounded so good. I grabbed the phone and dialed.

Louisa answered. "Hello?"

Oops. "Hi, honey – I'm staying over at Mom's, tonight. Got a seven to three, tomorrow."

"Peter!" Her voice was not happy.

I was still feeling shaky, so I just popped out with, "Listen, I gotta go. Talk to you later, okay."

Louisa let out a big sigh and said, "All right, then. Fine," And she hung up. Oh, she wasn't happy, but there was nothing I could do about it right then.

I did a quick re-dial.

"Ninth Precinct, Police Officer Shea."

"Johnny my man, it's your favorite paisan. Be a pal and leave a note on the sign-out sheet for Minguzzi to call me at mom's?" It's time for me to fill him in on what's what.

"Petey – hold on – you got a message from – Gina Franklyn – call her."

"...Okay – thanks."

I hung up, looked in my book and dialed the phone.

Gina's voice came on the line. "Hello?"

"Gina, hi, it's Peter Buono. Is everything okay?"

"Yes, I heard from my cousin in North Carolina. He has my brother's car. Anyway, his son wound up with it, and he found a couple rolls of film stuck between the seats. He's mailing them to me."

The film! Lou's film! Maybe...maybe...

"That is great news!" I said. "Call me soon as you have 'em. I got a guy to give it to. Don't even develop it. And Gina – Gina – don't tell anybody about this. I mean it – nobody, nobody."

" – Okay. Are you all right?"

"What d'you mean?"

156

"Your voice sounds shaky."

"I'm fine, now. I'm fine. Just a – a long day. Remember what I said, okay?"

"I'll call you soon as it arrives. Bye."

I hung up and sat at the kitchen table. This was better than great. If Lou hid it, that meant he got something, and now I could get them for him. Get the guys who set him up. I looked at the article about Sergeant Bruno – and crumpled it into a ball. Maybe Bruno's murder meant they were falling out and getting scared of each other. Maybe he was going to turn state's evidence on them. Man, so many great possibilities popped into my head. When Bobby called, I just asked him to sign me out. He grumbled, but he agreed to do it, then I went over to Catherine's and we took that great drive straight up the Hudson and back, then went back to her place. I got back to mom's just after midnight. That night I slept like a baby.

Just after dawn, the next morning, I headed out of mom's building, aiming for my car. It was just as the day was opening up and there was a fine mist in the air. Clean and beautiful and complimenting my mood. Yeah, I was gonna get 'em. Gonna get 'em, good. Once we had that film married up to my memo books and the evidence sign-out log from the Property Clerks Office, then they'll get and expert handwriting analysts, we'd have 'em all and –

I saw police car lights flashing under the Brooklyn Bridge, highlighted by the mist. A little bell went off in the back of my head, so I drove the one block to the scene, parked, got out and went over, holding my shield in one hand. A patrolman stood by the barrier tape.

"What's going on?" I asked him.

The patrolman shrugged and said, "Some guy took two in the head's all I know."

I noticed the patrol cars were surrounding a beat-up, three year-old florescent-colored mustang convertible. Aw, no. It couldn't be. It just couldn't.

"I think I know that car," I said. "Can I take a look?"

The patrolman shrugged and said, "Detective Lee's catching."

I hung my shield around my neck and headed over to this squat, round, intense-looking Asian guy – Detective Lee, all no-nonsense.

He saw me coming and frowned so I said, "I'm Buono. I – I know this car."

"Good," said Lee. "No I-D on the body and it's registered to some women in the Bronx, no phone listed at that address."

157

I looked in the Mustang and, sure enough, there sat Soto behind the wheel. His eyes were half-open. His lips almost curled into a smile. Two clean ones in, no exits.

I backed away, shaken, and looked around. My mother's apartment building was in clear view! This was a message. Done like a mob hit, but sloppy enough to show it wasn't one. Dammit. I slowly returned to Lee and said, "Victim's John Soto. Find out where Jose Mendoza was, last night – AKA Loco. He lives on Tenth Street. I'll call you at the Fifth. You got a direct line? And give you everything I have on him."

"Thanks. Makes my job easy." As he handed me a card.

"You wish," I almost laughed. Then I headed off.

I double-parked in front of mom's building and ran inside. Mom was just starting to get up.

"Peter, I thought I heard you leave?"

"Yeah, mom, just forgot something."

"You want breakfast?"

"No, I had some, thanks."

I quickly slipped a sheet of paper in my old high school typewriter and typed –

RE: BENCH TRIAL DOCKET #247981,
MENDOZA V. STATE OF NEW YORK.
DON'T HEAR THIS CASE. I HOPE YOU ENJOYED THOSE PASTRIES THAT WERE DELIVERED TO YOU SEVERAL YEARS AGO.

I removed the paper, folded it and slipped it into an envelope then wrote in big red letters on the outside – VERY URGENT.

The Criminal Courts building hasn't started to get busy, that time of morning, so I casually strolled up to Judge Lefkowitz's door, waited to make certain no one was around then slipped the envelope under the door and hurried away. I knew exactly what would happen.

Miss Weller would enter, see the envelope and put it on top of the mail without a thought. Then Judge Lefkowitz would come in, see the envelope and open it. He'd read the letter, put his coat back on, and exit. And as he headed out, Miss Weller'd look up, so he'd say something like, "Be right back." And vanish.

So I stuck around by a phone booth and waited till I saw him exit the Criminal Courts Building and hail a cab. For sure, Loco won't walk on the gun charge, not now. I couldn't help but smile...then I placed a call. It was like about eight-forty-five, but better late than never, right?

158

A woman answered the phone, "Chief Fitzer's office."

"Hello, this is Police Officer Buono. May I speak to Chief Doug Fitzer?"

"The Chief – hold on, who is this?"

"Uh – Police Officer Buono."

"Hold on."

A moment later, this growl of a voice came on the line. "Detective Gruber, can I help you?"

This sounded wrong, so I played it cagey and just said, "I'm Police Officer Buono, I was told to call today."

"You were supposed to call a couple hours ago."

"I was told to call after I turned out." Lame but it was all I could think of.

He huffed. "The chief wants me to tell you that you and your partner'll be transferred downtown within the week."

"Transferred!" I said. "Won't that send up a red flag?"

"Your C-O will be told it's a headquarters security detail, since we're finally clearing out the last of the offices. Nice and normal, no one will know, so don't worry. It'll be discreet. Orders'll be cut by the end of the day. Make sure you show up on time."

He hung up without another word.

I set the phone back on its hook, thinking. Yeah, there came that bad feeling, again. Something about this was just too visible and out in the open. So I made myself make another call.

I got an answering machine. "This is Gina Franklyn. Please leave a message."

I didn't like doing anything on tape like that, but I still said, "Gina, this is Peter B. If you would – don't call me at the precinct. Call Detective Marc Lampedusa at Cannel-6-5704. See he gets the film. Just in case. I think it is better that way."

Then I hung up and looked around. It seemed like everyone walking by me was casting me weird glances, like my fly was open or something. Maybe it's because I was shaking, again. I dunno. I just finally took in a deep breath and headed for my car. It was finally at the point where things would play out, and all I could do was hope for the best.

****

So that night I pulled my car into the driveway, got out and entered the house. Louisa was nursing the baby. So I sat by her. Put my arm around her. Pulled her close; all but clung to her. She shifted around, smoothed my hair. But her eyes were tight and wary.

"Did you get any sleep, last night?" she snapped.

"Yeah," I said, suddenly scared about her anger. "It's just been a long day."

"Has it?"

I nodded and leaned myself deeper into her arms, trying to hide from her stabbing eyes.

She hesitated then said, "What're you keeping from me?"

I tensed, and I know she felt it. "What d'you mean?" I asked; my voice cracking.

"Peter, the last few months, you've been growing more and more distant. More and more afraid of something; what is it? What're you keeping from me?"

I couldn't handle that, right then. I wasn't prepped for it, so I got up and headed for the bathroom, saying, "I gotta take a leak."

"Pete!" Her voice cut into me, it was so angry.

"It's nothing, Louisa."

"The hell it's not! You're gone all sorts of hours. Staying at your mother's more and more."

"How can you get on me about that?" I fired back, close to losing it. "I'm working two jobs to keep us going and – ."

"Is it another woman? Are you tired of me, already?"

"Aw, Jesus, how can you even ask me that, now, when I'm going through so damned much?"

"Going through what, Pete? You don't talk to me. You don't talk to anybody."

"I can't!"

"Why not?!"

I was about to explode when the phone rang. I grabbed it, all but yelling, "Hello?"

"Hi, Buono," Moretti's voice sniped back at me. "Soto says he can't wait to see you. He's waiting for you, in hell."

He hung up.

I almost collapsed. The son-of-a-bitch was taunting me. Calling me at home to let me know he knew where I was and doing it

160

just moments after I got there, to show me I was being watched. I leaned against the wall to steady myself.

"That is what I'm talking about, Pete," Louisa snapped at me. "Who were you talking to on the phone?"

I didn't say a word to her.

The doorbell rang. She carried Billy to the door, still spouting, "That is exactly what I'm talking about. You get these calls and you go white as a sheet and – ."

Moretti on the phone, now the doorbell? She's headed for the door? She's headed for the door! No, no, no – I spun around, screaming, "Aw, no! No!"

I jumped for her as she opened the door and blinding light and dust and noise filled the room and slashed against me and seared my skin and threw me back, flying through the air in slow-motion as I twisted and turned and tried to figure out the best way to land and I thought I was dying and –

I slammed against the front door.

It was solid.

Everything was intact.

No bomb.

No dust or splinters or fire.

Nothing.

Louisa was still seated on the couch, staring at me, wide-eyed, the baby crying. She didn't move, just whispered, "Peter."

Oh-my-god, oh-my-god, what just happened? What just happened? What'd I just do? That wasn't right. That wasn't normal.

I slid to the floor, shaken. It took me a minute but I finally choked out, "I – I'm sorry. I – I thought – I don't know what I thought. I – I didn't hurt you, did I?"

She shook her head, wary.

I made myself stand up and said, "I – listen, I'll go back to the doctor. I – I think those tranqs are messing with me in some way."

She gave me a hint of a nod, her eyes locked on me and holding Billy as if protecting him. I sort-of staggered over to the couch and gave her and the baby a kiss. She flinched at my touch. I can't say I blame her.

I wandered into the bathroom and closed the door and looked at myself in the mirror. My eyes were hollow. They looked kind of haunted. Lines slashed through my face, showing me how I'd look when I was ninety, probably. I felt like I'd aged a hundred years in the last twenty-four hours. I guess that's what Louisa was talking about.

161

I opened the medicine cabinet. I took a prescription bottle from inside and took one. My fingers shook like crazy so I had to use both hands to get it into my mouth. It was the same for drawing a glass of water. I spilled half of it before I had it to my lips.

What the hell was wrong with me? I'd really felt the heat when that bomb went off. Really felt the sting of splinters and shrapnel flying through the air and into my skin. Felt the force of the blast. I was blinded by it. All of it too real for me to ignore it.

Until I hit the door and it was still solid. Then everything just vanished and I was back to reality. Like I'd gone into some Twilight Zone for an instant then been dropped into my normal world just as quickly. I was almost afraid to ask Louisa if there'd really been a phone call. Hell, I was even wondering if we'd been arguing, before, because thinking about it, the baby wasn't crying over the anger.

Jesus, was it that easy to lose your mind? Get a little pressure on and suddenly you go from a Mr. Normal-Everyday kind of guy to loony tunes? I know I've always had an active imagination, but was this what it led to? No, no, I have several years of notes in my memo books showing what'd really happened. I had Lou knowing I was right and trying to help me get something on the cops who were dirty. Dammit...he was backing me up and I didn't protect him, in return. I'd warned him. I'd tried to get him to see the reality of it. But what it still boiled down to was I hadn't kept them from killing him. And now I knew I couldn't protect anybody, not even my family.

A shadow passed behind me. I spun around – but no one was there. Of course. Still, I checked the shower to make sure it was empty, then locked the door, set the water to going and undressed, shaking.

I was in the shower I don't know how long. I washed my hands and then my body. And then I washed my hair. But I started all over again washing my hands and then my feet. But my hands seemed unclean so I washed them again. Then I couldn't remember if I'd washed my hair so did it, again. And finally I washed my hands. The steam felt good in my lungs. Felt clean and real and safe. Then the water ran cold and I stopped.

I dressed in gym shorts and a t-shirt and combed my hair. And then I combed it again and again. Not because it wasn't right or I'd forgotten if I did it, but because the comb felt good on my scalp. Like it was reminding me there was a real world to feel and be part of and appreciate in tiny ways. I didn't stop till I started getting cold.

I slipped into the bedroom and put my service revolver under my pillow. Louisa noticed but pretended not to in this cute way she has of not moving anything except her eyes, thinking she's being subtle. I crawled under the covers and she held me close as we lay in the bed.

Finally, she said, "Honey...your father passing away, and then Lou and his partner getting killed...well, these past months...it's been tough on you. Hasn't it?"

I looked at her, but said nothing. She had no idea how tough things had gotten for me.

She kept on with, "Anybody would feel the pressure. Think that things had gone crazy."

Well...she was a right, in a way. I was feeling the pressure, but not in the way she thought. I was also remembering what happened to Fredo. I'd known what he was up to and how dangerous that was, and I'd done nothing to get him away from it. As a cop I'm supposed to protect people from that. Like I'm protecting Bobby from himself and Louisa with my lies. But I hadn't protected Fredo from being killed. I didn't protect Lou; or my dad by spilling my guts to him that killed him. Yeah, I had pressure on me. The belief that I'd failed everybody I knew who'd needed me.

She must've read some of that in my eyes, because she sighed and said, "Maybe this is some kind of mourning you're going through. All of this, it's...it's caught up to you and, well...why don't we take some vacation time? Drive up to Canada or something? Do nothing but...but nothing. Get away and relax. I'll even leave Billy with my mom. It'll be just you and me. Like a second honeymoon."

I just caressed her face. She had such a simple view of the world. Of life; just get away from the city and all will be fine. Who cares that your mind goes with you everywhere? How could she ever understand how lost I was? Catherine might, if I'd tell her what was what. But I couldn't put her or Bobby or anybody else in danger. I had to hold back, now. Hope Marc's guys would take the burden off me. Let me rest.

Louisa caressed my face. "Will you think about it, honey?"

I had to give her some kind of verbal answer, so I said, "Uh, I – Bobby and I – we're getting transferred. To a security detail at the old Police Headquarters. It's almost cleaned out. No many offices left. Dunno what my hours'll be – this transfer to Headquarters – but I think – I think it'll be better there. Not so much to deal with."

Louisa made me look at her, and I could see in her eyes she didn't believe me. But she decided to let it go and said, "I'm happy you're getting away from the Ninth; too many bad memories there." She kissed me on the cheek and snuggled next to me.

163

She also quietly snuck the pistol out from under my pillow. I knew she was doing it, and why...her now being afraid of me, a little too much. So I let her think she got away with it, and I held her close, my eyes open, thinking, hoping this was coming to an end soon.

It was. But not in the way I expected. Because a few days later; mom's doorbell rang. And when she asked who it was, the reply was, "Mrs. B, it's me, Ronnie – Millie's son, from next door at the old place."

Mom opened the door and Ronnie was there with a box of pastries from Patty's Pastry Shop.

He held them out, saying, "I brought these for you." He handed Mom the box and kissed her on the cheek.

"Ronnie, how nice of you," mom said. "I haven't seen you since the wedding. Come in. Have a cup of coffee."

"No, thanks – someone is waiting for me. When'll Pietro be here?"

"If he stops by, today, it'll be after four."

Ronnie pulled out a pen and wrote a number on the box, saying, "Ask him to gimme a call – four-thirty, five o'clock. I'll be waitin'."

"I will. You sure you won't come in? It's fresh coffee."

Ronnie smiled and kissed mom, again, as he said, "Wish I could but like I said, people are waitin', downstairs. Thanks. Bye."

"Goodbye. Say hello your mother for me."

He grinned, nodded and left.

Sounds all nice and easy, right?

But it was the beginning of the end.

****

Ronnie dropped off the pastries on the same day that I was headed into 240 Centre Street, the old police HQ. Sure enough, new orders were cut so Bobby and I were sent downtown for a security detail, effective immediately. Yeah, no red flags, none at all.

It's funny, even though it's half-abandoned, that building still had this haughty attitude like what you'd find uptown on Park, Madison or even Fifth Avenue, with its windows glaring down at you like you're nothing. I entered the Grand Lobby carrying a hang-up bag with my uniform and a smaller bag holding my other stuff. There was a large marble circular desk situated near the entrance, and thanks to some tall windows and the sun being out, everything was bright and glorious despite the emptiness of it all.

I stopped at the desk, where this hair bag sat, seeming oblivious to everything.

"P.O. Buono," I said. "I'm – ."

Before I could finish, he cut me off with, "Lockers're down the corridor, first door on the left." Then he pointed to the back right rear of him.

I headed down it and saw two men exit the first door on the left, both looking straight at me. Turned out they were a couple of lieutenants, both in cheap Robert Hall suits, with years of duty ringing their eyes. If one guy hadn't had silver hair while the other was salt-and-pepper, with a Roman nose instead of a pug, they'd have looked exactly alike. Guess the old hair bag called 'em up and gave them fair warning.

"Good morning, Officer Buono," said the pug, his voice ringing in the hall. "I'm Lieutenant Doherty. This is Lieutenant Rinaldi, this way."

They led me into a large waiting area what was just as empty as everything else, except for rows of temporary lockers set up across from a series of doors with frosted glass windows.

Doherty was talking the whole way as they directed me to a particular locker.

"Effective tomorrow, you and your partner'll be working steady four to twelves, here. Because after 1600 hours this place is totally empty and that the best time we can you know each other. We will have you inside and your partner outside, and nobody'll be the wiser."

165

"Plus, to give you better cover," said Rinaldi, "we let it out that this is a punishment of a sort."

"Punishment for what?" I asked, suddenly wary at how easily he'd said that.

"Let's just say you two haven't been choir boys. Do you want the laundry list?"

"We do our jobs and keep crime minimized in our sector."

"I know how the system works, and looks like you two knew how to work it. This way we're sending out a message – Don't try playing the system...too much."

"I did not create the system. All I want is to get things right."

He just looked at me and said, "That's up to whether or not you play by our rules."

"Do I get a handbook for these rules?"

"No, you get me," Doherty chimed in. "Here's your locker; put your things away."

He motioned to the corner one of a half-dozen metal doors.

"Here?" I asked.

Rinaldi nodded. "Got a lock?"

"Yeah," I said, so then I went down to the end of the row, found an empty bin.

"This one too good for you?" asked Rinaldi.

I looked at him with my best innocent expression and asked back, "Don't I get to choose my own locker?"

Doherty shrugged and said, "When you're done, meet us in room one-twenty-five."

I put my things away and locked the door, I walked into room 125.

This was as plain as rooms come – but along the back wall were 5 tape recorders...you know the old reel to reel kind, they were spinning. Just inside the entrance was a large desk and four chairs, overhead lighting, blank walls on the other three sides. I sat at the desk, opposite Rinaldi and Doherty. There was another tape recorder same type but with a wire and microphone attached that sat on this sort of stand. I notice it to start to spin. Then Doherty said, "Police Officer Buono has entered the room. The time is 1431 hours. With that said, this is the New York State Special Prosecutor's Office. I am Lieutenant Doherty, with the Internal Affairs Division. With me is Lieutenant Rinaldi. He is assigned to this office. Okay, officer Buono, would you please state your full name rank and command, for the record?"

I did.

166

"Now we just have a few questions today," Doherty continued. "To start with; prior to your appointment as a patrolman you were with the police trainee program. Is that correct?"

"Yes," I said, leaning forward a bit to make sure the mike got my answer clear.

"After the academy where were you assigned?"

"I first went to personal investigations and then to the Narcotics bureau."

"How were you able to get such a high profile assignment? Did you ask someone for help getting there?"

"What? Yeah, I wish I had a Rabbi. You think I be on patrol in the 9th my entire time on the job? So I'll let you Detective Lieutenant's figure that out, but if you cannot -- my orders were cut and I went, just like coming here."

"A little testy. No need for that. Maybe your Rabbi died and his connections went with him. If that is not a fact, why did you get those commands?"

"Because I type faster that most people can talk. That's why, I was told." Are they implying Big Joey was my hook?

"Let me ask you this – of the two-hundred and forty men and women assigned to the narcotics bureau, how many do you know by first name basis?"

"I don't know. I was there for eighteen, nineteen months, so most of 'em. Why?" I knew almost everybody because once I got all that old arrest information updated it only took me two to three hours to transfer the daily arrests onto the index cards. Sargent Bruno knew that and used my time on the switchboard freeing up Darla to do paperwork in the U/C office. Well, paydays was when I got to meet and talk to most everyone. Every other Thursday, the payroll checks were delivered and kept at the switchboard, and the honest cops were always there, first. Some guys had checks sitting around for months before they picked them up. Guess they didn't need the money.

"We looked at your assignments before your steady seat with Patrol Officer Minguzzi, and noticed you worked a number of occasions as a fill-in with Patrol Officer William Castle."

"Yeah," I said. "At the Ninth, I worked with a lot of good cops before hooking up with Bobby. I don't understand what – ."

"Just listen and answer," Rinaldi said. "Castle made sixteen Grand Larceny Auto collars in less than four months, while you were working together."

"So?" I said.

167

"And they were all rental cars," said Doherty.

"We did our job – ."

"Was there any incentive involved?"

"What do you mean Incentive?" I asked, completely confused. "What does that have to do with cops pilfering drugs from the evidence locker? We got some collars out of it and a decent arrest record but – ."

"Did the rental car companies pay you?" Rinaldi cut in.

I just looked at them, in shock.

"Officer refuses to answer," Doherty said. "When you weren't with Castle, you were the steady fill-in with P-O's Charles Hurrell and Bernardo Russ in sector Adam. Is that correct?"

"Yes, so what about that?" I snapped. "I worked with a dozen cops before Bobby and I partnered up. Why're you talkin' about this? Where are you going with this?"

"Just answer the questions," Rinaldi snapped.

"But why're you asking me about this?" I snapped right back at him. "What's it got to do with cops stealing drugs and puttin' 'em back on the street!?"

Doherty held up his hand and said, "C'mon, cool it, guys.

Aw, c'mon – the "good-cop-bad-cop" routine? Seriously. On ME!? I bolted up and started pacing. "I don't understand what's going on. That's not what I'm here for. I – I – I – I'm here about the Property Clerk's Office, not any old bullshit about guys I partnered with years ago and – ." I walked toward the back wall while I was pacing and noticed cards next to the spinning recorders the first 3 Had SIU-1 SIU-2 and SIU-3. I remembered while working the switchboard that the C. O. and SUI did not have connections; they had direct lines. The other two had cards in front with PC-1 and PC-2. I had heard that SIU was the most corrupt office, not only in the NYPD but in all of America. What a reputation. But the prince of the city did work there.

My mind was drifting. What if I'd took that offer to work undercover? Would I have wound up there at SIU at some point?

"Sit down, Officer Buono," said Doherty. "What are you daydreaming, or dreaming up some excuses? We have a lot more to cover with you."

"Am I under investigation? Is that why I'm here? Why's this the first I'm hearing of this? Nobody's ever accused me of anything, before!"

Rinaldi glared at me and snarled, "You weren't on our radar, before."

I stopped and looked at him. "But remember I came to you."

168

"You didn't come to us," said Doherty.

"That pervert in the 17th squad got the P C and us involved when Nassau County locked him up. Imagine a city detective going around raping women and stealing drugs from the property clerk's office. So you didn't come to us."

"Yes, I did!" I yelled at him. "I worked it through a buddy to keep low-key about what I knew. Marco Lampedusa! He'll verify it! You remember that – I came to you!"

Rinaldi stood up and growled, "We'll decide how it works and if – ."

"How it works?" Oh, man, this was not going right. "I come to you about dirty cops, about cops putting drugs back on the street, something that's wrong and evil and – and here you are trying to make me believe you got something on me, instead?! That I'm the one who's really under investigation? I'm here on my own free will, trying to stop something that's wrong and – !"

"And maybe you're throwing off a smoke screen to protect yourself." That came from Doherty in this smooth and icy voice.

That cut into my anger. I dropped back onto a chair, numb. "You – you think it's me who's dirty. You think I'm trying to pull some kind of crap to get away with something."

Doherty took in a deep breath and said, "Buono, we just need to clear these allegations up so they can't be used against you when – ."

"Allegations?!" I bolted to my feet. "Somebody's makin' allegations against me!? You – you know what? This set-up is illegal. If I'm under investigation, you're supposed to tell me and I'm allowed to have an attorney present. So I'm calling my delegate before I say another word."

"Won't do you any good," Rinaldi snapped. "This office does not exist."

Okay, my only choices right then were hit the smug son-of-a-bitch or get out. So I stormed from the room and down the hall and through the lobby and out of the building and down the street and into my car. I kicked it to life and peeled away. And in the rearview mirror, this guy who I later learned was Gruber came out and watched me drive off.

I almost drove to Cathy's but she was still working so I wound up in front of mom's building, instead. I parked and sat there, shaking. So now I had a new little something to worry about – me getting sent to jail over something that meant nothing. The rental agencies had come to us to ask us to do what they couldn't do themselves. And we had.

169

And they'd just shown us their appreciation. But now that was being used to make me seem like the criminal. They didn't seem interested in the guys who were helping to poison kids and rip families apart. They were fighting dirty and I wasn't sure why. Dammit.

It probably took me a while, but I finally forced myself to regain control then got out and headed inside, glad as hell I didn't have to report for actual duty till tomorrow. I saw the pastry box on mom's kitchen table the second I walked in the door. Knew instantly it was one of Patty's, just like those I'd blocked...Jesus, almost a decade ago.

Mom was chattering on about something; what, I got no idea because I didn't hear a word. I was totally focused on that box, like there was a bomb, inside it. And I don't mean the kind that explodes. The phone number written on it, alone, was indication of a whole new level of trouble. Well, staring at the damned thing wasn't going to do anything, so I made myself grab a glass of milk then casually stroll over to it and open it...and grimace.

"Hey, mom," I said, fighting to keep my voice steady as I helped myself to one, "you walk over for these today?"

"Oh, sorry, baby, I forgot," she said, all unaware. "Ronnie came by. He asked you to call. There's a phone number written on the box. I said you'd be here about four. You're a little early."

Assorted pastries; just like Patty would ask me to box for Judge Lefkowitz, all those years ago. Minus the envelope, of course.

Oh, shoot what did I expect who else was he going to run to, the local priest or rabbi? But this is the sit down that I needed.

This was from Rizo no doubt; Ronnie is just the messenger me and him – he hardly said anything to me at the wedding, other than remember this and forget that. We hadn't talked since I got his cousin off the hook. But now I've got to call him? The first day I'm hit by IAD he makes contact? Now I had a clue as to how deep in the dirt I was in.

I ripped off the top of the box with the number then said, "Back in a little while, mom. I forgot something in the car."

I headed down to the street to a public phone, not the one just downstairs I walked a block to the next one. I dialed Ronnie's number. It rang once and he picked but said nothing, so I popped off with, "Hey, Ronnie, what's what?"

He was at another phone booth; I could tell from the crackle and the background traffic. His voice was cool and controlled as he asked, "What's what with you?"

"Good. It's good."

170

"How are Louisa and the baby?"

"Good."

"Good. Y'know, you're early, callin'."

"Yeah. I know."

"Okay. A guy'd like to see you. Can you come by the club?"

Oh, not the club no way.

"Not the club Ronnie?" And I was damn proud my voice didn't shake when I said it. "I don't think that's good. Tell you what; let's meet at – at the Lime House, about six."

"Hold on."

I heard him dial another phone. He must be at a bank of them. He talked, softly, and then came back to me.

"Make it Patty's shop at seven."

"Ronnie, I want to meet in a more public place, and Patty's won't do. No offence, but that's the way it's gonna be."

Ronnie talked into the other phone then said, "Vincent's at six."

Vincent's Clam House, on Mott and Grand. Not all that public, but it was the best I was gonna get, so I just said, "See you then."

He hung up. Not even a "Later" to me. Yeah, things were beginning to make sense. Like hell they were.

Mom made her famous eggplant parmesan, and she had the good bread. I kept eating because of nerves. Made one sandwich, and then another. Got the bottle opener and took the cap off of a Pepsi. And every bit of it tasted perfect. Was this my last meal maybe? Then I tried to relax and clam myself and at a quarter to six, I kissed mom and headed over.

The positive thing about being a cop back then -- back in the good old days, you know, before meter maids -- was you can park anywhere, even by a fire hydrant. You just pop an NYPD ID on your dashboard and as long as you were not all night, you got no problems. And since Vincent's was only a few blocks from mom's, I was there early. This is one of those spots famous for its seafood and really spicy sauce. They said it's Cajun, but I never was able to verify that. Plus it's rumored that Rizo owned a piece of it...which it now looked like was true.

I checked the place out, didn't see anything that looked off...not even a Caddy parked nearby. Not many people out, either, it being pretty chilly. I smelled garlic in the sharp air; after all, it's still

171

little Italy, where the leaves blowing by come from the trees up the block.

I unclipped my revolver with holster from my belt and slipped it under the front seat. Can't go into this packing. Then I rubbed my face to make sure I wasn't sweating and –

Ronnie appeared by the passenger door. It took everything I had in me to keep from jumping at seeing him, and I still couldn't keep from crossing myself. Then I got out, locked the car and followed him inside.

It wasn't till we were inside that he shook my hand and kissed me on the cheek with a hug. I did the same back. I knew what he was really doing was feeling for a wire or gun. I also noticed there was nobody else in the place, just two waiters and the guy behind the counter that shucked the clams. I thought back to Frankie Bats and the body in the ice, and got angry. They couldn't...wouldn't do that to me? Or would they? Having this Judge is important to them; bench trial in his courtroom case dismissed, that simple. Big Joey wanted a bench trial but the D A prosecuted Big Joey's case, personally. He couldn't get a bench trial, therefore no fix.

Once Ronnie was happy I was clean, he stepped back and said, "Gotta check."

"I understand."

"So what's what?"

I shrugged. "What's what, yourself?"

He shrugged back. "You look good."

"Not as good as you. Never did."

"I got no responsibilities."

He wrapped his arm over my shoulders and guided me to a large round table in the back, like old friends. Rizo sat there like a king, half in shadows. Another mountain of a guy I'd never seen before was with him, along with this other guy, all looking like murder. Rizo stood and gave me a big hug and a kiss, then said, "That was a great wedding reception, but I mostly remember you as a kid from Patty's, taking every opportunity to charm the ladies."

I nodded and smiled.

"Have you always charmed your way in and out of things?"

"I always believed in being nice and trying to reason with everyone.

"Well, then," he said as he eyed me, nodding, "this is different. You must face up and explain this note."

172

Face up to? Perfect. I just gave him a shrug. The smile was gone and he motioned for me to sit. I did, my mind going a mile a minute.

"My friend is worried he thinks I lost control of things."

"Some friend," I shot back without thinking. "He's one you might have to worry about, yourself."

Rizo's eyes narrowed. "What do you mean?"

"The people he helps. And I'm betting without your okay. He's getting greedy and careless."

He stiffened and frowned. "What exactly are you talking about"?

Meaning, either Rizo didn't know about the Judge making outside deals, which was possible, or he just wanted me to believe that. So I jumped in, feet first.

"You think a low-life-junkie-smack-dealer who'd kill his own mother for a fix is a guy your friend ought to help?"

Rizo leaned back, his eyes sharp on me. "Explain me."

"He gets locked up, this junkie, on a burglary. No big deal. Has a bench trial with your guy and it gets dismissed. That's none of my business."

"That a fact? My guy cut him loose?"

"No question. Reason I know is I know the cop that locked up this low life, good, real good to the point he did me a big favor for a friend."

I could almost feel Ronnie tense up, thinking I'll mention his cousin, and then exhale as he realized I wasn't going to use his family to protect myself.

"Anyway, the cop asked me later, 'Who does this junkie know?' And he went on to explain how he had him cold, but the judge dismissed the case without an explanation."

"So do you know how my guy knows this low-life?"

Sure I knew, but I wasn't going to mention it. I still wasn't sure if Moretti was doing business with Rizo directly or not. Big Joey could have hooked the two of them up, and it still could be that Rizo'd had a hand in Loco getting cut loose. But taking the tactic that he's too "right" a guy to mess with scum would show him I held him in esteem and couldn't believe he'd associate himself with someone who's from the gutter.

"That's why the letter," I said. "I figured, this guy can't be with you, and you should know about it, this street junkie might get high and tell someone who tells someone and then it blows up."

173

Whether or not Rizo believed me, I couldn't say. He just breathed in deep, let the information filter through and finally his eyes cut over to me. "So he walked before, so why the letter now?"

"He, this low life, got another bench trial in front of your man, again. But I want this prick. I just want an equal playing field to get him a year on a gun rap, that's all."

"Why do you what him so bad?"

"He's responsible for clipping someone," I said, letting anger slip into my voice. "Just another junkie, but he did in right in front of my mother's apartment. To send me a message, that's why."

Rizo tightened then turned in his chair to think, his gaze focused on something across the room even as his boys and Ronnie all kept theirs locked on me. I forced myself to sit still.

I was playing all my cards, here. When it comes to guys like this, made guys, if you want a favor, you ask for it yourself. Or ask another made member to ask for you. It's like the American Indians and their pow-wows; I guess they couldn't call it a powwow, so it's called a sit down. Besides, Dad once told me. "You need a favor, Pietro? Ask for yourself, like a man." So here I was, using that to turn the tables back on Rizo. He calls me in for a sit-down because he's got a problem? I ask him for a favor because I got one.

Finally, Rizo looked back at me. "How does this affect me?"

"Okay, maybe I'm wrong. Maybe this junkie is with you, if so I back off. But if he isn't, you tell the judge not to take the trial, very simple. And with all due respect, Rizo, you really gotta smarten this Judge up. 'Cause to me, it looks like he's gettin' greedy and sloppy."

I felt Ronnie tense and look at Rizo. No one should talk to a guy like Rizo in the way I just did, but I couldn't show weakness. What I did was show respect by saying I'd back off if the guy was one of his. I felt he knew I would not cross him.

Rizo eyed me. "You sure that's what's going on?"

"No question."

"I see." He didn't move for what seemed like an hour but was probably only a minute or two, and then he said, "I talk to people. They tell me what a good kid you were, and that you're still a good kid. You do what you can to help good people."

Whoa – maybe he did know about Ronnie's cousin. "I – I try to help everyone when I can. But this thing here; Rizo, its gettin' personal. It's gettin' aimed at my family."

174

"Understood," he said. "That junkie ain't with me, and you can bet I'll get that little Jew, coke-snorting judge in line or he'll be using a wheel chair to get around."

Rizo looked at Ronnie and got a big nod, in answer, and then he leaned forward. I really had to work to keep myself still.

"As for the rest...you know more than you let on; the quiet ones always do. But it stays with you, right?"

"Always has, Rizo. Always will."

His eyes dug into me, almost begging me to react in some way to give him an excuse to take me out, but I just looked back in as off-hand a manner as I could. And then he nodded.

"I just wanted to be sure there are no long-term problems to worry about."

"There aren't. Not from me. You have my word."

"Patty's right," he smiled, "you are a good kid. Ain't he, Ronnie?"

Ronnie just nodded, but I could see a proud smile hiding behind his eyes. Damn, maybe this wasn't going to be it, after all.

"Thanks," I said to Rizo. "It means a lot, comin' from you."

He stood up; so did I.

"Good to see you, Pietro," he said. "Take care. And give your baby a kiss from me. One thing – you mind if I send him a little something?"

"I'd be honored."

Then he shook my hand and kissed my cheek, and suddenly I had the feeling that this'd all been too easy. That he didn't really believe me. That he was letting the waiters see us part on good terms and give himself cover. So when Ronnie escorted me to the front door without another word, just a kiss goodbye on the cheek, I didn't know for sure either way if anything was fixed by this sit down.

I made myself walk to my car, get in, start it up and coolly drive away, all under Ronnie's gaze. But soon as I got two streets away I stopped and slammed the door open and hurled every bit of food I'd shoved down my throat onto the pavement. My stomach was flipping harder and faster than the roller coaster at Coney Island. Once I was into dry heaves, I pulled back into the car, dug for the pistol and clipped the holster back onto my belt. Then I popped some Dentyne turned left on Canal Street and headed for the Manhattan Bridge so I could get to the Long Island Expressway.

The L.I.E. is quieter this time of night, and dark. Barely even enough light to see by as cars whisper along like coffins on a gentle

175

river. Gliding down the never-ending concrete, the median hiding approaching headlights as your own lights did nothing more than shine on the red, red, red brake lights ahead of you. All gleaming bright and knowing and warning you, "Take care; take extra care," in time with the "thu-thutt, thu-thutt-thu-thutt" of tires passing over separations in the pavement.

There's light glowing everywhere beyond the barriers on both sides; highlighting trees and dark buildings and phone poles. It's like being on a deep black forest path you have to follow, cutting past occasional street lamps and over or under growling traffic, with no way to get off except for the occasion fork in the road that leads to a slower pace filled with cars that wouldn't move aside even for ambulances, let alone their fellow man.

I was driving that '68 Charger in military green, slap-stick trannie and this great sound system I popped in thanks to Louisa's cousin, Derek. It had a 318, not the 340, but it purred along the road, like it was warming up and ready to shoot for the moon. It can lull you into a haze of comfort, the soft thrumming of that engine. It can make you feel safe and secure and ready for anything. Floating along like that, you're king of the world.

Some of the guys had wondered how I could afford this car and that gas-guzzler of a Chevy wagon Louisa drove, on top of a house in Garden City (and rumors of a high-class girl friend on the side). I guess some of the gossip was getting back to IAD and that's what led to them questioning me about those rental cars. He's gotta be on the pad to be able to pay for all that and -- .

A black car rolled up behind me. At first I paid no attention but it seemed that it was tailing me. It had two headlights burning on the left side, driver's side, and only one on the right.

Oh, man not again.

I couldn't see the driver but there was a passenger with him this time, for sure. And neither one of them was moving, like they were focused on my car and nothing else.

I cut into the lane left of me and sped up. It kept pacing me. I sped up more. It stayed right with me, like it was tied to my car. I went faster, faster. It kept pacing me. I was weaving in and around traffic, not bothering to be nice in how I drove. I couldn't shake him. So I slowed to the speed limit. So did they; for a minute. Then he approached on the left – and made a sharp turn to the right, cutting me off!

176

I slammed across traffic to the shoulder, cars screaming at me with their horns and drivers' curses echoing after me, and then I skidded to a halt, barely missing sideswiping the wall. When I finally stopped, I was at an angle to the road and dust was swirling around me.

The other car stopped down the expressway, on the shoulder.

Then it backed up to me.

I couldn't believe it. There were no taillights. No light over the license plate. I think I actually blinked and rubbed my eyes.

The car got closer and closer. I had to think fast.

I killed my engine and crawled over to the passenger side to get out, then bolted to the trunk. I popped it open and pulled out a shotgun. I'd put it in months ago, when I was close to freaking out over the threat to me and mine. I was never a boy scout but I always heeded their motto – Be prepared.

I kept the shotgun hidden by the Charger's tail as I waited. I tried to peek through the windows of my car, through the space under the end of the trunk lid, to see what the other car was doing.

It stopped, its engine still running, steamy exhaust billowing from the tailpipe like the smoke from hell. It looked like a Ford Galaxy, maybe. Or the Mercury version, two men got out and walked towards me, both of them big and beefy, their hands behind their backs.

Okay, cowboys, you wanna see what daddy's got waiting for you? Here.

I stepped from behind the Charger, holding up my badge with my left hand as I yelled, "Police! Let me see the hands."

They keep coming, smiling, not even looking at each other.

I raised the shotgun with my right hand, holding it at the ready, in full view. "Lemme see the hands!"

Needless to say, the men stopped. In fact, they scurried back to their car in this really funny retreat, bumping into each other at least once, and then burned rubber to get the hell away from me. I think I laughed, but it wasn't from joy or ease or pleasure or anything like that.

No, it's because now I knew – all bets were off and I was on my own.

177

****

I got back to the house in less than ten minutes, the tires all but screaming as I skidded to a halt. I bolted from the car and slammed inside, shoved the shotgun behind the couch, locked the front door and closed all the blinds, then I double-locked the back door and closed the kitchen blinds, too. If anybody was going to try and come in, they'd find it harder than –

Louisa appeared out of nowhere, scaring the hell out of me.

"Honey, what're you doing?"

I tried to act casual by grabbing her in a big hug, something I haven't done in a while.

"Nothing, listen – tomorrow, I'm starting those four to twelves. Would it be okay with your sister if – if you and the baby visited her for a day or two?"

Louisa looked at me, wary. "Why?"

She'd been dropping more hints, lately about my weird schedule and being out all hours, like she knew about Catherine, but that wasn't something I could face, just yet.

"I – I'll be tied up late," I muttered, lamely, "and I – I figure I'll stay at mom's, again, and I prefer that you not be home alone." Man, I wasn't even convincing myself that I was convincing. So I popped up with, "You're looking really good. Let's open a nice bottle of wine tonight." Having two or three glasses holding hands and hugging help clear my mind then I took her to bed.

I gotta say having to focus like that helped me calm down, a lot. I even got to sleep, a serious sleep, for the first time in weeks with decent dreams and –

I bolted awake. Something didn't sound right. Some kind of shuffling noise, like someone trying to keep quiet and –

A shadow moved, a figure of some kind scurrying by the open bedroom door. Dammit, I know I locked this place down! How could anyone get in? Dammit. I grabbed my revolver from under my pillow and snuck out of the bedroom.

First thing I did was check on Billy. Still sound asleep; I could just hear his breathing. Poor little guy, getting born into my crap of a life. What the hell was I gonna tell him when things finally came to a head with everything? How was I going to explain Louisa and Catherine? How could I make him see none of this was his fault, just

178

his father's? Louisa'd help, if we got divorced; I could even hear her telling him, "Daddy was a bastard and left you."

Leave him? How could I do that to my son? My father hadn't. Hell, I'd never even seen him look at another woman besides mom. But if I was to shift my world to Catherine, it'd mean leaving all of this. I would betray everything I'd promised at the wedding. Before god and everybody, I couldn't protect my marriage, my family and my partners. No wonder I was on the way to hell.

I sat by Billy's bed, watching him sleep, unable to move until I heard that shuffling sound, again. I smiled, this time. I could at least protect my son from the scum the earth put out. So I readied my pistol...and then I went through every room in the rest of the house.

Nothing was there, no one else around. But I'd heard it. I'd seen it. What the hell was it? I finally returned to the baby's bedroom, spooked, and did not sleep the rest of the night.

That's where Louisa found me, the next morning, but she didn't say anything as I returned the shotgun to the Charger's trunk, and then packed her station wagon, keeping a watchful eye on anyone passing who I didn't know.

Once it was done, I guided her and the baby into the car, saying. "I'll follow you. Don't go directly to the parkway."

"Peter – you're scaring me."

"Look, it's no big deal," I said, trying to be comforting. "It's just – just – humor me. Okay?"

I kissed Billy before putting him in the car seat and gave Louisa a long hug while looking around. They drove off, and I followed, still keeping a wary eye out. Like those idiots were dumb enough to pull something in broad daylight.

Later that afternoon, I met up with Bobby outside Centre Street before I even changed into my uniform.

"Running a little late, today. Is everything OK?"

"Bobby, last night going home – two guys in a black car ran me off the road."

"No, no shit!" he said. "Did you run the plate number?"

"No, it happened too fast. I never looked for it, I'm just glad I had my shotgun in the car."

"Petey, wait, wait, back up a minute. You're a cop. Gettin' the license plate should be the first thing you do. And you didn't get it?"

"I know but – ."

"No excuses! I'll back you up all the way, but c'mon, buddy, this has got to make sense first."

179

"What do you mean?"

"You don't know what I mean? You don't talk to me about anything and you're actin' so weird, and maybe this could be..." His voice trailed off.

"Could be what?" I spit out, getting pissed.

"This could be like Lou's funeral."

"Come on man, it was real."

"Then why weren't you actin' like a cop? You're smarter'n that, what the fuck – ?"

"Yo!"

We jerked around to see this big, thick, grey-haired guy in a suit that was maybe two sizes too small for him, approaching us. He looked a bit familiar as he held up his gold Detective shield and snapped, "Buono?"

"That's me," I said, not liking him from the first second.

"I'm Gruber. You're needed inside." Then looking right at Bobby, he said, "Officer your post is the entire perimeter of this building take a walk around it and keep us safe."

Bobby walked up to him and got about six inches from him and said with a snarl.

"Who the fuck're you givin' orders?"

"I'm the cop who'll have you on a lifetime fixer in Staten Island, that's who the fuck I am."

"Why don't we talk about this after work tonight?" Bobby shot back.

I snuck between them and said, "Bobby, it's cool. I know who he's with. I'll see you a little later."

He yanked me to one side, snarling, "What is it? You better tell me what the fuck's going on here before I – ."

"I can't."

"Bullshit! I'm your partner. You can tell me anything."

"Bobby, please trust me. Just – just keep calm out here – and I'll see you when I'm done and – and you're right; once I'm done, I'll explain everything. Fill you in, complete."

Bobby snarled and huffed, but he headed off. Then Gruber and I returned to the front of the building.

"Your partner's hot-headed," he said.

"He's just worried about me."

Gruber didn't say another word; just lead me inside and down to room 125. I took a deep breath and entered.

180

There they were, again, Doherty and Rinaldi. Still at the same table with the same tape recorder, but this time both with the same sneer on their faces. No good cop or bad cop from these two; it was gonna be all bad. So I sat across from them at the table, Gruber behind me, and as soon as the tape recorder started running and they'd made their opening spiel, I said, "You have a leak."

Doherty snapped to attention, then, and snarled, "A leak – what do you mean?"

"I was run off the road by two guys, last night," I said. "They were cops and they were serious."

"How do you know they were cops?" Rinaldi asked.

"The way they drove, the way they walked, they way they dressed. Just look in the mirror and you'll know what I'm talking about."

"This is bullshit," Doherty shot at me. "Only ten people know we're here."

"Well," I said, "that narrows down the suspects."

Gruber shook his head. "I don't think it was cops."

"I'm telling you, people say you can smell a cop. Well, being one makes it easier for me, and they stunk of bad cop."

"So what," asked Gruber, "you want somebody assigned to you?"

"Like you did for Serpico?" I snapped at him. I wasn't gonna give this Nazi one inch, if I could help it.

Doherty waved his hand, irritated. "Let's get back to business. Every bit of drug evidence has been retested in the property clerk's office, and to the embarrassment of this Department almost everything with a voucher number dated before three months ago is baking soda, quinine, or some other white powder. Even the French Connection drugs are gone."

I rolled my eyes at that one. "Aren't you guys paying any attention? Those drugs were gone way before I was ever on the job. Hell, two good guys in SIU made that bust over ten years ago. What do you think the shelf life is on pure heroin? Especially in an environment like the Property Clerk's office. No air conditioning in the summer, humid and sticky, and in the winter more steam heat that most saunas. How long?"

"How did you know about all this?" asked Gruber. "And how well, did you know Big Joey, The Baker?"

I had to take a deep breath on that. "Joey who?" I said then remembering the relationship Big Joe had with Moretti. It was a

181

powerful one. Joey could come up with a million in cash instantly. The Property Clerk's office was run by cops that were on restricted duty. Most had drinking problems; some others were complete wrecks with gambling and or domestic problems. In Big Joey's neighborhood, seemed like everybody knew everybody.

Patrolman La Rocco grew up there and still lived there. The year was 1964; La Rocco had about 19 years with NYPD earning almost $10,000 a Year. (That was the salary for a cop in 1964.) La Rocco had bad gambling habits along with a drinking problem. He knew Moretti and the relationship he had with Big Joe, and in a sober moment he conceived a plan to make more than 5 years' pay in a day. He approached Moretti with the deal.

At one point the French Connection Drugs were shipped off to a federal lab. Then in 1964 the 50 Kilos were returned to the Property Clerks Office. Patrolman La Rocco was there the day it was returned and Moretti was the first to be told. The deal -- bring $50,000 in large bills along with 50 kilo bungles of powder wrapped like drugs. They were to arrive at The Property Clerks Office on a Wednesday evening at 6 PM. Most Judges Adjourned court at 4PM, 99% of evidence was returned before 5PM. The Property Clerks office would have one limited duty cop stay until 6PM. Just in case something ran late, Patrolman La Rocco was the late man on Wednesdays, he and only he manned the entire Property Clerks office from 5PM until the doors were locked for the day, around 6PM. I could see it as if I were dreaming.

Two guys each carrying two large leather travel cases, are to walk into 400 Broom Street, nod at the cop on security at the building front door, walk over to the elevator and go up to 2nd Floor. The dummy drugs in kilo packages and $50,000 in cash are in the bags. It took about 3 minutes to make the transfer. La Rocco gave them the real goods. They left the 50 thousand and the dummy drugs and two guys walked out with the four leather travel bags, one in each hand, with a total of 50 bundles 2.2 pounds each of pure heroin. The worthless powder was placed back in storage and remained there untouched, untested for years.

Patrolman La Rocco retired. The next week he paid off some debts and left for parts unknown. Big Joey got 50 kilos of pure heroin for $200 thousand -- four-thousand per key, it would be cut 4 to 5 times and resold for between 10 and 12 thousand a key. Moretti and Kowalski made 75 thousand each, and Big Joey's crew made millions.

I seemed to be in a daze then heard yelling.

182

"Don't hand us that crap," he shot back. "Everybody in the Fourth Ward knew who he was."

"There were a dozen guys there when I grew up there. Because I speak Italian does than mean I know Sinatra?"

Gruber started to flare, but Doherty stepped between us. "Cut the pissing contest. Let's get back to the property clerk's office."

I shook my head. "The department runs it like a candy store. It's a total joke, and you gotta know it. If not I'm wrong about you guys actually being cops. Hell, I wouldn't be surprised if the expensive art and jewelry evidence haven't already been replaced with copies."

Doherty, Rinaldi and Gruber looked at each other.

"See if we can get an expert check it out," said Doherty. Gruber hesitated then started from the room as Doherty turned back to me.

I knew who they had to call, the NYPD's foremost authority on art, a detective that I had several conversations with in early 1969 when he would come in for his paycheck. He was assigned to Narcotics and was cleaner than snow white, and at the time he could not wait to get out of narcotics. He figured he could do it on his own, but needed to call his uncle -- a former governor and now a cabinet member in the Nixon administration. Talk about a Rabbi or hook. His transfer came in and I think I was the first person he told. Needles to say, he was so happy to get out of Narcotics and into The Major Case Squad.

"We have dates when the drugs were signed out and switched. Seems like most of the activity was from 1969 until just the day before the P C's men went in. You got your tin in '69, didn't you"?

"That's right May of '69 so what"?

"This stinks of you, all over."

"Tell you what why don't you and this office GO FUCK YOURSELVES." I couldn't take it anymore; I got up and headed toward the door.

"Police officer Peter G Buono, I have the authority to suspend you, right here and now! I know you understand this. Calm down and it won't happen. Listen to what I have to say and it will be your move, it will be up to you." I was handed a legal pad page with dates hand written. "Regarding these dates if you were in the building on those days, we want to know who else was there and what if anything did you see?"

"I'll check my old memo books."

And finally I caught their attention.

"Memo books?" Gruber asked, halfway through the door, trying not to look like he was too interested, but it was obvious he was.

"Yeah," I said. "I made entries every time I was at that office when something didn't seem right – names, dates, you name it."

The three of them exchanged looks.

"When can you bring them in?" Rinaldi asked.

"Tomorrow, I keep them in a safe place."

"Be better if he got them now," said Gruber.

"Right," said Doherty. "Will it take long?"

"Forever," I said. "Rush hour is not completely over."

"Do it." That was Rinaldi, giving me his patented snarl.

I glanced between the three of them and left. It didn't feel right – first the, "We're gonna get you, you little rat," attitude then bringing up Big Joey then this sudden rush for my memo books. So I played it safe.

Dark was already setting in, so I didn't head straight for the Bridge. I figured I cut through some side streets; make sure I wasn't being followed.

When I arrived at Delancy Street it seemed like a morgue after sundown. Dark and desolate, even with late rush hour traffic. Think I was surprised I didn't make it?

Steam started spilling from under the Charger's hood as I made the approach. If I'd been following my usual route home, who knows where I would be, on the bridge or somewhere else with no phone booths. Not that this place was so much better, but at least it had a couple streetlights and phones on every corner.

I pulled off to the right, staying on Delancy, and parked under a streetlight, near a fire hydrant, got out and checked under the hood. The radiator spewed steam and fluid; the hose had been cut. Half-scared-half-angry, I pulled the shotgun from the trunk and hurried down to a phone booth on the next corner.

The second I got there, that black car with the two men approached. Had to be the one from the other night, no light over the tag on a car that's all but new. That's when I started thinking I'd maybe outsmarted myself, because all the traffic was headed up to the bridge, by-passing where I was. I could hear the engines and horns and tires squealing and everything. I backed into a shadow, keeping the shotgun ready. They kept on driving.

I tried to catch the license plate but the streetlights didn't help and it was too dark to see it on its own. Well, that explained why I

184

couldn't get the number. I waited till they were gone, then I hopped in the booth and dialed.

"Ninth Precinct, Roberts."

"Joe, Pete Buono, I need a favor. My car's got problems and I think I might have one too."

"Where are you?"

"I'm in the 7th on Delancy Street, just east of Ridge. Call a tow for me and – and ask a sector car to meet me here, forthwith."

"I'll take care of it."

I slipped over to a building near the Charger and stood in the shadows. Watching. Waiting. The night seemed to get darker; the traffic farther and farther away. Somebody, someplace, was picking at a guitar, like they were just learning the chords. I could smell a steak being broiled, and damn it smelled good. Made me remember I hadn't eaten since noon, and here it was going on – wait, it was past seven? Where the hell did the time disappear to? Jeez, whoever was cooking that steak must have already – .

The Galaxy passed, again. Had it been by before? I mean, after I saw it the first time? I couldn't be sure. It stopped and the passenger door opened.

I pushed back into the shadows, the shotgun ready. No shaking, this time. My family was safe; Catherine was still a secret to everybody but Bobby, so she was protected; mom was in a secure building; so c'mon, you bastards, I'm ready for anything.

A guy started to get out. Dark overcoat, even in the dark I could tell it was not an expensive one. And he was white, very Anglo.

I tensed. My bet was he's from some sort of hit squad protecting other rouge cops, and that almost made me laugh. He's being pretty dumb about it if he was. He was all confident even in that cheap overcoat, in control. Sure he's what it takes. I'd never had that, not really. Never did. Just acted like it so people'd feel better.

He walked around the Charger, looking in through the windows. He seemed upset that he couldn't see anything. He was about to try opening a door when headlights flashed over him. The sector car had arrived. The second he saw it, he slipped back to the black car, hopped in and they drove away.

I headed over just as the sector car and tow truck arrived.

"Hey, Jimmy, thanks!" I said. "I need a ride back to Centre Street."

"What's with the heavy artillery?"

185

"Aw, I forgot I had it in the trunk," I said. "I don't want it to fall into the wrong hands, y'know."

As they jacked my Charger up, I got a business card from the tow truck driver then hopped in the back of the RMP.

When we got back to 240 Centre Street, I saw Doherty leaving the building so tapped Jimmy on the shoulder.

"Here's fine. Can I leave my shotgun with you? Put it in your locker. I'll pick it up, tomorrow."

"I guess. What's up?"

"Just can't take it inside. Thanks."

I jumped out of the sector car and ran over to Doherty, calling, "Hey, Lieutenant."

He looked around, seeming startled. "That was quick."

"We need to talk."

"You got your memo books?"

"I never made it. My car was sabotaged."

He gave me that sneer, again, as he said, "Sabotaged? And exactly where do you think that happen?"

"Here. Someone cut the radiator hose. This place is compromised."

"Wasn't your partner watching your car outside while you're in here?"

"It's a big block, unless he stood right by the car at all times, how could he or anyone prevent anything?"

"What kinda crap're you pullin'?"

"I'm not pulling anything! I'm telling you – !"

"You're giving us a line of bull, Officer! You give us nothing but delays and excuses. Y'know what? Go back on post. We'll deal with you on Monday. I'm going to talk to the Chief, first thing Monday morning, when you come in you damn well better have those books with you."

I pulled out the repair shop's business card. "You don't believe me? My car's at this shop. Call them." I shoved it in his pocket then stormed off to change into my uniform.

A little later, Bobby and I were walking around the perimeter of the building. And I'd quietly filled him in on everything, including how far things have gotten with Catherine. And he was real quiet and deep in thought.

"I'm telling you, my car was messed with," I said. "Did I imagine that? And the same car – a new Ford Galaxy – came by but the bulb over the plate was out."

186

"And you never told me any of it," he said, sounding hurt. "Me. I'm your partner."

"Bobby, I wanted to protect you," I said. "In hindsight that was stupid on my part. If I'd been talking to you, also, instead of just Marc and Lou..." My voice trailed off. Things might have been better and maybe I wouldn't be in this situation.

I guess Bobby sensed the turmoil in me, because he put a hand on my shoulder and said, "Partner; listen I'm with you. I didn't mean anything, earlier. I just wonder – how's the best way I can help you?"

But something about how he said it was...I dunno...wrong, I felt like he was humoring me. Meaning he didn't believe me. Nobody believed me, not even my partner. Yeah, it's cool he's still willing to back me up...but that knocked the wind out of me.

Now I had to prove it to God and everybody. And all I had was my memo books. Sure, they could be cross-referenced with when drugs were checked out and duty records, showing who was doing what when. But that'd take weeks, if not months, and I'd be on the firing line the whole time. Under investigation, a sitting duck. If it ever did go to trial, Moretti and Velasquez and all of them would be innocents who were wrongly accused by a low-life piece of scum who didn't know right from wrong and was playing the system to get vindicated at the expense of the good guys.

Finally, I said, "Listen to me carefully, if they -- remember if they ask you anything – I never said anything about anything to you."

"Petey, what? Who's gonna ask?"

"Bobby, trust me – they twist your words. They make stuff up. They act like you're dirty. So you – you don't know a thing about anything. Remember that. Make sure. Okay?"

Bobby nodded. At least I could keep him out of it. Hope the taint didn't mess up his career. As for mine I'm fucked. Wish he gets another partner willing to protect him from himself.

Then we saw Gruber approaching.

"Aw, shit," Bobby muttered, "here is that scumbag again. Watch out for him."

Oh, Bobby...it was too late for that.

Gruber didn't even say hello, just started in with, "Minguzzi, handle it out here. Understand?! I need to speak to your partner. We'll be back in a bit."

Bobby bit his tongue. I hesitated then followed Gruber to this bar right around the corner on Kenmare Street. It was one of those big time cop bars, when Headquarters here was in full swing; probably the place where the NYPD version of a sit-down occurred. They'd talk about stuff like, "They pay this every month or we close them down," and, "You send us our cut," and basic stuff like that. Just like the wise guys. Just like the politicians all over. All of them so damned much alike. It's as if the whole idea of laws and justice were only thrown up as smoke screens to keep the stooges and marks clueless as to what was really going on.

We sat at a table in the back, a partition separating us from the bar. I was reminded of my meeting with Rizo the night before. It looks like I was now carrying on the tradition with Gruber.

"You hungry?" he asked. Gonna play good cop, huh?

"No, thanks," I said, even though I was. Because I have to admit, I was still a little shaky. I was finally realizing that if that RMP hadn't shown when it did, earlier, I'd be the latest cop being shot by the Black Panthers or caught in a drug war or committing suicide.

"Then what you drinking?" said Gruber. "No waiter this late."

The question startled me, and it took me a moment to wake up. "Uh – Scotch and water," I said. "Thanks."

Gruber went to the bar and ordered as I sat at the table and tried to collect my thoughts. This was threatening to go worse than bad. If it didn't get me killed, it'd probably get me kicked off the job. How the hell could I explain that to mom and my sisters, let alone Louisa and Catherine? No income. No health insurance, no nothing. I should've just kept my mouth shut. I'd have protected my family that way. It's not like I could change the world with my stupid, limited ways. I am a total loser and –

Gruber set the drink in front of me, breaking my chain of thought.

"Those guys inside," he said. "Rinaldi's an asshole, and Doherty? Well, neither one of 'em ever did a day on patrol. They don't know what it's like to be a cop – a real cop."

He raised his glass and downed his drink. I took a good swallow. It felt just right as it hit my gut. It slammed the thoughts away from me.

"Drink up," he said. "I'll get you another."

"Thanks, not just yet," I said, and then I leaned forward. "Y'know, I – I just don't get it. I – I'm trying to help but they act like – .""

"They see one guy wrong; they think we're all bad. It's their job, squeezing cops."

188

I took another sip. Let it sit on my tongue for a moment before sliding down my throat. Then I noticed Gruber eying me in a way that made me uncomfortable. It seemed like he was happy about something. A smile started crossing his face.

"Y'know, I heard your mother still lives here in the Fifth," he said.

I leaned back on the seat. He was making me really uncomfortable. "My mother -- what's she got to do with this?"

He shrugged, his grin getting even wider. "And you're hooked up good with big Joey's old crew from downtown."

What the hell? "What're you gettin' at? Tryin' to do Rinaldi's crap for him?"

"Just want to point out that it could prove...embarrassing if this ever goes to trial. Did you know a Sergeant Bruno?"

Oh, shit. The bells started sounding a warning. "A little, why?"

"Right, you worked under him for – what – a year and a half?"

"I worked under Goldberg and...and filled in on the, the switchboard." And I stared into Gruber's dead, dead eyes and went cold.

Oh, my god, no wonder I don't got a gold shield.

"You're fucking the leak."

Gruber's face twisted into this vicious snarl as he leaned in close, his voice low, eyes cold and mean as he growled, "Try tellin' anybody that. You think they'll believe you? A nut job seeing' a shrink? Who's on meds and gettin' worked over for being dirty? Who worked under a dirty cop?"

Oh, my god, "Bruno was part of it."

Gruber silently chuckled, and swear to god, I could see the devil in him as he said, "You could say that. Seems the pressure got to be too much for him. But then, for all his bullshit – he was a pussy. You're not a pussy are you, Pete? Petey or your dago-wop name Pietro? You're not the kind of pussy that puts cops in jail, are you?"

"You're killin' people!"

"They're killin' themselves! I don't go stickin' needles in nobody's arm! So get this straight – this is gonna end, right here, right now. You're gonna tell those two up-tight little ass-wipes inside that you never had any memo books. That it was all just smoke to save your ass or I promise you, there's gonna be more like your cousin, Fredo, on your conscience. Like maybe Louisa's brother or Catherine's – ."

189

I whipped my fist into his fat ugly face. I didn't even think about it. And when he crashed to the floor, I piled on top of him, screaming, "You know what you did to my family, you prick!? You know what you did to my dad?! My cousin! I'll fuckin' kill you, you son-of-a-bitch!" And I was whaling away, nonstop. They said it took three people to pull me off him and drag me back to the bar.

Gruber just laughed, his nose flowing with blood. "You fuckin' psycho – you're full of shit!"

"I got proof, you – ."

"You got shit, you fuckin' guinea!" he snarled as he got to his feet. "You never saw nobody; do nothing with nobody, never. You were just blowing smoke 'cause you heard they were looking into cops being on the pad!"

"I got my – ."

He jolted up into my face, his blood flicking onto my cheeks along with his spit as he growled, "Hey, is your mom safe? How are Louisa and little Billy? Where are they? Her sister's, right?"

"No, no, I was told – I was promised – ."

"Fuckin' shit, you asshole, you think some dumb-fuck capo's gonna make us back off? We're the fuckin' N-Y-P-D! We break assholes like Rizo for breakfast!"

People were still holding me back, so I kicked him in his fat, ugly gut then shook everybody off and staggered to the exit.

Gruber's choking laughter followed me. "You're a dumb shit, Pietrooo!"

I bolted outside, my stomach heaving. He was right; I'd assaulted him. I'd beat the shit out of a fellow cop, in front of witnesses. I'd ruined everything, stupid, stupid!

I heard the door snap open behind me and Gruber yell, "You stupid fuck, listen to me! You'll let 'em give you a slap on the wrist as punishment and you'll keep on being quiet, like a good boy – or I guarantee you, we WILL end it."

I started to run, Gruber's voice echoing after me. I heard gunshots, but knew he wouldn't be stupid enough to shoot me now. Not here. Not in the back. Not without provocation. No, he'd be getting the names of witnesses to use against me. And while I didn't think of him as brilliant, he's a cop and any cop'd be at least that smart.

So now I knew. There it was – all out on the table and out of control. Rizo couldn't help me. IAD couldn't do shit. Nobody could. It was all on me – and I didn't know what to do.

190

I stopped running, winded, and pulled out a handkerchief and wiped his blood off my face as I rounded a corner and nearly slammed into Bobby. I was shaking like crazy. I couldn't stop.

"What's wrong?" he asked. "What'd that scumbag do to you?"

I understood what he said, but for some reason I couldn't understand him, so I just grunted, "Huh?"

"Partner, what'd he say to you? Petey, you look like shit."

I finally found my voice and said, "You – you're right. He is a scumbag."

Bobby and I headed away, with him leading and keeping a tight eye on me. That was a good thing, because I was feeling weirder and weirder. Like the world wasn't mine, anymore. Like the sky was getting blacker and blacker and farther away, but then it would be, it being close to midnight. I mean, I think it was.

Man; that drink wasn't sitting right with me.

Bobby finally asked, "Pete – what's wrong?"

"Huh?"

"You're hummin' some tune...half-singin' words like 'Mack's back in town' or something. What the fuck?"

"I – I dunno what's what," I said. "I – I must be comin' down with somethin'."

We rounded the corner and even though my legs turned my body didn't and I nearly fell over the curb. Bobby caught me, and suddenly I saw Catherine sitting in her convertible Caddy, the radio playing, her mink wrapped tight around her, its hood covering her golden hair. She looked so much like something out of a movie, so perfect, just seeing her...I'd never felt so happy in my life. I forgot all about Bobby and stumbled over to lean against the car, like I was drunk.

"Baby," I said, beginning to sort of mutter my words. "What you doing here?"

She looked at me with her bright, shining eyes and said, "Bobby said your car broke down. I came to pick you up. Take you home. You look like – like you need the ride."

And a cloud passed over her.

"You don't mind, do you?" said Bobby as he came up behind me. "I knew you had no car and since you gave me her number in case of emergency I figured this is one besides I wanted to introduce myself. Talk to her."

"No, it – it's great," I said, making myself stay calm. There was plenty of time to explain my new reality to them both. "Just great, makes it easier, lots easier."

Catherine looked at me, worried. "Sweetie, you look so – kind off, you look flush."

I looked around, suddenly really nervous, and I was having a hard time forming a thought. "It – it's not – you – you – you have a good day at work?"

Catherine shot a glance at Bobby and said, "Always."

Suddenly, I was near tears. I crouched by the car and touched her face, making certain she was real. "Oh, baby, I'm so glad to see you."

Bobby's voice took on a careful tone as he said, "Should I should leave you two alone? Why don't I go in to change?"

I grabbed him suddenly terrified. "No! No – uh, Bobby – will you let me – uh, you stay with her make sure everything is alright till I'm back?"

He looked at me, just as wary as Catherine was. "I should come in with you."

"No, please – I – I'll be out in a few minutes. Stay here with her. Just want my – my – my heavy coat."

I backed away from them. They didn't move. And yet they did. Gently, Bobby to the left, her to the right, both closer, made no sense. Not with their voices echoing around me.

I turned and staggered towards the entrance, sweating and trembling. The street weaved. Shadows loomed. Images shifted together. Middle of the night makes everything worse. It seemed like everything around me going to hell. Even across from Police Headquarters, this city is not safe. And now, now it seems no place in the world was safe. No place. Not anymore.

I looked back to see Catherine still parked waiting. Bobby right there, standing guard, beside her, Bobby gave me a thumbs up indicating he had things under control he wanted to make sure I knew I wasn't alone, or something. Put an ache in my heart to know that he had my back and she was safe.

I should not have gone in there. Should've just got in that Caddy and let her drive me to my mom's or home to Louisa and shown her I was screwin' around on her or just gone driving up the Hudson. Gone anyplace else but in there and I thought about it for half a second. It's just, even with all the crap that'd just happened, I still couldn't

192

believe how bad off I was. Didn't realize what evil could be waiting for me inside.

But like a robot I started across the street. And once again, HQ's old, baroque, snotty looks glared down at me like I was some piece of trash blowing past in the wind, even though it was just about abandoned and going to trash, itself. Nothing but those offices left by the lockers still in use, including the one involving me. Well – not including it; that office did not exist. It seems like I didn't really exist either.

Climbing the steps to the main doors, I had to hold onto the banister. That meant thrashing through crumbled up bags and broken bottles and newspapers flapping against the posts, but it kept me from falling backwards down to the pavement. And half the lights seemed to be either busted or missing, making being there even more like a Hitchcock movie.

It felt older and darker, inside. Lights burned out. There was trash on the floors, shadows twisting everywhere. There was still that cop at the reception/security desk. Like always, and would be till the last piece of furniture was gone. And like always, he didn't look up as I entered and said, "Hey, what's what?" My voice cracked. I could hear it, but he didn't.

"How ya doin'?" was all he said.

"I – I been better," I said, "but thanks, been a long day. All these lights missin' – don't maintenance care, anymore?"

He just grunted and kept reading whatever it was he had in his hands. He had a lamp on his desk and a cushion under his butt, so he was set.

I just sighed and headed down a corridor. In the direction of the locker area next to the office that was crushing my life. Didn't even care how quiet it was, or how nobody else was around. Why would they be? It's near midnight, right? Or had they already moved everybody over to the new place and not told me? That'd be crazy...but wouldn't surprise me, the way things'd gone the last couple weeks. Never even thought about how I'd been there just a few hours ago, getting beat all to hell. So I kept on going.

The corridor seemed to grow longer and darker as I went. And there were these shuffling sounds, fresh and new, echoing from everywhere. My breathing quickened. My eyes darted about, wary. Why were so many fixtures missing light bulbs, completely? That didn't make sense, unless they'd been removed, deliberately. Make it harder to see into the darkness, are they setting me up.

193

I got to the first door on the left and hesitated. Undid the safety on my holster then carefully looked toward my locker. The free-standing lockers seemed to be glowing a little. The rest of the room was so dark and dirty and empty and quiet, even my breathing seemed to echo.

Or was it mine I was hearing?

I started to shake. I carefully slipped inside and crept past the lockers, getting closer and closer to mine. I saw nothing. There was no one, just shadows filling the room, drowning it.

I was sweating now, even though the building was cold. I noticed my breath whispering in and out, like it was trying to escape. I wondered if my nose could get frostbite, grinned and giggled. What is going on what's happening to me?

I finally reached my locker and leaned against it and looked down. And even though my hand was shaking, I could see this thin trail of blood whisper over the skin.

Aw, no – no – maybe Gruber had fired at me. Could I have been shot and not know it? Or knifed when we were fighting? Had Gruber done this to me? I didn't feel any pain. Then again, I wasn't feeling anything right then.

I almost fainted but caught myself by slamming my head against the locker, twice, Again, back in control, I fumbled with the lock's combination, running through it three times and smearing blood all over it before I was able to work it right. When it popped open, the noise bounced off the walls.

I heard that shuffling sound, again, and froze to listen. There was nothing but silence, not even breathing.

I slowly pulled off my coat. It didn't hurt, but something was pulling sharp against my left shoulder. I checked it and saw my shirt was soaked with sweat – and blood. I wiped my face. Blood smeared over it.

Oh shit, something HAD happened. Oh, God. No wonder I was feeling so out of it. I was in shock and needed to hit the ER and –

The shuffling sound whispered up, again. It was closer, much closer. I started to quake, inside.

"Bobby?" I tried to call, "Bobby, that you?"

Then again nothing, not even the shuffling. Until this hint of a noise came from my right and I turned to find –

A gunman standing at the end of the lockers, raising a pistol!

Everything clicked into slow-motion as I yanked out my service revolver, dropped to one knee and fired at him.

194

My first shot hit his left knee. The second ripped through his thigh. Two more hit an arm and a shoulder.

He got a couple of shots off at me and I felt a punch in my side, but then he crashed against an office wall and landed in a sitting position, his leg twisted under him.

I rose slowly, carefully, in complete disbelief, and inched up to the guy, pistol ready but shaking in my bloody hands. Barely under control and hoping to God he wasn't gonna make another move.

I heard voices and footsteps approaching from a thousand miles away.

The guy lifted his gun, unsteady.

I fired, again! Hit him in the forehead. The bullet exploded through his skull.

Blood splattered over me, covered me. I dropped to my knees, about ready to pass out – then I saw it. I saw the gunman's gold shield. He was a cop. A detective! A cop had just shot a cop in police headquarters!

And it was GRUBER!

"Man, was there gonna be hell to pay for that," I thought as I quietly drifted towards darkness...but then these sharp, screaming pictures flashed before me of –

Fredo being killed.

Lou and his partner getting executed.

Bobby Bats and his bodyguard dead in the trunk.

The body in the box of ice on the ferry.

The black car following me.

The bomb killing Louisa and the baby.

My dad dying.

The cops at Lou's funeral trying to shoot me and Bobby.

And dogs and jackals began tearing at my limbs, demons laughing at me.

I screamed from the onslaught and –

Bobby was there in front of me, shaking me, jolting me from the loop of visual death. I grabbed onto him like a man who's drowning and caught a flash of the wall and –

Gruber's body had vanished!

Bobby's face was white and he was yelling, "Petey, Petey what the hell – ?"

I looked at my hands and body and I was covered in sweat only it was turning the color of blood and Gruber's body was back there, again, but nobody else seemed to care about it and shadows were

195

jumping everywhere and blood was trailing down the wall and the demons screeched with laughter as the dogs tore at my legs and arms and –

I slammed my head back against the wall – twice, again – and caught about two seconds worth of clarity so I could mutter, "Bobby – drink – Gruber bought drink – in drink – ."

And I was jolted by Bobby screaming, "CALL AN AMBULANCE!"

I kept muttering, "Gruber. I killed him. Tried to kill me and – and – Gruber – he – he – Bobby – my memo books – ."

Bobby leaned in close and whispered, "Memo books? Right – where are they?"

I could barely talk, but I made myself mutter, "Louisa – her mom – her mom – she knows – she's – aw, man – get 'em to Marc. Nobody else. You be sure and – and – ." And the demons were screaming and the dogs howling and I was shrieking, "All the blood, the blood!" Over and over and over as it flowed down my arms and from my chest and I was drowning in it and trying to wipe it off my hands but it won't come off. "But it's not mine. It's not mine! It's not mine!"

And it won't come off.

It won't come off.

And then there was darkness.

Blesséd darkness.

Blesséd...

****

Well...it seems I did not shoot Gruber; he was nowhere near HQ when I lost it. Looks like all I shot at was shadows. But then, he already had all he needed to push for a Department hearing – to have me terminated for assaulting him.

Bobby told me what happened, next, when he came to visit me, with Marc. He was pissed off about it, but Marc explained, "It was more than just the assault that made them agree to it; you also had this unlawful discharge of a fire arm, at 240 Centre Street no less. Besides that, your erratic behavior and not telling the department you were on medication? Word came down straight from the state prosecutor's office – put him on ice. They need to distance themselves from you, and the part they played in this."

Even having incriminating photos of Moretti handing drugs over to the black guys in that Caddy weren't enough to make them back off.

"Well," Bobby snarled, "it wasn't enough till I handed your memo books over. That's when they started seeing not just the connections, what with work schedules and handwriting analysis, but who it might've been taking them out. Once that got going, they knew it was a real catastrophe in the making."

Only took four dead cops and god knows how many dead junkies to show them what was what. And once they'd pulled everything together, Marc had headed the file over to Police Plaza and taken an elevator up to the Fourth floor, where Gruber was waiting for him. He handed the bastard the envelope of evidence and punched the elevators down button as he said, "Get this to Chief Fitzer."

Then Marc got on the elevator and the doors closed.

I can fill in the rest, no problem. Gruber carried the file into the men's room. He went into a stall, looked through every one of the pictures, and then ripped up any that showed Moretti in a uniform getting into a new city car and driving up to the club and carrying the red bag inside. After all, how could he explain doing that when he's a gold shield? Then Gruber flushed them down the toilet while the photos of the black guys in the Cadillac were returned to the file.

It wasn't a stupid move, not really. You see, the chief wouldn't have known he was missing any photos for days or weeks, even. Would've been a nice delaying tactic to give everyone a chance to get their stories in order or get the hell out of Dodge. Only problem

197

was, when Gruber exited the stall, Marc and Bobby were waiting – along with Doherty and Rinaldi.

Marc says he smiled when he told Gruber, "Lab results came back. Buono had LSD in his system, a double dose. Doctors think it may have fried his brain. You have any idea how it got there?"

That is when Gruber made a stupid move by reaching into his jacket. Bobby just snapped and with one punch knocked him out.

"I broke his nose and cheek bone," said Bobby. "Blood was everywhere."

He still had my back. Man, did that make me feel good.

That is when the whole thing busted wide open...well, as wide as it was going to get. The city wasn't gonna have another situation like Serpico, no way in hell. Too much would've had to be explained. Too much would've had to change. Too many people would've been held up as part of the problem and the only solution would've been to bring in someone from the outside to clean things up. "That would've hurt morale."

So it took them five minutes to officially certify me as crazy, drug-induced or not. That was the way to get rid of me. Now nobody talked about me being that rolling-your-eyes kind of crazy...well okay, maybe some people did a little, at first. But c'mon – when you consider what happened, of course people would want that to be the excuse. It makes it all so easy. He's a nut-case; a little psycho. Like it's my fault I lost my marbles, or it's because of something inside me that was inherently flawed. It must have been, because very few people get that screwed up by Acid. So that lets the people who should've been there, the brass guys with time and experience – lets them off the hook for not doing their jobs...if they ever intended to. Who hadn't heard the rumors that Serpico getting shot was really a setup? Even he believed it, and he got the hell out of the country. But that's what happens to anybody who breaks the brotherhood's code of silence, who won't protect the guys he works with; no matter what kind of evil they're pulling. It can mess you up, that shit. Can add to your confusion, make you even crazier.

But you want to know what really convinced everybody absolutely and positively that I was a freak job? Get ready for it. I could type 135 words per minute; 160 when I was really on. I'm talking a manual typewriter without errors. Girls can do that, not guys; not if they're normal. Swear to god, a couple of the guys from my trainee class offered that up as proof. Yeah, top typing skills mean you're nuts. Who can do that and be human?

198

Paranoid-schizophrenic's what they finally settled on as they nodded their heads in a way that says they're oh-so-sure of themselves. And who'm I to argue with guys who've got a diploma that cost a hundred-K to put on their wall? Sometimes when I dream I'm awake it is so real. What'd one guy I met in the nuthouse say? Insanity's not a state of mind; it's a consensus by people who are too crazy to know they're just as nuts as you are.

So they forced me onto disability at a third of my pension; it was that or they'd press disciplinary charges and I'd wind up losing everything, including my health insurance, not just for me but for my wife and kid, too. I had to have that. I had to stay under the care of a doctor.

And I still am, even now, forty plus years later. Not many people look the same after 40 plus years, but what do you think the likes of hardcore anti-hallucinogenic drugs do to you?

I don't want people to recognize me anyway, so maybe it is good that I look nothing like I did in the past.

Acid trips don't last forever, though some say one time can wreck you up for life. There are others who insisted my illness was caused by fear, a fear that manifested in me seeing my wife and child die, according to the evidence they'd gathered, and the drugs only released it from my deepest psyche. But now it could be healed...and on and on and on.

None of it mattered. I was still institutionalized, for a while, and worked over by doctors trying a hundred different drug cocktails in some idiotic attempt to figure out which one would keep me under control – and that I could put in me without hurling, keeling over from a heart attack, or losing my liver.

But you know, the only thing that makes me think I might've been crazy the whole damn time is I wanted to believe somebody, anybody would care and not put the almighty buck first.

It didn't help that I had the background of a guy who knows what he knows and knows people know he knows. But getting smacked around by a girl when you're young makes you want to keep secrets, but now after 40 plus years it was time to speak about all those things I know about that have been eating me up for all these years.

So to finish this up – About 20 guys were arrested, most resigned first, none convicted of the actual thefts. Seems since I didn't testify they really did not have enough proof. But several were locked up by the feds, you know Internal Revenue. They could not hide all that money and left a trail of spending that was way above what their W-2 provided.

Moretti must have made some enemies or a bad deal. He was killed after he got out of federal prison. I once thought about asking Ronnie if he knew what happened, but what would be the point?

Kowalski vanished the second things blew up. He's still considered a fugitive and they say they're still looking for him...but something tells me, not very hard. My feeling is they ought to check the bottom of Upper Bay halfway between Bayonne and Gowamus.

Velasquez did federal time, seems his sister bought a very expensive Italian sports car for over $100,000 in cash (small bills I understand). Jonas was quick to cooperate; turning state's evidence. That still did not help the State's case. He'd struck me from the start as somebody you couldn't trust to hold your coat while you pissed.

Interesting that Jonas died in a freak car wreck. His body was burned to a crisp. They say it was an accident, but it seemed like too much of a coincidence, to me. This thing was far and wide, and it was too easy. The Detective from the 17th figured it out; he just took drugs and other high value items that guys from the 17th locked up, so a simple check of the blotter everyday got him the voucher number along with the arresting officer's name. I was wondering how many others (cops) all over the city were doing this.

For some reason, no criminal charges were filed against Gruber. He was just demoted back to patrolman and fined two week's pay. Guess they didn't want any connection between him and what happened to me to come out. He retired soon after. I wasn't surprised.

Marc did his full tour and retired, then died of "natural causes" a little while ago. I didn't even know till after he was buried. What a good man I miss him.

Without me, Bobby's temper finally got him into too much hot water. He beat the hell out of a guy that he and his new partner caught raping a twelve year-old girl on the roof of a building on Ninth Street. Broke both of the guy's arms and his jaw, plus the guy lost most of his teeth. They arrested Bobby and he almost went to jail over that scumbag; instead, he got suspended...and then terminated. He dropped out of sight. I haven't seen him in twenty-five years.

Rizo died in jail, calling shots until the day he passed.

Of course, it came out that I'd been seeing Catherine. So I lost my wife. Oh, Louisa stayed with me...well, helped me while I was trying to recuperate, for several years. We did not divorce so she could keep access to my health benefits for her and the baby. She was entitled to do that. But then she dropped me completely, and was lucky enough to marry, again. A good stable provider

Man, I never wanted anybody to get hurt.

Oh, and just to be clear – I'm not in a nut house. Not anymore. But I am still under a doctor's care. As for work, sometimes I'm fine and can do some things for guys I'm still connected to. Like Ronnie; he'll throw me a bone for old time's sake, now and then. Other times, I can't even tie my shoes. Don't even leave the house for weeks at a time.

Oh, I got my pension, but it's nowhere near enough to live on, these days. Of course, no one, me included, thought I would live this long, because now I'm a senior citizen. I got a Single Room Occupancy apartment (one room) in an undisclosed location.

On the days I can leave my place.

I am very careful, because I just know somebody's out there waiting for me to appear so they can finish me off. I never know when that fear will overwhelm me; it just jumps on my back out of nowhere for no reason.

Because the fact is, from the time of its inception up until 1973, the New York City Police Property Clerk's office had no cameras. And no matter how hard the New York City Police Department swears only three-hundred and ninety-eight pounds of hard drugs went missing, that's right 398 pounds that is 288 pounds above and beyond the French Connection drugs. The exact amount will never be known. Nor will they ever really know just how many people were involved. Nor are they even trying to figure that out. But there's no question it was way more than the guys I knew about. Look at the Cop from the 17th Squad, He did not even work at the Narcotics Office and was able to simply figure it out. Remember Cops are human, most are honest and caring; others...a small few...will take advantage of any Inherent Flaw in a system. It was so easy, it was almost entrapment. And what happened was the easy money, well if you can call ruining thousands of people's lives easy money.

What's even worse is, there's still some cops that think what I was trying to do was wrong – helping to bring down fellow cops. I wonder how, even though they were the worst of the worst. I don't care what they think, when I look in the mirror, I know what I did was right. Still, I was a cop, and cops don't rat on their brothers. No matter what they do. So they will get even. And sometimes that can mean murder. That's why Serpico wound up in Switzerland; they won't go that far to get you.

201

I always felt one of these creeps would bump into me somewhere and try to take me out. I've been waiting for almost forty years now; but I think I outlived them all.

This theft of drugs has been referred to as the biggest heist in America; remember the street value of the almost 400 pounds was in excess of seventy million dollars.

So let me end this by saying up front – I'm glad I told my story. The department and some cops want you to think this "Buono" guy never existed. That he's a figment of some warped imagination. That he was just some psycho kid who couldn't handle being a real cop. Who fucked around on his wife and had an appetite that was too big. And who let that take him over so that nothing he said was real or to be believed.

But I am real. I did exist. I do. And still do, especially in my own mind, and that's despite everything they tried and are still trying. Now it was time to tell my story, before life slips away and I'm lost forever.

So there it is.
And here I am.
What a hell of a way to end up.

Good luck and GOD bless!

CPSIA information can be obtained
at www.ICGtesting.com
Printed in the USA
LVHW081443270222
712142LV00011B/262